The International Tribunal for the Law of the Sea

ELEMENTS OF INTERNATIONAL LAW

Series Editors

Mark Janis is William F. Starr Professor of Law at the University of Connecticut.

Douglas Guilfoyle is Associate Professor of International and Security Law at UNSW Canberra.

Stephan Schill is Professor of International and Economic Law and Governance at the University of Amsterdam.

Bruno Simma is Professor of Law at the University of Michigan and a Judge at the Iran-US Claims Tribunal in The Hague.

Kimberley Trapp is Professor of Public International Law at University College London.

Elements of International Law represents a fresh approach in the literature of international law. It is a long series of short books. *Elements* adopts an objective, non-argumentative approach to its subject matter, focusing on narrowly-defined core topics in international law. Eventually, the series will offer a comprehensive treatment of the whole of the field. At the same time, each individual title will be a reliable go-to source for practising international lawyers, judges and arbitrators, government and military officers, scholars, teachers, and students engaged in the discipline of international law.

The International Tribunal for the Law of the Sea

Kriangsak Kittichaisaree

OXFORD
UNIVERSITY PRESS

OXFORD

UNIVERSITY PRESS

Great Clarendon Street, Oxford, OX2 6DP,
United Kingdom

Oxford University Press is a department of the University of Oxford.
It furthers the University's objective of excellence in research, scholarship,
and education by publishing worldwide. Oxford is a registered trade mark of
Oxford University Press in the UK and in certain other countries

© Kriangsak Kittichaisaree 2021

The moral rights of the author have been asserted

First Edition published in 2021

Impression: 1

Crown copyright material is reproduced under Class Licence
Number C01P0000148 with the permission of OPSI
and the Queen's Printer for Scotland

Published in the United States of America by Oxford University Press
198 Madison Avenue, New York, NY 10016, United States of America

British Library Cataloguing in Publication Data

Data available

Library of Congress Control Number: 2020945215

ISBN 978-0-19-886529-2 (hbk.)
ISBN 978-0-19-886534-6 (pbk.)

DOI: 10.1093/law/9780198865292.001.0001

Printed and bound by
CPI Group (UK) Ltd, Croydon, CR0 4YY

Preface

This book is part of the Oxford University Press's *Elements of International Law* series to provide readers with a highly reliable, objective, readable, and in-depth account of the subject using an objective, non-argumentative, approach. The author mainly focuses on the analysis of the important rules and procedures of the International Tribunal for the Law of the Sea and the Tribunal's own case law, referring to the jurisprudence of other international courts and arbitration tribunals insofar as it has been alluded to by the Tribunal itself.

The Registry of the Tribunal has produced voluminous research papers for internal discussion among the judges of the Tribunal. The author hereby shares some of the information from these papers only where it is also intended to be accessible to the general public.

Due to the limited length of this book, readers may find it useful to also consult treaty provisions, Rules, and other documents on the International Tribunal on the Law of the Sea's website at www.itlos.org.

The author is grateful to Elzbieta Mizerska-Dyba, Head of Library and Archives, and Svenja Heim, Library Assistant, of the International Tribunal for the Law of the Sea for their research assistance. Thanks are also owed to Arron Nicholas Honniball, Research Fellow (Ocean Law and Policy) at the Centre for International Law/National University of Singapore, for sharing useful information. Douglas Guilfoyle, law of the sea editor of the series, as well as Merel Alstein, John Smallman, Eleanor Hanger, and Jack McNichol of the Oxford University Press duly deserve the author's sincere gratitude for their invaluable guidance and advice to enable this book see the light of day.

This book is the author's own work and is not an official publication of the International Tribunal for the Law of the Sea.

Hamburg
October 2020

Contents

Table of Cases

Tables of Treaties and Conventions

Table of International Instruments

Table of Statutes and Rules of International Tribunal

Abbreviations

Area, the	seabed and ocean floor and subsoil thereof, beyond the limits of national jurisdiction
Authority, the	International Seabed Authority
BBNJ	marine biological diversity of areas beyond national jurisdiction
Doc	Document
ETS	European Treaty Series
EU	European Union
FAO	Food and Agriculture Organization
FSA	1995 UN Agreement for the Implementation of the Provisions of the UN Convention on the Law of the Sea of 10 December 1982 relating to the Conservation and Management of Straddling Fish Stocks and Highly Migratory Species Fish Stocks
GATT	1994 General Agreement on Tariffs and Trade
ICGJ	Oxford Reports on International Courts of General Jurisdiction
ICJ	International Court of Justice
ICLQ	International and Comparative Law Quarterly
ILM	International Legal Materials
IMO	International Maritime Organization
Implementing Agreement	1994 Agreement relating to the Implementation of Part XI of the United Nations Convention on the Law of the Sea of 10 December 1982
Int'l	International
Int'l & Comp L Rev	International and Comparative Law Review
ISBA	International Seabed Authority
ITLOS	International Tribunal for the Law of the Sea
IUU fishing	illegal, unreported, and unregulated fishing
J	Journal
JIL	Journal of International Law
L	Law
MCA Convention	Convention on the determination of the minimum access conditions and exploitation of fisheries resources within the maritime zones under the jurisdiction of SRFC Member States

MPA	marine protected area
nm	nautical miles
ODIL	Ocean Development and International Law
OJ	Official Journal of the European Union
OUP	Oxford University Press
PCIJ	Permanent Court of International Justice
Rep	Reports
Rev	Review
RFMO	Regional Fisheries Management Organization
RIAA	Reports of International Arbitral Awards
Rules	Rules of the International Tribunal for the Law of the Sea
SPLOS	Meeting of States Parties to UNCLOS
SRFC	Sub-Regional Fisheries Commission
Statute	Statute of the International Tribunal for the Law of the Sea
Third Conference	Third United Nations Conference on the Law of the Sea (1973–1982)
UN	United Nations
UNCLOS	1982 United Nations Convention on the Law of the Sea
UNESCO	United Nations Educational, Scientific, and Cultural Organization
UNTS	United Nations Treaty Series
Virginia Commentary	Myron H Nordquist, Shabtai Rosenne, and Louis B Sohn (eds), *United Nations Convention on the Law of the Sea 1982: A Commentary* (Brill 1989) vol 5
WTO	World Trade Organization
WWF	World Wildlife Fund for Nature
YB	Yearbook
YBIL	Yearbook of International Law
ZaöRV	Zeitschrift für ausländisches öffentliches Recht und Völkerrecht

1

ITLOS and the Dispute Settlement System under UNCLOS

Oceans cover approximately 70 per cent of the earth's surface. The sea comprises living and non-living natural resources as well as serves multifarious purposes such as navigation, routes for submarine cables for telecommunication and oil and gas pipelines, and maintaining the climate balance. A stable legal regime governing the uses and management of the ocean is thus an important feature of international relations. From 1973 to 1982, representatives of 160 sovereign States participated in the Third United Nations Conference on the Law of the Sea to negotiate a comprehensive international agreement on the law of the sea, culminating in the adoption of the 1982 United Nations Convention on the Law of the Sea ('UNCLOS'),[1] with 320 Articles in 17 Parts plus nine Annexes, on 10 December 1982. As of this writing, UNCLOS has 168 parties, including the European Union, State of Palestine, Cook Islands, and Niue. Crafting an agreement of such scale and complexity obviously required considerable compromise among the negotiating States.

One of the significant achievements of the Third Conference is the development of a comprehensive system for the settlement of the disputes that may arise with respect to the interpretation or application of UNCLOS.[2] The dispute settlement system under UNCLOS was drafted with the main purpose of achieving the uniform and effective interpretation and application of UNCLOS, as the compromises it embodied would otherwise be vulnerable to unilateral interpretation. UNCLOS sets up two international organizations: the International Seabed Authority ('Authority') and the International Tribunal for the Law of the Sea ('ITLOS'). The Authority is the organization through which States Parties to UNCLOS organize and

---

[1] 1833 UNTS 3.

[2] Myron H Nordquist, Shabtai Rosenne, and Louis B Sohn (eds), *United Nations Convention on the Law of the Sea 1982: A Commentary*, vol 5 (Brill 1989) ('Virginia Commentary') 5.

control activities in the seabed and ocean floor and subsoil thereof, beyond the limits of national jurisdiction ('the Area'), particularly with a view to administering the resources of the Area.[3] ITLOS, the dispute settlement mechanism specifically created by UNCLOS, is composed of 21 judges elected by States Parties to UNCLOS, each for a nine-year renewable term.

The dispute settlement system as established is flexible and contains a variety of mechanisms. It allows urgent issues to be tackled swiftly through seeking provisional measures of protection from a court or tribunal as well as a functional approach. The functional approach includes special provision for fisheries, including the prompt release of detained fishing vessels and crews, and the establishment of the Seabed Disputes Chamber within ITLOS to deal with disputes related to activities in the Area administered by the Authority.

Part of this flexibility is that States are free to choose the forum in which to settle their disputes under UNCLOS—the principal choices being ITLOS, the International Court of Justice ('ICJ'), and arbitration, as will be explained below. Beyond these, States Parties are permitted to choose another forum to settle their disputes by agreeing to adopt their own arrangements for dispute settlement at any stage thus opting out of the general arrangements. As a result, the residual dispute settlement regime under UNCLOS becomes applicable only where no settlement has been reached and where any agreement between the parties does not exclude any further dispute settlement procedure under UNCLOS. Thus, Part XV of UNCLOS governing dispute settlement requires the disputing parties to exchange views on the means to settle their dispute as well as provides some exceptions to compulsory dispute settlement under UNCLOS.[4]

The rest of this introductory chapter therefore considers ITLOS's place within the dispute settlement regime under UNCLOS, entities with access to ITLOS, other international agreements besides UNCLOS that confer jurisdiction on ITLOS, ITLOS's relationship and interaction with the other

---

[3] UNCLOS Arts 1(1) and 157(1).

[4] Virginia Commentary (n 2) 331–40; David H Anderson, 'Peaceful Settlement of Disputes under UNCLOS' in Jill Barrett and Richard Barnes (eds), *Law of the Sea: UNCLOS as a Living Treaty* (British Institute of Int'l & Comp Law 2016) 385, 388–92, 405–08; Rosemary R Rayfuse, 'The Future of Compulsory Dispute Settlement under the Law of the Sea Convention' (2005) 36 Victoria U Wellington L Rev 683; Dominik Zimmermann, *The Independence of International Courts: The Adherence of International Judiciary to a Fundamental Value of the Administration of Justice* (Hart 2014) 215–21; Philippe Gautier, 'The Settlement of Disputes' in David Joseph Attard, Malgosia Fitzmaurice, and Norman A Martinez Gutierrez (eds), *The IMLI Manual on International Maritime Law*, vol I (OUP 2014) 533. For an overview of the drafting history of Part XV of UNCLOS, see Virginia Commentary (n 2) 5–15.

principal choices of dispute settlement mechanisms, and the pros and cons of using ITLOS instead of other forums.

1. ITLOS's place within the dispute settlement regime under UNCLOS

UNCLOS provides for two types of jurisdiction—contentious jurisdiction to settle disputes between disputing parties, and advisory jurisdiction to render advisory opinions requested by entities entitled to seek such opinions.

The jurisdictional provisions of Part XV, covering Articles 279 through 299, are complex and must be set out here in some detail. Section 1, under the heading 'General Provisions', covers Articles 279 through 285. Article 279 stipulates the obligation among States Parties to settle 'any dispute between them concerning the interpretation or application of this Convention' by peaceful means in accordance with the UN Charter[5] and, to this end, they shall seek a solution by such means including negotiation, mediation, arbitration, or judicial settlement.[6] Article 280 of UNCLOS gives the disputing parties the autonomy to select their preferred means of dispute resolution by providing that nothing in Part XV of UNCLOS impairs the right of any States Parties to agree at any time to settle a dispute between them concerning the interpretation or application of UNCLOS by any peaceful means of their own choice.

By virtue of Article 281, if the States Parties which are parties to a dispute concerning the interpretation or application of UNCLOS have agreed to seek settlement of the dispute by a peaceful means of their own choice, the procedures provided for in Part XV apply only where (1) no settlement has been reached by recourse to such means; and (2) the agreement between the parties does not exclude any further procedure. Moreover, if the parties have also agreed on a time limit, this article applies only upon the expiration of such time limit. The rationale behind Article 281 is that

---

[5] 1 UNTS XVI. UN Charter Art 2(3): 'All Members shall settle their international disputes by peaceful means in such a manner that international peace and security, and justice, are not endangered.'

[6] UN Charter Art 33(1): 'The parties to any dispute, the continuance of which is likely to endanger the maintenance of international peace and security, shall, first of all, seek a solution by negotiation, enquiry, mediation, conciliation, arbitration, judicial settlement, resort to regional agencies or arrangements, or other peaceful means of their own choice.'

it prioritizes the right of States Parties to UNCLOS to resort to some other means of dispute settlement outside UNCLOS, but if such a settlement is not reached through the alternative procedure chosen by the disputing parties, Part XV of UNCLOS will become applicable and any disputing party will be entitled to resort then to its specified procedures.[7] Furthermore, the disputing parties that have agreed to resort to some other means of dispute settlement outside UNCLOS must clearly express their intention to exclude the application of Article 281.[8] Thus, in *Land Reclamation in and around the Straits of Johor (Malaysia v Singapore)*, ITLOS held that once Malaysia accepted Singapore's invitation to the meetings after Malaysia had already instituted arbitral proceedings under Annex VII to UNCLOS, with both parties agreeing that the meetings would be *without prejudice* to Malaysia's right to proceed with arbitration or to request ITLOS to prescribe provisional measures, then Article 281 of UNCLOS did not apply to bar recourse to UNCLOS dispute settlement.[9]

Article 282 also potentially limits recourse to Part XV measures. According to this Article, if the States Parties which are parties to a dispute concerning the interpretation or application of UNCLOS have agreed, through a general, regional, or bilateral agreement or otherwise, that such dispute shall, at the request of any party to the dispute, be submitted to a procedure entailing a binding decision, that procedure shall apply in lieu of the procedures provided for in UNCLOS, unless the parties to the dispute otherwise agree. This provision responds to the prevailing view at the Third Conference that parties would normally prefer to have the dispute settled in accordance with a procedure previously agreed upon.[10]

ITLOS has construed Article 282 narrowly. In one case, ITLOS held that the fact that the 1993 Convention for the Conservation of Southern Bluefin Tuna[11] applies between the parties and provides only for *consensual* dispute resolution does not preclude recourse to the compulsory proceedings

---

[7] Virginia Commentary (n 2) 22–23.

[8] The arbitral tribunal in *South China Sea Arbitration, Philippines v China* rules that the overall object and purpose of the system for dispute settlement as an integral part of UNCLOS requires the disputing parties to exclude the applicability of Art 281, which is a pivotal part of UNCLOS, by clearly expressing an intention to do so (Award, PCA Case No 2013-19, ICGJ 495 (PCA 2016) para 225).

[9] *Land Reclamation in and around the Straits of Johor (Malaysia v Singapore)* (Provisional Measures, Order of 8 October 2003) ITLOS Reports 2003, 10, 20–21 [53]–[57].

[10] Virginia Commentary (n 2) 25–26.

[11] 1819 UNTS 360.

entailing binding decisions in Part XV of UNCLOS.[12] In a subsequent case, ITLOS ruled that even if other agreements contain rights or obligations similar or identical to the rights or obligations set out in UNCLOS, the rights and obligations under those agreements have a separate existence from those under UNCLOS.[13] Moreover, the application of international law rules on interpretation of treaties to identical or similar provisions of different treaties may not yield the same results, having regard to, inter alia, differences in the contexts, objects, and purposes; subsequent practice of parties; and *travaux préparatoires*.[14] In any event, insofar as a dispute concerns the interpretation or application of UNCLOS and no other agreement, only the dispute settlement procedures under UNCLOS are relevant to that dispute.[15]

---

[12] *Southern Bluefin Tuna (New Zealand v Japan; Australia v Japan)* (Provisional Measures, Order of 27 August 1999) ITLOS Reports 1999, 280, 294 [55]. See also P Chandrasekhara Rao and Philippe Gautier, *The International Tribunal for the Law of the Sea: Law, Practice and Procedure* (Edward Elgar 2018) 115–18.

[13] *MOX Plant (Ireland v United Kingdom)* (Provisional Measures, Order of 3 December 2001) ITLOS Reports 2001, 95, 106 [50] and see also 106 [48]–[49]. Followed in *South China Sea Arbitration, Philippines v China*, PCA Case No 2013–19, Award on Jurisdiction and Admissibility of 29 October 2015 para 177.

[14] *MOX Plant* (n 13) 106 [51].

[15] ibid 106 [52]. See also Nigel Bankes, 'Precluding the Applicability of Section 2 of Part XV of the Law of the Sea Convention' (2017) 48 ODIL 239, 242–45; Alan Boyle, 'Litigating Climate Change under Part XII of the LOSC' (2019) 34 Int'l J Marine & Coastal L 458, 475–77. cf Barbara Kwiatkowska, 'The Ireland v UK (MOX Plant) Case: Applying the Doctrine of Treaty Parallelism' (2003) 18 Int'l J Maritime & Coastal L 1; Miguel García García-Revillo, *The Contentious and Advisory Jurisdiction of the International Tribunal for the Law of the Sea* (Brill/Nijhoff 2015) 53–76, 277–87. The International Court of Justice has also construed the scope of Article 282 narrowly in *Maritime Delimitation in the Indian Ocean (Somalia v Kenya)* (Preliminary Objections). Kenya's optional clause declaration pursuant to Art 36(2) of the ICJ's Statute (33 UNTS 993) provides, in relevant part, that Kenya accepts the ICJ's jurisdiction 'over all disputes … other than … [d]isputes in regard to which the parties to the dispute have agreed or shall agree to have recourse to some other method or methods of settlement'. In the ICJ's opinion, the *travaux préparatoires* of UNCLOS make clear that the negotiators gave particular attention to optional clause declarations when drafting Art 282, ensuring, through the use of the phrase 'or otherwise', that agreements to the ICJ's jurisdiction based on optional clause declarations fall within the scope of Art 282. Therefore, UNCLOS Art 282 should be interpreted so that an agreement to the ICJ's jurisdiction through optional clause declarations under Art 36(2) of the ICJ's Statute falls within the scope of UNCLOS Art 282 and applies 'in lieu' of procedures provided for in section 2 of Part XV of UNCLOS, even when such declarations contain a reservation to the same effect as that of Kenya. The contrary interpretation, opines the ICJ, would mean that, by ratifying a treaty which gives priority to agreed procedures resulting from the aforesaid optional clause declarations (pursuant to UNCLOS Art 282), States would have achieved precisely the opposite outcome, giving priority instead to the procedures contained in section 2 of Part XV of UNCLOS. Consequently, under Art 282, the optional clause declarations of the parties constitute an agreement, reached 'otherwise', to settle in the ICJ disputes concerning interpretation or application of UNCLOS, and the procedure before the ICJ shall thus apply 'in lieu' of procedures provided for in section 2 of Part XV: [2017] ICJ Rep 3, 46–50 [119]–[133].

The *EU–Chile Swordfish* dispute shows how ITLOS's jurisdiction under UNCLOS may exist in parallel with that of other international dispute settlement body, as a unilateral ban against access, landing, and transshipment in a port may implicate not only the law of the sea but also international trade law.[16]

In order to alleviate overfishing of swordfish, a highly migratory species, Chile prohibited the unloading and transit in Chile's ports of swordfish catches taken from the high seas bordering Chile's exclusive economic zone by foreign and Chilean vessels in contravention of Chilean conservation rules. Considering the European Union to have failed to cooperate with Chile to ensure the conservation of swordfish under UNCLOS, Chile denied fishing vessels of EU Member States operating in the South East Pacific access to Chilean ports to unload their swordfish catches either to land them for warehousing or to trans-ship them onto other vessels. Such access to Chilean ports was for the purpose of re-exporting swordfish to the markets of Member States of the North American Free Trade Agreement,[17] especially the USA. The EU considered Chile's denial of access to Chilean ports a violation of the 1994 General Agreement on Tariffs and Trade ('GATT').[18] After failing to settle the dispute by means of bilateral consultations, exchange of notes, and a bilateral technical commission, the EU brought the dispute before the World Trade Organization ('WTO') in April 2000, contending that Chile's ban on unloading of swordfish in its ports was inconsistent with GATT's Articles V (providing for freedom of transit for goods through the territory of each contracting party on their way to or from other contracting parties) and XI (prohibiting quantitative restrictions on imports or exports, subject to some exceptions for imports of agricultural or fishery products). However, it could be argued, the WTO's *Guide to GATT Law and Practice*[19] expressly excludes fishing vessels from GATT provisions. Also, Article XX(g) of GATT on the conservation of exhaustible natural resources arguably allowed Chile to undertake the measure in dispute. Yet, Chile considered the dispute to be a law of the sea dispute rather than a trade dispute. At Chile's invitation, the EU also subsequently

---

[16] Peter-Tobias Stoll and Silja Vöneky, 'The *Swordfish* Case: Law of the Sea v Trade' (2002) 62 ZaöRV 21, 26–28, 33–35; Marcus Rau, '*Comment:* The *Swordfish* Case: Law of the Sea v Trade' (2002) 62 ZaöRV 37; Marcos Orellana, 'The Swordfish Dispute between the EU and Chile at the ITLOS and the WTO' (2002) 71 Nordic JIL 55.

[17] (1993) 32 ILM 289.

[18] 1867 UNTS 187.

[19] *Guide to GATT Law and Practice*, vol 1 (World Trade Organization 1995) 213–17, 214 n 1.

agreed to settle the dispute under UNCLOS. Both sides invoked provisions of UNCLOS concerning: cooperation in ensuring conservation of highly migratory species (Art 64), conservation of the living resources of the high seas (Arts 116–19), dispute settlement (Art 297), good faith and non-abuse of right (Art 300), freedom of the high seas including freedom of fishing, subject to conservation obligations (Art 87), and prohibiting any State from subjecting any part of the high seas to its sovereignty (Art 89). On the request of the parties, ITLOS formed a Special Chamber comprising five ITLOS judges to decide, among other things, whether the European Community had complied with its obligations under UNCLOS to ensure conservation of swordfish in the fishing activities undertaken by vessels flying the flag of any of its Member States in the high seas adjacent to Chile's exclusive economic zone, and whether the Chilean Decree which purported to apply Chile's conservation measures relating to swordfish on the high seas violated UNCLOS. Nonetheless, both sides reached an agreement in January 2001 to suspend the proceedings at the WTO and at ITLOS by reactivating a bilateral technical commission to bridge the differences between the two sides, allowing port access for fish caught under a new scientific fisheries programme, and setting up a multilateral conservation forum for the Southeast Pacific. Both sides eventually agreed on an Understanding on 16 October 2008 to cooperate for the long-term conservation and management of the swordfish stocks in the South Eastern Pacific; and for Chile to allow EU vessels fishing for swordfish in the high seas access to designated Chilean ports for landings, trans-shipments, replenishing, or repairs. Once this Understanding was reached, the case was removed from ITLOS's docket.[20]

On the whole, two situations may be distinguished. The first situation is where separate cases relate to the law of the sea matters—it may then be appropriate for each forum with competent jurisdiction to carefully delineate the dispute before it under the respective international agreements so as to avoid conflicting decisions. The second is where the same facts give rise to two disputes concerning different matters, one concerning the law of the sea and submitted to the compulsory dispute settlement mechanism under Part XV of UNCLOS, and the other concerning another legal matter and submitted to a compulsory dispute settlement mechanism under another international agreement. When called upon to adjudicate on certain

---

[20] *Conservation and Sustainable Exploitation of Swordfish Stocks (Chile/European Union)* (Order of 16 December 2009) ITLOS Reports 2008–09, 13.

issues not strictly falling within its usual area of competence, each competent court or tribunal should bear in mind considerations of mutual respect and comity between international judicial bodies.[21]

The final provisions of section 1 concern a range of matters. Article 283 provides for the obligation of the disputing States Parties to exchange views on the means to settle their dispute, whereas Article 284 allows States Parties to submit their disputes to conciliation, if the disputing parties so agree. By virtue of Article 285, Articles 279 through 284 also apply to any *dispute* which pursuant to Part XI, section 5, governing the jurisdiction of the Seabed Disputes Chamber, is to be settled in accordance with procedures provided for in Part XV, and if an entity other than a State Party is a party to such a dispute, section 1 of Part XV applies *mutatis mutandis*.

Importantly, section 2 of Part XV, covering Articles 286 through 296, of UNCLOS regulates compulsory proceedings entailing binding decisions. Pursuant to Article 286, any dispute concerning the interpretation or application of UNCLOS shall, where no settlement has been reached by recourse to section 1, be submitted at the request of any party to the dispute to the court or tribunal having jurisdiction under this section. ITLOS has mandatory jurisdiction over prompt release of detained vessels and their crews under Article 292 and prescription of provisional measures under Article 290(5) (pending the establishment of an arbitral tribunal to which the dispute is being submitted), whereas its Seabed Disputes Chamber has mandatory jurisdiction over disputes related to activities in the Area. Otherwise, ITLOS's jurisdiction is shared with other forums for dispute settlement, as will be explained below.[22]

According to Article 287(1) of UNCLOS, when signing, ratifying, or acceding to UNCLOS or at any time thereafter, a State shall be free to choose, by means of a written declaration, one or more of the following means for the settlement of disputes concerning the interpretation or application of UNCLOS: (a) ITLOS; (b) the ICJ; (c) an arbitral tribunal constituted in accordance with Annex VII; (d) a special arbitral tribunal constituted in accordance with Annex VIII for one or more of the categories of disputes specified therein; namely, fisheries; protection and preservation of the marine environment; marine scientific research; or navigation, including pollution from vessels and by dumping. Article 287(2) adds that

---

[21] Rao and Gautier (n 12) 22–24.

[22] The relevant provisions on ITLOS's non-mandatory and non-exclusive jurisdiction are UNCLOS Arts 286, 287, and 288(1), (2), and (4), and the ITLOS Statute Art 21.

a declaration made under paragraph 1 shall not affect or be affected by the obligation of a State Party to accept the jurisdiction of ITLOS's Seabed Disputes Chamber to the extent and in the manner provided for in Part XI, section 5. By virtue of Article 287(3), a State Party to UNCLOS, which is a party to a dispute not covered by a declaration in force, shall be deemed to have accepted arbitration in accordance with Annex VII. According to Article 287(4), if the parties to a dispute have accepted the same procedure for the settlement of the dispute, it may be submitted only to that procedure, unless the parties otherwise agree. Pursuant to Article 287(5), if the parties to a dispute have not accepted the same procedure for the settlement of the dispute, it may be submitted only to arbitration in accordance with Annex VII, unless the parties otherwise agree.

Article 287 accommodates the competing positions at the Third UN Conference on the Law of the Sea. One group of States argued for conferring jurisdiction over law of the sea disputes on the ICJ, which had already rendered several important judgments on such disputes. These States emphasized the need for uniformity of international jurisprudence and the danger of having too many tribunals which might render conflicting decisions. A second group of States preferred a special Law of the Sea Tribunal, desiring a tribunal which would be less conservative than the ICJ, would better understand the new law of the sea, and would be more representative of various legal systems and the different regions of the world. As also pointed out by the latter group, the ICJ was only open to States, and in some law of the sea matters it would be important to allow international organizations, corporations, and individuals to have access to the tribunal. A third group of States opposed the establishment of such a tribunal because standing tribunals were too rigid, as the parties could not choose the judges most knowledgeable on the subject of the dispute and had to accept a pre-established procedure, which was ponderous and slow. In the view of some of those in the third group, arbitration was a more flexible procedure since parties were allowed to select the arbitrators and could therefore ensure a proper balance in the tribunal, and because parties could also design an expeditious arbitration procedure, allowing a prompt decision of their dispute, thus preventing a dangerous deterioration of relations between parties, which often resulted from protracted disputes. A fourth group of States advocated a more functional approach by having a special procedure for each main category of disputes (eg, those relating to seabed mining, navigation, fisheries, marine pollution, and marine scientific research), contending that as many law of the sea disputes were likely to relate to technical matters, it would not be appropriate for the tribunal to be composed only of lawyers; instead it should be selected primarily from lists of experts nominated by technically competent agencies. Lastly, a few States completely opposed the idea of binding third-party decisions and expressed preference for an optional protocol for the settlement of disputes.[23]

Arbitration is the residual, or 'default', dispute settlement mechanism under Article 287(5) applicable where the parties have not otherwise agreed as to the forum. However, Article 287(1)(d) also provides for special arbitral tribunals under Annex VIII to be heard by scientific and technical experts. This provision reflects two concerns at the Third Conference: first, the significance of scientific and technical considerations, and, second, the establishment of facts to settle disputes of technical or scientific nature.[24]

Pursuant to Article 288(1), a court or tribunal referred to in Article 287 shall have jurisdiction over any dispute concerning the interpretation or application of UNCLOS which is submitted to it in accordance with this Part XV. Article 288(2) adds that such court or tribunal shall have jurisdiction over any dispute concerning the interpretation or application of 'an international agreement related to the purposes of [UNCLOS], which is submitted to it in accordance with the agreement'. In this connection, Article 21 of the Statute provides that ITLOS's jurisdiction comprises all disputes and all applications submitted to it in accordance with UNCLOS and all matters specifically provided for in any other agreement which confers jurisdiction on ITLOS. Under Article 22 of the Statute, if all the parties to a treaty or convention already in force and concerning the subject matter covered by UNCLOS so agree, any disputes concerning the interpretation or application of such treaty or convention may, in accordance with such agreement, be submitted to ITLOS. This provision differs from Article 288(2) of UNCLOS in two respects: the treaty under which the dispute arises must already be in force at the time of the institution of proceedings, and the parties to that treaty or convention must agree to submit the dispute to ITLOS.[25]

Under Article 288(3), the Seabed Disputes Chamber and any other chamber or arbitral tribunal referred to in Part XI, section 5, shall have jurisdiction in any matter which is submitted to it in accordance therewith.

---

[23] Virginia Commentary (n 2) 40–45.

[24] ibid 439–43.

[25] Christopher Staker, 'Art 22 Annex VI' in Alexander Proelss (ed), *The United Nations Convention on the Law of the Sea: A Commentary* (Hart 2017) 2384.

Pursuant to Article 288(4) of UNCLOS, in the event of a dispute as to whether a court or tribunal has jurisdiction, the matter shall be settled by decision of that court or tribunal.

Several States Parties to UNCLOS have declared their preference for dispute settlement mechanism(s) as set out in Table 1.1.

Portugal and Timor-Leste have accepted all the mechanisms listed in Article 287 without indicating their preference. Cuba and Guinea-Bissau reject the ICJ's jurisdiction for any type of disputes, but have not declared their preference for the other mechanisms, either.

The following States Parties have chosen ITLOS as their first choice in specific disputes: Bangladesh (for maritime boundary disputes with Myanmar and India in the Bay of Bengal), Nigeria (for the settlement of disputes with Switzerland concerning the arrest and detention of the M/T 'San Padre Pio'), Panama (for the settlement of the dispute with Italy concerning the arrest and detention of the M/V 'Norstar'), and Saint Vincent and the

Table 1.1 First choices of UNCLOS dispute settlement mechanism at time of writing

ITLOS	ICJ	Annex VII arbitration	ITLOS, ICJ, and Annex VIII arbitration	ITLOS and ICJ	ITLOS and Annex VII arbitration
Algeria, Angola, Argentina, Austria, Bulgaria, Capo Verde, Chile, Croatia, DR Congo, Fiji, Germany, Greece, Hungary, Madagascar, Montenegro, Switzerland, Tanzania, Trinidad and Tobago, Tunisia, and Uruguay	Denmark, Honduras, Nicaragua, Norway, Sweden, and the UK	Belarus, Egypt, Russia, Slovenia, and Ukraine	Ecuador and Mexico	Australia, Belgium, Estonia, Finland, Italy, Latvia, Lithuania, Netherlands, Oman, Spain, and Togo	Canada

Grenadines (for the settlement of disputes concerning the arrest and detention of its vessels).

While Belarus, Russia, and Ukraine accept an Annex VII arbitral tribunal as their 'first choice' dispute settlement mechanism they will use a special arbitral tribunal constituted in accordance with Annex VIII for the settlement of disputes concerning fisheries, protection and preservation of the marine environment, marine scientific research, or navigation, including pollution from vessels and by dumping. They recognize ITLOS's jurisdiction over questions concerning the prompt release of detained vessels or their crews, as envisaged in Article 292 of UNCLOS.

Numerous parties to UNCLOS have not made any declaration under Article 287.[26]

Where two States Parties to UNCLOS select more than one common forum but in a different priority, there would be more than one forum jointly selected and the choice of forum would be left to the applicant.[27] In this respect, the Netherlands has made it clear in its declaration that in the event another State Party has chosen the ICJ and ITLOS without indicating precedence, the Netherlands should be considered as having chosen the ICJ only.

Obligations under UNCLOS for the 'prompt release' of certain vessels upon posting a reasonable bond, especially fishing vessels, have been

---

[26] Afghanistan, Albania, Antigua and Barbuda, Armenia, Azerbaijan, Bahamas, Bahrain, Barbados, Belize, Benin, Bhutan, Bolivia, Bosnia and Herzegovina, Botswana, Brazil, Brunei, Burkina Faso, Cameroon, Chad, China, Comoros, Congo, Cook Islands, Costa Rica, Cote d'Ivoire, Cyprus, Czech Republic, DR Congo, Djibouti, Dominica, Dominican Republic, Equatorial Guinea, Eswatini, European Union, France, Gabon, Gambia, Georgia, Ghana, Grenada, Guatemala, Guinea, Guyana, Haiti, Iceland, India, Indonesia, Iraq, Ireland, Jamaica, Japan, Jordan, Kenya, Kiribati, Kuwait, Laos, Lebanon, Lesotho, Liberia, Luxembourg, Malawi, Malaysia, Maldives, Mali, Malta, Marshall Islands, Mauritania, Mauritius, Micronesia, Monaco, Mongolia, Mozambique, Myanmar, New Zealand, Niger, Niue, North Macedonia, Pakistan, Palau, Papua New Guinea, Paraguay, Philippines, Poland, Qatar, Republic of Korea, Romania, Saint Kitts and Nevis, Saint Lucia, Samoa, Sao Tome and Principe, Saudi Arabia, Senegal, Serbia, Seychelles, Sierra Leone, Singapore, Slovakia, Solomon Islands, Somalia, South Africa, Sri Lanka, State of Palestine, Sudan, Suriname, Thailand, Tonga, Tuvalu, Uganda, UAE, Vanuatu, Vietnam, Yemen, Zambia, and Zimbabwe.

[27] Rao and Gautier (n 12) 102. According to former ITLOS Judge Treves (Tullio Treves, 'Article 287 Choice of Procedure' in Proelss, *The United Nations Convention on the Law of the Sea* (n 25) 1857), '[i]n case of declarations choosing more than one adjudicating body without stating a preference between them, the party that makes such multiple choice increases the possibility that the other party to the case has made the same choice.' He adds that there does not seem to be a real difference in effect between declarations choosing more than one adjudicating body without expressing a preference and those in which such preference is expressed, although in practice it may be prudent for plaintiff States to start proceedings before the court or tribunal indicated as the first preference by the defendant State.

contentious in practice. Article 292(1) stipulates that where the authorities of a State Party have detained a vessel flying the flag of another State Party and it is alleged that the detaining State has not complied with the provisions of UNCLOS for the prompt release of the vessel or its crew upon the posting of a reasonable bond or other financial security, the question of release from detention may be submitted to any court or tribunal agreed upon by the parties or, failing such agreement within 10 days from the time of detention, to a court or tribunal accepted by the detaining State under Article 287 or to ITLOS, unless the parties otherwise agree.

ITLOS is also available to States as an ad hoc consent-based forum. According to Article 54(5) of the ITLOS Rules, when the applicant proposes to found ITLOS's jurisdiction upon a consent thereto yet to be given or manifested by the party against which the application is made, the application shall be transmitted to that party. It shall not, however, be entered in the List of cases, nor any action be taken in the proceedings, unless and until the party against which such application is made consents to ITLOS's jurisdiction for the purposes of the case. This provision copies almost verbatim Article 38(5) of the Rules of the ICJ and is known as consent a posteriori or *forum prorogatum*,[28] based on the principle that while the consent of the parties confers jurisdiction on a court or tribunal, neither the Statute nor the Rules require(s) this consent to be expressed in any particular form.[29] As of this writing, no State Party to UNCLOS has expressly availed itself of the *forum prorogatum* option in any case before ITLOS. However, a special chamber of ITLOS has held, in *Dispute Concerning the Delimitation of the Maritime Boundary between Ghana and Côte d'Ivoire in the Atlantic Ocean (Ghana/Côte d'Ivoire)*, that the parties in dispute have implicitly broadened the scope of the dispute submitted to it, so that their 'dispute concerning the delimitation of their maritime boundary in the Atlantic Ocean' also embraces a dispute on international responsibility deriving from hydrocarbon activities in the disputed area. After concluding that its jurisdiction to decide on the final submission of Côte d'Ivoire concerning the alleged international responsibility of Ghana is not covered by the special agreement by which the dispute concerning delimitation was submitted to it, the ITLOS

---

[28] See *Anglo-Iranian Oil Co* (Jurisdiction) [1952] ICJ Rep 93, 113–14; *Certain Questions of Mutual Assistance in Criminal Matters (Djibouti v France)* (Merits) [2008] ICJ Rep 177, 181 [2]–[4]; *Corfu Channel (UK v Albania)* (Preliminary Objection) [1947–48] ICJ Rep 15, 27; *Armed Activities on the Territory of the Congo (New Application: 2002) (Democratic Republic of the Congo v Rwanda)* (Jurisdiction and Admissibility) [2006] ICJ Rep 6, 18–19 [21].

[29] *Corfu Channel* (Preliminary Objection) (n 28) 27.

special chamber finds that the parties, following institution of the proceedings, have 'implied by their conduct in the pleadings on the merits' that they have accepted its jurisdiction to deal with the claim concerning Ghana's international responsibility. The special chamber alludes to international jurisprudence to the effect that the jurisdiction of an international court or tribunal may be broadened by the conduct of parties in the proceedings (*forum prorogatum*), provided the attitude of the respondent State must be capable of being regarded as an unequivocal indication of the desire of that State to accept the broadened jurisdiction in a voluntary and indisputable manner.[30] Indeed, according to the jurisprudence of the ICJ and the Permanent Court of International Justice, the ICJ's predecessor, regarding the forms which the parties' expression of their consent to its jurisdiction may take, neither their respective Statutes nor Rules require this consent to be expressed in any particular form, and there is nothing to prevent the acceptance of jurisdiction from being effected by two separate and successive acts, instead of jointly and beforehand by a special agreement.[31]

Section 3 of Part XV on the limitations and exceptions to the applicability of section 2 of Part XV has only three articles—Articles 297 through 299. Articles 297 and 298 will be analysed in Chapter 3 below. By virtue of Article 299 on the right of the parties to agree upon a procedure, a dispute excluded under Article 297 or excepted by a declaration made under Article 298 from the dispute settlement procedures provided for in section 2 of Part XV may be submitted to such procedures only by agreement of the parties to the dispute, and nothing in section 3 impairs the right of the parties to the dispute to agree to some other procedure for the settlement of such dispute or to reach an amicable settlement. The purpose of Article 299 is to clarify that even in the case of exclusions and exceptions, the parties to a dispute retain the right to submit a dispute to the procedures of section 2 entailing a binding decision—this rule derives from the general provision in Article 280 according to which the parties to a dispute may at any time agree to settle it by any peaceful means of their own choice.[32]

---

[30] (Merits) ITLOS Reports 2017, 4, 148–50 [545–54]. For a criticism of this reasoning, see Bin Zhao, 'The Curious Case of Ghana/Côte d'Ivoire: A Consistent Approach to Hydrocarbon Activities in the Disputed Area?' (2020) 10 Asian JIL 94.

[31] *Armed Activities on the Territory of the Congo (New Application: 2002)* (Jurisdiction and Admissibility) 18 [21], quoting *Corfu Channel* (Preliminary Objection) (n 28) 27–28; *Rights of Minorities in Upper Silesia (Minority Schools)* (Merits) PCIJ Rep Series A, No 15, 23.

[32] Virginia Commentary (n 2) 142–43. cf Andrew Serdy, 'Art 299' in Proelss, *The United Nations Convention on the Law of the Sea* (n 25) 1932.

Section 5 of Part XI of UNCLOS regulates settlement of disputes and advisory opinions by the Seabed Disputes Chamber related to the activities in the Area. In addition to its contentious jurisdiction as expressly provided for in Part XV of UNCLOS, the full bench of ITLOS has ruled that, by virtue of Article 21 of its Statute, which is Annex VI to UNCLOS, ITLOS may give advisory opinions on 'all matters specifically provided for in any other agreement which confers jurisdiction on [ITLOS]', as will be explained in detail in Chapter 4 below.

2. Entities with access to ITLOS

Article 291(1) of UNCLOS provides that the UNCLOS Part XV dispute settlement procedures shall be open to States Parties. Pursuant to Article 291(2), the UNCLOS dispute settlement procedures shall also be open to entities other than States Parties only as specifically provided for in UNCLOS.[33] In this connection, Article 20 of the Statute of ITLOS stipulates, in paragraph 1, that ITLOS 'shall be open to States Parties' and, in paragraph 2, that ITLOS

shall be open to entities other than States Parties in any case expressly provided for in Part XI or in any case submitted pursuant to any other agreement conferring jurisdiction on the [ITLOS] which is accepted by all the parties to that case.[34]

In the event of a dispute as to whether ITLOS has jurisdiction *ratione personae* under Article 20 of its Statute, the matter is to be settled by ITLOS's decision, as provided in Article 288(4) of UNCLOS.

The authors of the highly regarded Virginia Commentary examine the drafting history of Article 20(2) of the Statute in some detail and reach the following conclusions.[35] The entities that can become parties to UNCLOS include intergovernmental organizations to which Member States have

---

[33] For a drafting history of Article 291, see Virginia Commentary (n 2) 60–65.

[34] See also Budislav Vukas, 'The International Tribunal for the Law of the Sea: Some Features of the International Judicial Institution' (1997) 37 Indian JIL 372, 380; Dolliver Nelson, 'The International Tribunal for the Law of the Sea: Some Issues' (1997) 37 Indian JIL 388, 395; Gudmundur Eiriksson, *The International Tribunal for the Law of the Sea* (Brill/Nijhoff 2000) 115; García-Revillo (n 15) 288–94.

[35] Virginia Commentary (n 2) 368, 374–78, 392–93.

transferred competence over UNCLOS matters.[36] Other entities listed in Article 305(1)(b), (c), (d), and (e)[37] may also become parties to UNCLOS. These provisions principally concern self-governing territories that are either not yet fully independent States or are associated States. All of these entities have access to ITLOS in appropriate cases and thus may be parties to a dispute, since any reference to States Parties in UNCLOS would include all of these categories of entities. By contrast, 'entities other than States Parties' would include States which are not parties to UNCLOS, the entities listed in Article 305 that have not become parties, other international intergovernmental organizations, the Authority (including the Enterprise and its other organs given separate juridical personality), State enterprises, and natural or juridical persons. However, such entities must be specified in the agreement by which all the parties to a case have accepted ITLOS's jurisdiction or in a case expressly provided for in Part XI concerning activities in the Area (which in principle restricts access of the entities other than States Parties to the Seabed Disputes Chamber only, where such cases may involve mining companies or consortia), as will be elaborated in Chapter 3 below.

It may be recalled that under Article 288(2) of UNCLOS a court or tribunal chosen by the parties to settle their disputes 'shall also have jurisdiction over any dispute concerning the interpretation or application of an international agreement related to the purposes of [UNCLOS], which is submitted to it in accordance with the agreement'. In addition, Article 21 of ITLOS's Statute stipulates that its jurisdiction comprises all disputes and all

---

[36] As contemplated under UNCLOS Article 305(1)(f), in accordance with Annex IX. Annex IX of UNCLOS Art 1 reads: 'For the purposes of article 305 and of this Annex, "international organization" means an intergovernmental organization constituted by States to which its Member States have transferred competence over matters governed by this Convention, including the competence to enter into treaties in respect of those matters.' To date, only the European Union fits this definition.

[37] Art 305(1):

(b) Namibia, represented by the United Nations Council for Namibia; (c) all self-governing associated States which have chosen that status in an act of self-determination supervised and approved by the United Nations in accordance with General Assembly resolution 1514 (XV) and which have competence over the matters governed by this Convention, including the competence to enter into treaties in respect of those matters; (d) all self-governing associated States which, in accordance with their respective instruments of association, have competence over the matters governed by this Convention, including the competence to enter into treaties in respect of those matters; (e) all territories which enjoy full internal self-government, recognized as such by the United Nations, but have not attained full independence in accordance with General Assembly resolution 1514 (XV) and which have competence over the matters governed by this Convention, including the competence to enter into treaties in respect of those matters ...

applications submitted to it in accordance with UNCLOS 'and all matters specifically provided for in any other agreement which confers jurisdiction on [ITLOS]'. The word 'agreement' in Articles 20 and 21 of the ITLOS Statute is broader than 'an international agreement' referred to in Article 288(2) of UNCLOS.[38] In broadening access to ITLOS, the Third Conference found it necessary to extend the possible ranges of jurisdictional bases of ITLOS by using the expression 'any other agreement' in these two articles of the Statute. Article 20 of the Statute specifies the States or other entities to which ITLOS shall be open, whereas Article 21 of the same establishes the scope of the jurisdiction of ITLOS *ratione materiae* in respect of all entities to which ITLOS is open. Due to the specific provision in Article 20(2) of the ITLOS Statute, the procedures available under Part XI and ITLOS's Statute are thus available to other entities to the extent accepted by all the parties to the agreement the interpretation or application of which may be in dispute; however, the Part XV restrictions applicable to disputes relating to the interpretation or application of UNCLOS itself (as discussed in Chapter 3) are not applicable to disputes arising under such separate agreements.[39]

By virtue of Article 31 of the ITLOS Statute, only a State Party to UNCLOS has a right to intervene in a dispute before ITLOS. This results from strong objections to giving the right to intervene to entities other than States Parties to UNCLOS.

3. Other international agreements besides UNCLOS that confer jurisdiction on ITLOS

It is apparent from the preceding discussion that other international agreements besides UNCLOS may confer jurisdiction on ITLOS. The following

---

[38] In the Third Conference President's first text, the international agreements which could confer jurisdiction on ITLOS were described as being public or private. Subsequently, the catalogue of entities was reduced, and the reference to territories and the reference to 'public or private' international agreements was deleted. Nevertheless, deletion of the word 'international' before 'agreement' implied that the particular definitions of 'treaty' in the 1969 Vienna Convention on the Law of Treaties (1155 UNTS 331) and in the 1986 Vienna Convention on the Law of Treaties between States and International Organizations or between International Organizations [(1986) 25 ILM 543] would not be applicable to the agreements envisaged by Arts 20 and 21 of the ITLOS Statute. See Virginia Commentary (n 2) 378–80.

[39] Virginia Commentary (n 2) 375.

are some of the major examples of such treaties as regards fisheries management, pollution, and protection of underwater cultural heritage.

Under Article IX(3) of the 1993 FAO Agreement to Promote Compliance with International Conservation and Management Measures by Fishing Vessels on the High Seas,[40] any unresolved dispute with regard to the interpretation or application of the provisions of this Agreement shall, with the consent of all parties to the dispute, be referred for settlement to the ICJ, ITLOS, or arbitration.

Another major treaty in the field of fisheries management is the 1995 UN Agreement for the Implementation of the Provisions of the UN Convention on the Law of the Sea of 10 December 1982 relating to the Conservation and Management of Straddling Fish Stocks and Highly Migratory Species Fish Stocks ('FSA').[41] It contains a detailed dispute settlement regime with a number of points of interaction with UNCLOS. Article 30 of the FSA stipulates that the provisions relating to the settlement of disputes set out in Part XV of UNCLOS apply *mutatis mutandis* to any dispute between States Parties to the FSA concerning the interpretation or application of the FSA, whether or not they are also parties to UNCLOS. Likewise, the UNCLOS dispute settlement provisions apply *mutatis mutandis* to any dispute between States Parties to the FSA concerning the interpretation or application of a subregional, regional, or global fisheries agreement relating to straddling fish stocks or highly migratory fish stocks to which they are parties, including any dispute concerning the conservation and management of such stocks, whether or not they are also parties to UNCLOS.

Any procedure accepted by a State Party to both the FSA and UNCLOS pursuant to Article 287 of UNCLOS shall apply to the settlement of disputes under the FSA, unless that State Party, when signing, ratifying, or acceding to the FSA, or at any time thereafter, has contracted out by accepting another procedure pursuant to Article 287 of UNCLOS for the settlement of disputes under the FSA.

A State Party to the FSA which is not a party to UNCLOS shall be free to choose, by a written declaration, one or more of the means set out in Article 287(1) of UNCLOS for the settlement of disputes under the FSA. Article 287 of UNCLOS shall apply to such a declaration, as well as to any dispute to which such State is a party which is not covered by a declaration in force. Any court or tribunal to which a dispute has been submitted under

---

[40] 2221 UNTS 91.
[41] 2167 UNTS 88.

Part VIII (Peaceful Settlement of Disputes) of the FSA shall apply the relevant provisions of UNCLOS, of the FSA, and of any relevant subregional, regional, or global fisheries agreement, as well as generally accepted standards for the conservation and management of living marine resources and other rules of international law not incompatible with UNCLOS, with a view to ensuring the conservation of the straddling fish stocks and highly migratory fish stocks concerned.

As regards urgent provisional measures, pursuant to Article 31 of the FSA, the court or tribunal to which the dispute has been submitted under Part VIII of the FSA may prescribe any provisional measures which it considers appropriate under the circumstances to preserve the respective rights of the parties to the dispute or to prevent damage to the stocks in question, as well as in the circumstances referred to in Articles 7(5)[42] and 16(2)[43] of the FSA. However, a State Party to the FSA which is not a party to UNCLOS may declare that, notwithstanding Article 290(5) of UNCLOS on the prescription of provisional measures by ITLOS pending the establishment of an arbitral tribunal to which the dispute is being submitted, ITLOS shall not be entitled to prescribe, modify, or revoke provisional measures without the agreement of such State.

Several regional fisheries agreements allow their respective States Parties to resort to the compulsory dispute settlement procedures entailing binding decisions provided for in section 2 of Part XV of UNCLOS irrespective of whether or not the parties to the dispute are also parties to UNCLOS.[44]

---

[42] FSA Art 7(5) reads:

> 5. Pending agreement on compatible conservation and management measures, the States concerned, in a spirit of understanding and cooperation, shall make every effort to enter into provisional arrangements of a practical nature. In the event that they are unable to agree on such arrangements, any of the States concerned may, for the purpose of obtaining provisional measures, submit the dispute to a court or tribunal in accordance with the procedures for the settlement of disputes provided for in Part VIII.

[43] FSA Art 16(2) stipulates in its pertinent part that 'States' shall act in good faith and make every effort to agree without delay on conservation and management measures to be applied in the carrying out of fishing operations in the area of the high seas surrounded entirely by an area under the national jurisdiction of a single State. If, within a reasonable period of time, the fishing States concerned and the coastal State are unable to agree on such measures, they shall make every effort to enter into provisional arrangements or measures of a practical nature. Pending the establishment of such provisional arrangements or measures, the States concerned shall take measures in respect of vessels flying their flag in order that they not engage in fisheries which could undermine the stocks concerned.

[44] eg, 2000 Convention on the Conservation and Management of Highly Migratory Fish Stocks in the Western and Central Pacific Ocean (2001) 40 ILM 277, Art 31; 2001 Convention on the Conservation and Management of Fisheries Resources in the South East Atlantic Ocean

Article 16(3) of the 1996 Protocol to the Convention on the Prevention of Marine Pollution by Dumping or Wastes and Other Matters[45] allows States Parties to this Protocol that are parties to a dispute to agree to use one of the procedures listed in Article 287(1) of UNCLOS, whether or not they are also States Parties to UNCLOS.

According to Article 25 of the 2001 UNESCO Convention on the Protection of the Underwater Cultural Heritage,[46] if mediation to settle a dispute is not undertaken or if there is no settlement by mediation, the provisions relating to the settlement of disputes set out in Part XV of UNCLOS apply *mutatis mutandis* to any dispute between States Parties concerning the interpretation or application of the 2001 UNESCO Convention, whether or not they are also parties to UNCLOS. Any procedure chosen by a State Party to the 2001 UNESCO Convention and to UNCLOS pursuant to Article 287 of the latter shall apply to the settlement of disputes under this article, unless that State Party chooses another procedure pursuant to Article 287 for the purpose of the settlement of disputes arising out of the 2001 UNESCO Convention. Besides, a State Party to the 2001 UNESCO Convention which is not a party to UNCLOS is free to choose, by means of a written declaration, one or more of the means set out in Article 287(1) of UNCLOS specifically for the purpose of settlement of disputes under this article, and Article 287 shall apply to such a declaration, as well as to any dispute to which such State is party, which is not covered by a declaration in force.[47]

4. ITLOS's relationship and interaction with the other principal choices of dispute settlement mechanisms

Judgments and reasoning by an international court or tribunal only bind the parties to the particular dispute before it. However, ITLOS and the other three choices of dispute settlement mechanisms strive to develop a

---

(2002) 41 ILM 257, Art 24; 2006 Southern Indian Ocean Fisheries Agreement (OJ L196/15) Art 20(1).

[45] (1997) 36 ILM 1.
[46] (2001) 41 ILM 37.
[47] See also 2007 Nairobi Convention on the Removal of Wrecks (IMO Doc LEG/CONF/16/ 19 of 23 May 2007) Art 15.

consistent and coherent jurisprudence in construing UNCLOS.[48] Examples are readily found in the field of maritime delimitation. ITLOS has cited the ICJ's jurisprudence on effects of islands on maritime boundary delimitation and the jurisprudence on maritime boundary delimitation process.[49] ITLOS has also alluded to the reasoning of an Annex VII arbitral tribunal regarding various adjustments which could be made within the relevant legal constraints to produce an equitable result,[50] and the view that there is in law only a single continental shelf rather than an inner continental shelf and a separate extended or outer continental shelf.[51] Where ITLOS faces new legal issues not previously decided by it, it seeks guidance from the ICJ's case law, such as the one on evidence of a tacit legal agreement[52] and the one on *forum prorogatum*.[53]

For its part, the ICJ has cited ITLOS's judgment in the *Dispute concerning Delimitation of the Maritime Boundary between Bangladesh and Myanmar in the Bay of Bengal (Bangladesh/Myanmar)* extending the line of the single maritime boundary beyond the 200-nm limit until it reaches the area where the rights of third States may be affected; it also agreed with ITLOS

---

[48] Anderson (n 4) 408–11, 415; Philippe Sands, 'Of Courts and Competition: Dispute Settlement under Part XV of UNCLOS' in Rüdiger Wolfrum, Maja Seršić, and Trpimir M Šošić (eds), *Contemporary Development in International Law: Essays in Honour of Budislav Vukas* (Brill/Nijhoff 2015) 796–99; Alexander Proelss, 'Contributions of the ITLOS to Strengthening the Regime for the Protection of the Marine Environment' in Angela Del Vecchio and Roberto Virzo (eds), *Interpretation of the United Nations Convention on the Law of the Sea by International Courts and Tribunals* (Springer 2019) 105.

[49] *Delimitation of the Maritime Boundary in the Bay of Bengal (Bangladesh/Myanmar)* ITLOS Reports 2012, 4, 47 [151], 56 [185], 66 [233]–[234], 72–73 [264], 81 [294]–[295], 87 [326], 88 [328] and [330]. See also *Dispute Concerning the Delimitation of the Maritime Boundary between Ghana and Côte d'Ivoire in the Atlantic Ocean* (Merits), ITLOS Reports 2017, 4, 71 [215], 74 [226], 82 [262], 88 [285], 116 [409], 127–28 [452–54], 131–33[469–77], 144 [533].

[50] *Delimitation of the Maritime Boundary in the Bay of Bengal* (n 49) 87 [327], citing *Arbitration between Barbados and the Republic of Trinidad and Tobago, relating to the delimitation of the exclusive economic zone and the continental shelf between them* (Award) PCA 11 Apr 2006 RIAA, vol XXVII, 147, 243 [373].

[51] *Delimitation of the Maritime Boundary in the Bay of Bengal* (n 49) 96–97 [362], quoting *Arbitration between Barbados and the Republic of Trinidad and Tobago* (n 50) 208–09 [213]. Reiterated by the special chamber of ITLOS in *Dispute Concerning the Delimitation of the Maritime Boundary between Ghana and Côte d'Ivoire in the Atlantic Ocean* (n 49) 136 [490].

[52] *Dispute Concerning the Delimitation of the Maritime Boundary between Ghana and Côte d'Ivoire in the Atlantic Ocean* (n 49) 70 [212], citing *Territorial and Maritime Dispute between Nicaragua and Honduras in the Caribbean Sea (Nicaragua v Honduras)* [2007] ICJ Rep 659, 735 [253].

[53] *Dispute Concerning the Delimitation of the Maritime Boundary between Ghana and Côte d'Ivoire in the Atlantic Ocean* (n 49) 150 [552], quoting *Armed Activities on the Territory of the Congo (New Application: 2002)* (Jurisdiction and Admissibility) 18–19 [21].

in making a 'clear distinction' under UNCLOS between the delimitation of continental shelf and the delineation of its outer limits.[54]

Arbitral tribunal constituted under Annex VII of UNCLOS also make use of ITLOS's jurisprudence. The Annex VII arbitral tribunal in *Bay of Bengal Maritime Boundary Delimitation (Bangladesh v India)* reasons that since Articles 74 and 83 of UNCLOS do not provide for a particular method of delimitation, the appropriate delimitation method—if the States concerned cannot agree—is left to be determined through the mechanisms for the peaceful settlement of disputes and, in this connection, the arbitral tribunal recalls the principles enunciated by ITLOS in *Dispute concerning Delimitation of the Maritime Boundary between Bangladesh and Myanmar in the Bay of Bengal (Bangladesh/Myanmar)* as part of international case law which constitutes an *acquis judiciaire*, a source of international law under Article 38(1)(d) of the Statute of the ICJ, and should be read into Articles 74 and 83 of UNCLOS.[55] This reasoning is, in turn, cited by a special chamber of ITLOS in a subsequent case.[56] Such interaction is unsurprising. Other than the desire of different bodies to promote a unified approach to the law of the sea, ICJ and ITLOS judges have frequently been appointed as arbitrators in Annexe VII cases.

Nonetheless, ITLOS does not treat the ICJ's or Annex VII arbitral tribunals' reasoning and decisions as binding precedents. For example, in its application to ITLOS for the prescription of provisional measures in *Detention of three Ukrainian naval vessels (Ukraine v Russian Federation)*, Ukraine cited the ruling of the Annex VII arbitral tribunal in *South China Sea Arbitration, Philippines v China*[57] to support its argument that the dispute pending before ITLOS did not concern military activities excluded from compulsory dispute settlement in accordance with Article 298(1)(b) of UNCLOS if the party whose actions were at issue characterized them as non-military in nature.[58] ITLOS did not refer to that arbitral award in its reasoning on this point[59] even though two of the ITLOS judges in *Detention*

---

[54] *Territorial and Maritime Dispute (Nicaragua v Colombia)* [2012] ICJ Rep 624, 668 [125], citing ITLOS's Judgment in *Delimitation of the Maritime Boundary in the Bay of Bengal* (n 49) paras 462 and 376–94, respectively.

[55] *Bay of Bengal Maritime Boundary Delimitation (Bangladesh v India)* ICGJ 479 (PCA 2014) para 339.

[56] *Dispute Concerning the Delimitation of the Maritime Boundary between Ghana and Côte d'Ivoire in the Atlantic Ocean* (n 49) 86 [281].

[57] ICGJ 495 (PCA 2016) para 938.

[58] *Detention of three Ukrainian naval vessels (Ukraine v Russian Federation)* (Provisional Measures, Order of 25 May 2019) ITLOS Reports 2019 para 56.

[59] ibid paras 63–77.

of three Ukrainian naval vessels and two former ITLOS judges served as arbitrators in the *South China Sea* case.

5. The pros and cons of using ITLOS instead of other forums

Where disputing parties have not chosen a means for the settlement of disputes under Article 287(1) of UNCLOS or do not agree on the same choice of dispute settlement forum, they must accept arbitration in accordance with Annex VII of UNCLOS. According to the President of the Third Conference, the logic for this default mechanism is that 'whilst arbitration was not everyone's first choice, it was a method acceptable to all States because it is the parties to the dispute that choose the arbiters'.[60]

Some other possible advantages of resorting to an Annex VII arbitral tribunal could be that arbitration is more acceptable to domestic public opinion, especially for the losing party, since it is not a supranational body to which the disputing parties may be perceived to have ceded their sovereignty. In addition, the increased confidentiality available in arbitration and the bar to third-party intervention in arbitration may make arbitration a better option than either ITLOS or the ICJ, neither of which is as stringent as arbitration in this respect.[61]

Not infrequently, however, disputing parties have agreed to transfer their disputes already submitted to an Annex VII arbitral tribunal to ITLOS instead.[62]

Unlike an Annex VII arbitral tribunal, ITLOS and the ICJ have detailed standing rules of procedure and benches of elected judges at permanent

---

[60] Tommy Koh, *Building a New Legal Order for the Oceans* (NUS Press 2020) 43. See also Virginia Commentary (n 2) 421.

[61] Sicco Rah and Tilo Wallrabenstein, 'The International Tribunal for the Law of the Sea and Its Future' (2007) 21 Ocean YB 41, 53–54, cited in Douglas W Gates, 'International Law Adrift: Forum Shopping, Forum Rejection, and the Future of Maritime Dispute Resolution' (2017) 18 Chicago JIL 287, 305–06.

[62] eg, *M/V 'Saiga' (No 2) (Saint Vincent and the Grenadines v Guinea)* ITLOS Case No 2 in 1998; *Conservation and Sustainable Exploitation of Swordfish Stocks (Chile/European Union)* ITLOS Case No 7 in 2000; *Delimitation of the Maritime Boundary in the Bay of Bengal (Bangladesh/Myanmar)* ITLOS Case No 16 in 2009; *M/V 'Virginia G' (Panama/Guinea-Bissau)* ITLOS Case No 19 in 2011; *Dispute Concerning the Delimitation of the Maritime Boundary between Ghana and Côte d'Ivoire in the Atlantic Ocean (Ghana v Côte d'Ivoire)* ITLOS Case No 23 in 2014; *Dispute Concerning Delimitation of the Maritime Boundary between Mauritius and Maldives in the Indian Ocean (Mauritius/Maldives)* ITLOS Case No 28 in September 2019; and *M/T 'San Padre Pio' (No 2) (Switzerland/Nigeria)* ITLOS Case No 29 in December 2019.

premises whose costs are defrayed by their respective budgets.[63] Unless otherwise decided by ITLOS, each party shall bear its own costs[64]—namely, lawyers' fees, travelling, accommodation, and other expenses—while appearing before ITLOS. Annex VII arbitral tribunals have to be constituted and accommodated ad hoc as well as establish their own rules of procedures, including those on third-party intervention, use of experts,[65] approach to evidence, and availability of interim relief and interlocutory decisions. Parties to a dispute submitted to an Annex VII arbitral tribunal must pay the expenses incurred and fees charged by the arbitrators as well as pay for the secretarial services provided and premises used. Disputing parties frequently fail to agree on the remaining three arbitrators who have to be appointed by the President of ITLOS in consultation with the parties.[66]

The authoritativeness of the chosen forum and arbitrators/judges could be a factor for disputing parties in their choice of the forum. The ICJ has a longer record in international dispute settlement, including in the law of the sea, than ITLOS. However, ITLOS is a more specialized body than the ICJ in relation to the interpretation and application of UNCLOS.[67] ITLOS's 21 elected judges are more representative of the world's legal systems than the 15-judge ICJ, and, unlike the ICJ, is 'not umbilically connected to the UN Security Council'[68] and the UN General Assembly, the two principal political organs of the UN which proceed independently of one another to elect ICJ judges.[69]

To date, the ICJ, but not ITLOS, has been used to adjudicate law of the sea disputes where one or more of the disputing parties is/are not party to UNCLOS.[70] This is probably because States not party to UNCLOS may not be aware that they may resort to ITLOS to settle their disputes thanks to Articles 20(2), 21, and 22 of the ITLOS Statute, as explained above.

---

[63] According to ITLOS Statute Art 19, ITLOS's expenses shall be borne by the States Parties to UNCLOS and by the International Seabed Authority on such terms and in such a manner as shall be decided at meetings of the States Parties. When an entity other than a State Party or the Authority is a party to a case submitted to it, ITLOS shall fix the amount which that party is to contribute towards ITLOS's expenses.

[64] Statute Art 34.

[65] See also Lucas Carlos Lima, 'Use of Experts in the International Tribunal for the Law of the Sea and Annex VII Arbitral Tribunals' in Del Vecchio and Virzo (n 48) 407.

[66] Anderson (n 4) 404; cf Sands (n 48) 794–96.

[67] cf Zimmermann (n 4) 219.

[68] Sands (n 48) 793. Also, Zimmermann (n 4) 220–21.

[69] ICJ Statute Art 8.

[70] Anastasia Telesetsky, 'The International Tribunal for the Law of the Sea: Seeking the Legitimacy of State Consent' in Nienke Grossman and others (eds), *Legitimacy and International Courts* (Cambridge University Press 2018) 174, 181.

In general, an Annex VII arbitration and ITLOS take relatively much shorter time to dispose of cases in their respective dockets than the ICJ does.[71]

An analysis of the cases submitted to the forums listed in Article 287(1) of UNCLOS by subject matter reveals the frequency with which different forums hear similar types of cases. ITLOS hears every law enforcement prompt release case under Article 292 because UNCLOS grants ITLOS exclusive jurisdiction over those matters. Parties with cases tangentially dealing with the detention or confiscation of ships but not covered under Article 292 also tend to choose ITLOS as a forum because of its subject matter expertise in the field, including where the vessel is no longer detained and the applicant seeks damages for alleged violations of UNCLOS.[72] In other matters, such as boundary delimitation, fisheries, and marine environmental protection, there is competition between the forums. Additionally, States frequently resort to the provisional measures option under Article 290 to invoke the jurisdiction of both ITLOS and an Annex VII arbitral tribunal hoping one or both will render a favourable ruling.[73]

---

[71] Sands (n 48) 793–94.

[72] eg, *M/V 'Norstar' (Panama v Italy)*, which ITLOS rendered its judgment on the merits on 10 April 2019.

[73] Gates (n 61) 299–304, 320.

2

Overview of ITLOS's Composition, Organization, Structure, and Rules of Procedure

1. Introduction

The International Tribunal for the Law of the Sea, or ITLOS, is constituted and functions in accordance with the provisions of the 1982 United Nations Convention on the Law of the Sea[1] ('UNCLOS') and its Statute (which is Annex VI to UNCLOS). The seat of ITLOS is in Hamburg, Federal Republic of Germany, although ITLOS may sit and exercise its functions elsewhere whenever it considers this desirable.[2] ITLOS's premises are provided by the German Government free of rent. ITLOS's official working languages are English and French.

The United Nations recognizes ITLOS as an autonomous international judicial body with jurisdiction as provided for in the relevant provisions of UNCLOS and its Statute. For its part, ITLOS recognizes the UN's responsibilities under the UN Charter,[3] in particular in the fields of international peace and security, economic, social, cultural, and humanitarian development, and the peaceful settlement of international disputes. The UN and ITLOS each undertakes to respect the status and mandate of the other and to establish cooperative working relations pursuant to the provisions of the Agreement on Cooperation and Relationship between the UN and ITLOS.[4] With a view to facilitating the effective attainment of their objectives and the coordination of their activities, they shall consult and cooperate,

---

[1] 1833 UNTS 3, in force as of 16 November 1994.
[2] Statute Art 1.
[3] 1 UNTS XVI.
[4] The 1997 Agreement on Cooperation and Relationship between the United Nations and the International Tribunal for the Law of the Sea (2000 UNTS 467) Art 1.

whenever appropriate, on matters of mutual concern, and pursue, whenever appropriate, initiatives to coordinate their activities.[5] ITLOS also has an observer status in the UN General Assembly,[6] enabling it to participate in the UN General Assembly's meetings and work when matters of relevance to ITLOS are being considered. Moreover, ITLOS's Registrar transmits to the UN information and documentation relating to ITLOS's work, including documentation relating to applications, pleadings, oral proceedings, orders, judgments, and other communications and documentation before ITLOS.

2. Full-bench ITLOS

ITLOS is composed of 21 judges elected by secret ballot by the States Parties to UNCLOS[7] from among persons nominated by States Parties who enjoy the highest reputation for fairness and integrity and of recognized competence in the field of the law of the sea. Under the Statute, the body of judges taken as a whole shall represent the principal legal systems of the world and equitable geographical distribution shall be assured.[8] No two judges may be nationals of the same State.[9] There shall be no fewer than three members from each of the five geographical groups as established by the UN General Assembly.[10] The main rationale for having 21 judges instead of a smaller number is to ensure expeditious discharge of ITLOS's functions and to allow ITLOS to form the Seabed Disputes Chamber as well as special chambers referred to in Article 15 of the Statute which deal with particular categories of disputes if the parties so request.[11]

ITLOS judges are elected for nine years and may be re-elected. However, of the judges elected at the first election, the terms of seven members expired

---

[5] ibid Art 2.

[6] ibid Art 3(1).

[7] The European Union does not participate in the voting process, including the election of ITLOS judges, due to Annex IX to UNCLOS Art 4(4), which reads: 'Participation of [an international organization which is party to UNCLOS] shall in no case entail an increase of the representation to which its Member States which are States Parties would otherwise be entitled, including rights in decision-making.'

[8] Statute Art 2.

[9] Statute Art 3(1).

[10] Statute Art 3(2).

[11] Dominik Zimmermann, *The Independence of International Courts: The Adherence of International Judiciary to a Fundamental Value of the Administration of Justice* (Hart 2014) 239–40.

at the end of three years, and the terms of seven more members expired after six years.[12] The judges whose terms were to expire earlier were chosen by lot drawn by the UN Secretary-General immediately after the first election of judges in 1996. This means States Parties to UNCLOS now regularly elect one third of the 21 ITLOS judges every three years. A quorum of two thirds of the States Parties is required for the election of ITLOS judges, and those elected must obtain the largest number of votes and a two-thirds majority of the States Parties present and voting, provided such majority includes a majority of the States Parties.[13]

On 18 October 1996, the ceremonial inauguration of ITLOS was held in Hamburg, Germany, in the presence of the UN Secretary-General. On 13 November 1997, the first case, M/V 'Saiga' (Saint Vincent and the Grenadines v Guinea), concerning the application for the prompt release of an oil tanker flying the flag of Saint Vincent and the Grenadines and its crew being detained by Guinea, was submitted to ITLOS, which rendered its judgment in that case less than a month thereafter, on 4 December 1997.[14]

As regards the question of equitable geographical representation, the 2009 Meeting of States Parties to UNCLOS approved the following allocation of seats on ITLOS (effective 2011): five members of ITLOS shall be from the Group of African States; another five members shall be from the Group of Asian States; another three members shall be from the Group of Eastern European States; another four members shall be from the Group of Latin American and Caribbean States; another three members shall be from the Group of Western European and Other States; and the remaining one member shall be elected from among the Group of African States, the Group of Asian States, and the Group of Western European and Other States (the 'floating seat'). Responding to demands by the African Group and the Asian Group, the 'floating seat' arrangement reduces the automatic quota of the Western European and Other States in elections for the ITLOS judges by one seat in order to make the distribution of seats among geographical regions more equitable.[15] Yet, Professor David Joseph Attard from Malta was elected to serve for a nine-year term at the election held in June 2011 to fill this floating seat, after several rounds of voting in which he beat three candidates from Africa. While this arrangement was expressly

---

[12] Statute Art 5(1) and (2).

[13] Statute Art 4(4).

[14] M/V 'Saiga' (Saint Vincent and the Grenadines v Guinea) (Prompt Release) ITLOS Reports 1997, 16.

[15] Doc SPLOS/201 (26 June 2009). See further Zimmermann (n 11) 246–56.

without prejudice to future arrangements for elections it was nonetheless applied in the 2014, 2017, and 2020 elections.

The President and Vice President of ITLOS are elected by ITLOS judges by secret ballots for a period of three years.[16] The President presides over all meetings of ITLOS, directs its judicial work, supervises its administration, and represents ITLOS in its relations with States and other entities.[17] If ITLOS is not sitting, the President may exercise certain power in procedural matters on behalf of ITLOS.[18] However, no ITLOS judge who is a national of a party in a case, a national of a State member of an international organization which is a party in a case, or a national of a sponsoring State of an entity other than a State which is a party in a case, shall exercise the functions of the presidency in respect of the case.[19] In the event of a vacancy in the presidency or of the inability of the ITLOS President to exercise the functions of the presidency, these shall be exercised by the ITLOS Vice President or, failing him/her, by the Senior ITLOS Judge.[20]

All available incumbent judges of ITLOS shall sit; a quorum of 11 elected judges shall be required to constitute ITLOS.[21]

3. Funding

ITLOS's expenses are borne by the States Parties to UNCLOS and by the International Seabed Authority on such terms and in such a manner as decided at meetings of the States Parties. The contributions are calculated according to the UN scale of assessment, reflecting the size of the economy of each State Party to UNCLOS. ITLOS's approved budget for the years 2019–20 was €20,521,200, compared with €18,817,600 for the years 2015–16, and €21,119,900 for the years 2017–18. ITLOS's proposed budget for the years 2021–22 is €24,155,000. The salaries, allowances, and compensation of ITLOS judges, which shall be free of all taxation, are determined from time to time at annual meetings of States Parties to UNCLOS, taking into

---

[16] Rules Arts 10 and 11.

[17] Rules Art 12.

[18] As in, eg, Rules Arts 21(1), 59(3), 67(3), 105(3), and 106(3).

[19] Rules Art 16(1).

[20] Rules Art 13(1). Seniority of ITLOS judges is based on the date when each judge is elected. If judges are elected on the same date, the seniority is according to their respective ages.

[21] Statute Art 13(1).

account ITLOS's workload, but these may not be decreased during the term of office.[22]

States Parties to UNCLOS that are parties to cases before ITLOS do not incur any ITLOS fees or charges. Developing States party to a disputes before ITLOS may qualify for financial assistance from a voluntary trust fund, established by the UN General Assembly in 2000 and maintained by the Division for Ocean Affairs and the Law of the Sea of the UN Office of Legal Affairs, to assist them in covering, inter alia, their lawyers' fees and/or the cost of travel and accommodation of their delegation during the oral proceedings before ITLOS.[23] When an entity other than a State Party or the Authority is a party to a case submitted to it, ITLOS shall fix the amount which that party is to contribute towards ITLOS's expenses.[24]

4. Seabed Disputes Chamber

The Third UN Conference on the Law of the Sea entrusted with drafting UNCLOS considered setting up a tribunal as an organ of the International Seabed Authority with jurisdiction over disputes related to seabed activities in the Area (principally seabed prospecting, exploration, and mining). Eventually the Conference agreed to vest the Seabed Disputes Chamber of ITLOS with virtually exclusive jurisdiction over disputes concerning the interpretation of Part XI of UNCLOS and the relevant annexes and regulations that are the legal basis for the organization and management of activities in the Area.[25] The Chamber is a separate judicial

---

[22] Statute Art 18(5) and (8). For more information, see P Chandrasekhara Rao and Philippe Gautier, *The International Tribunal for the Law of the Sea: Law, Practice and Procedure* (Edward Elgar 2018) 43–44.

[23] Annex I to UN General Assembly resolution 55/7 of 30 October 2000, Doc A/RES/55/7 (27 February 2001). For example, in 2004, Guinea-Bissau was granted US$20,000 from the trust fund in connection with its participation as the respondent in *'Juno Trader' (Saint Vincent and the Grenadines v Guinea-Bissau)* (Prompt Release) ITLOS Reports 2004, 17.

[24] Statute Art 19(2). See also Zimmermann (n 11) 264–68.

[25] Myron H Nordquist, Shabtai Rosenne, and Louis B Sohn (eds), *United Nations Convention on the Law of the Sea 1982: A Commentary*, vol 5 (Brill 1989) ('Virginia Commentary') 405, 409; AO Adede, *The System for Settlement of Disputes under the United Nations Convention on the Law of the Sea: A Drafting History and a Commentary* (Martinus Nijhoff 1987) 137; David H Anderson, 'Peaceful Settlement of Disputes under UNCLOS' in Jill Barrett and Richard Barnes (eds), *Law of the Sea: UNCLOS as a Living Treaty* (British Institute of International & Comparative Law 2016) 391.

However, UNCLOS Art 188(1) provides that such disputes may be submitted to a special chamber of ITLOS to be formed in accordance with Arts 15 and 17 of Annex VI to UNCLOS or to an ad hoc chamber of the Seabed Disputes Chamber to be formed in accordance with Art 36 of that Annex VI. This provision represents a compromise at the Third Conference

body within ITLOS.[26] It comprises 11 members, selected every three years by a majority of the elected members of ITLOS from among them and with the principal legal systems of the world and equitable geographical distribution being assured. Members of the Chamber may serve for a maximum of two consecutive terms.[27] A quorum of 7 of the 11 members selected by ITLOS shall be required to constitute the Chamber.[28] A judgment given by the Seabed Disputes Chamber shall be considered as rendered by ITLOS itself.[29] Thus far, the Chamber has delivered one advisory opinion.[30]

5. Special chambers

By virtue of Article 15(1) of its Statute, ITLOS may form such chambers, composed of three or more of its elected judges, as it considers necessary for dealing with particular categories of disputes. Disputes shall be heard and determined by the chambers if the parties so request, and a judgment given by any of these chambers shall be considered as rendered by ITLOS itself.[31] Under Article 29 of ITLOS's Rules, whenever ITLOS decides to form a standing special chamber provided for in Article 15(1) of the Statute, it shall determine the particular category of disputes for which it is formed, the number of its members, the period for which they will serve, and the quorum for meetings. The members of such chamber shall be selected by ITLOS itself from among its judges, having regard to any special knowledge,

---

between those States in favour of ensuring the availability of the choices of dispute settlement procedure in UNCLOS Art 287 in all cases of interpretation or application of UNCLOS, on the one side, and those advocating unity of jurisdiction of the Seabed Disputes Chamber for all matters in Part XI and the related annexes, on the other side (Myron H Nordquist, Satya N Nandan, Shabtai Rosenne, and Michael W Lodge (eds), *United Nations Convention on the Law of the Sea 1982: A Commentary* vol 6 (Kluwer 2002) 625).

[26] *Responsibilities and Obligations of States with respect to Activities in the Area* (Advisory Opinion) ITLOS Reports 2011, 10, 23 [25].

[27] Statute Art 35(1)–(3). In practice, the ITLOS President invites ITLOS judges to express their wish as to whether they would like to become members of any particular standing chamber of ITLOS and he will then endeavour to take into consideration all relevant factors in nominating members of each chamber, including those of the Seabed Disputes Chamber, for ITLOS to approve.

[28] Statute Art 35(7).

[29] Statute Art 15(5).

[30] *Responsibilities and Obligations of States with respect to Activities in the Area* (Advisory Opinion) (n 26).

[31] Statute Art 15(4) and (5).

expertise, or previous experience which any of the judges may have in relation to the category of disputes the chamber deals with.

ITLOS has established the following three standing special chambers: the Chamber for Fisheries Disputes, the Chamber for Marine Environment Disputes, and the Chamber for Maritime Boundary Delimitation Disputes. Members of each Chamber serve for a three-year renewable term. Each of the chambers is composed of nine to ten members. To date, no dispute has been submitted to any of these Chambers because disputing parties prefer to resort to either the full bench of ITLOS or the special chamber stipulated in Article 15(2), which is a chamber for dealing with a particular dispute submitted to it where the parties so request and whose composition is determined by ITLOS with the approval of the parties.

It is possible that the flexibility of Article 15(2) special chambers is preferred by some parties as it gives the parties some control in its establishment and composition.[32] The first case in which a special chamber referred to in Article 15(2) was utilized was *Conservation and Sustainable Exploitation of Swordfish Stocks (Chile/European Community)*. However, the case was subsequently discontinued by agreement of the parties and removed from ITLOS's docket. The second, but the first to reach the merits phase, was *Dispute Concerning Delimitation of the Maritime Boundary between Ghana and Côte d'Ivoire in the Atlantic Ocean (Ghana/ Côte d'Ivoire)*.[33] The third one was *Dispute Concerning Delimitation of the Maritime Boundary between Mauritius and Maldives in the Indian Ocean (Mauritius/Maldives)*, submitted to ITLOS in 2019.

In the second case mentioned above, Ghana instituted an Annex VII arbitral proceeding against Côte d'Ivoire, but the parties subsequently transferred the dispute to a special chamber of ITLOS by virtue of a special agreement. The special chamber comprised five judges—three permanent judges of ITLOS and two judges ad hoc appointed by each of the parties. In the third case, on 18 June 2019 Mauritius instituted an Annex VII arbitral proceeding against the Maldives. Both parties failed to appoint the three remaining arbitrators within the time limit prescribed under Article 3 of

---

[32] Edwin E Egede and Lawrence Apaalse, 'Dispute Concerning the Delimitation of the Maritime Boundary between Ghana and Côte d'Ivoire in the Atlantic Ocean: Lesson from Another Maritime Delimitation Case Arising from the African Region' (2019) 29 Indiana Int'l & Comp L Rev 55, 63; Millicent McCreath and Zoe Scanlon, 'Prospects for the Future Use of ITLOS Ad Hoc Special Chambers after the *Ghana/Côte d'Ivoire Case*' (2018) 17 Law & Practice of Int'l Courts and Tribunals 309.

[33] (Merits) ITLOS Reports 2017, 4.

Annex VII of UNCLOS and had to request the President of ITLOS to make the necessary appointments within a period of 30 days and in consultation with the parties. The President then persuaded the parties to submit the dispute to ITLOS instead of the Annex VII arbitral tribunal, and they agreed. However, one of the parties strongly preferred the dispute to be submitted to an Article 15(2) special chamber, and not a full bench of ITLOS. As a compromise, the ITLOS President suggested, and the parties accepted, that such special chamber be established and composed of nine members, with seven judges chosen by the parties from among the 21 ITLOS judges plus two judges ad hoc appointed by each of the parties. On 24 September 2019, the parties transmitted a special agreement and notification to ITLOS to submit their aforesaid dispute to a special chamber of ITLOS to be constituted pursuant to Article 15(2) of the ITLOS Statute. The special chamber was constituted on 27 September 2019.[34] Thus, in practice, the Article 15(2) procedure has proven flexible and adaptable.

With a view to the speedy dispatch of business, the Chamber of Summary Procedure is annually established by ITLOS pursuant to Article 15(3) of the ITLOS Statute to hear and determine disputes by summary procedures. It is composed of the President and Vice-President of ITLOS, acting ex officio, and three other ITLOS judges. The quorum for meetings of this Chamber is three members. Two alternative members are selected for the purpose of replacing members unable to participate in a particular proceeding. This Chamber has never been used despite the request of certain applicants, as the respondents preferred the full-bench ITLOS.[35]

6. Registry

ITLOS is assisted by the Registry, an international secretariat which provides legal, administrative, financial, library, conference, and information services. The Registry comprises an international staff recruited by ITLOS. ITLOS has concluded an agreement with the UN to allow ITLOS's staff members to have recourse to the UN Appeals Tribunal in administrative matters.[36] Since 1997, the staff of the ITLOS Registry participate in the

---

[34] ITLOS Order 2019/4 (27 September 2019).

[35] eg, M/V 'Louisa' (Saint Vincent and the Grenadines v Kingdom of Spain) (Provisional Measures) ITLOS Reports 2008–10, 58, 60 [7]–[9]; M/V 'Norstar' (Panama v Italy) (Preliminary Objections) ITLOS Reports 2016 paras 5 and 10.

[36] Agreement between the United Nations and the International Tribunal for the Law of the Sea extending the competence of the United Nations Appeals Tribunal to the Tribunal with

UN Joint Staff Pension Fund and, since 2016, ITLOS is a participant in the International Civil Service Commission, an independent expert body established by the UN General Assembly in 1974 to regulate and coordinate the service conditions of staff in the UN common system.

According to its Statute, ITLOS shall appoint its Registrar to head the Registry and may provide for the appointment of such other officers as may be necessary.[37] The Registrar is elected by the judges of ITLOS by secret ballot from among candidates nominated by the judges. The Registrar serves for a term of five years and may be re-elected.[38] The Registrar is the regular channel of communications to and from ITLOS and any request made by a party to proceedings before ITLOS shall be addressed to the Registrar unless made in open court in the course of the oral proceedings.[39] The Registrar is assisted by a Deputy Registrar, who is elected by the same process to serve a five-year (re-electable) term.[40]

7. Proceedings in contentious cases

This part will deal with proceedings in contentious cases only. Initiation of a request for an advisory opinion from ITLOS or the Seabed Disputes Chamber and the proceedings involved deserve a separate analysis in Chapter 4 so that readers can better understand them in the overall context of the advisory jurisdiction of ITLOS and that of the Chamber.

Disputes are submitted to ITLOS either by notification of a special agreement or by written application, addressed to the ITLOS Registrar. In either case, the subject of the dispute and the parties shall be indicated. The Registrar shall forthwith notify the special agreement or the application to all concerned as well as all States Parties to UNCLOS.[41]

---

respect to applications alleging non-compliance with the terms of appointment or contracts of employment of staff members of the Registry, dated 1 July 2009 <www.itlos.org/fileadmin/itlos/documents/basic_texts/itlos_un_appeals_tribunal_eng.pdf> accessed 20 March 2020.

[37] Statute Art 12(2).
[38] Rules Art 32(1).
[39] Rules Art 51.
[40] Rules Art 33. Although this provision allows ITLOS to elect an Assistant Registrar by the same process to serve for a five-year renewable term, ITLOS has not exercised this option so far.
[41] Statute Art 24.

All communications to the parties shall be sent to their agents. Therefore, in their respective initial communications by the parties to ITLOS each of them shall also notify ITLOS of the appointment of its agent. The communications to a party before that party has appointed an agent and to an entity other than a party shall be sent as follows: (a) in the case of a State, ITLOS shall direct all communications to its Government; (b) in the case of the International Seabed Authority or the Enterprise, any international organization, and any other intergovernmental organization, ITLOS shall direct all communications to the competent body or executive head of such organization at its headquarters location; (c) in the case of State enterprises or natural or juridical persons referred to in Article 153(2)(b) of UNCLOS,[42] ITLOS shall direct all communications through the Government of the sponsoring or certifying State, as the case may be; (d) in the case of a group of States, State enterprises, or natural or juridical persons referred to in Article 153(2)(b) of UNCLOS, ITLOS shall direct all communications to each member of the group according to subparagraphs (a) and (c) above; (e) in the case of other natural or juridical persons, ITLOS shall direct all communications through the Government of the State in whose territory the communication has to be received. The same provisions apply whenever steps are to be taken to procure evidence on the spot.[43]

When proceedings before ITLOS are initiated by means of an application (*requête*), the application shall indicate the party making it, the party against which the claim is brought, and the subject of the dispute. The application shall specify as far as possible the legal grounds upon which ITLOS's jurisdiction is said to be based; it shall also specify the precise nature of the claim, together with a succinct statement of the facts and grounds on which the claim is based. The original of the application shall be signed by the agent of the party submitting it or by the diplomatic representative of that party in Germany where ITLOS has its seat or by some other duly authorized person. The ITLOS Registrar shall forthwith transmit to the respondent a certified copy of the application. When the applicant proposes to found ITLOS's jurisdiction upon a consent yet to be given or manifested

---

[42] According to Art 153(2)(b) of UNCLOS, the activities in the Area shall be carried out in association with the Authority by States Parties, or State enterprises, or natural or juridical persons which possess the nationality of States Parties or are effectively controlled by them or their nationals, when sponsored by such States, or any group of the foregoing which meets the requirements provided in Part XI (The Area) and in Annex III (Basic Conditions of Prospecting, Exploration, and Exploitation).

[43] Rules Art 52.

by the party against which the application is made unilaterally (*forum prorogatum*; see Chapter 1), the application shall be transmitted to that party, but shall not however be entered in the List of cases, nor any action be taken in the proceedings, unless and until the party against which such application is made consents to ITLOS's jurisdiction for the purposes of the case.[44]

When proceedings are brought before ITLOS by the notification of a special agreement (*compromis*), the notification may be effected by the parties jointly or by any one or more of them. If the notification is not a joint one, a certified copy of it shall forthwith be communicated by the ITLOS Registrar to any other party. In each case the notification shall be accompanied by an original or certified copy of the special agreement. The notification shall also, insofar as this is not already apparent from the agreement, indicate the precise subject of the dispute and identify the parties to it.[45]

8. The conduct of proceedings

The proceedings after the submission of a dispute consist of two parts: written and oral. In general, the written proceedings consist of the communication to ITLOS and to the parties of memorials, counter-memorials, and, if ITLOS so authorizes, replies and rejoinders, as well as all documents in support. The oral proceedings consist of the hearing by ITLOS of agents, counsel, advocates, witnesses, and experts.[46] As a guiding principle, the proceedings before ITLOS shall be conducted without unnecessary delay or expense.[47] Thus, in every case submitted to ITLOS, the ITLOS President shall ascertain the views of the parties with regard to questions of procedure and, for this purpose, he may summon the agents of the parties to meet him as soon as possible after their appointment and whenever necessary thereafter, or use other appropriate means of communication.[48] Time limits for the completion of steps in the proceedings may be fixed by assigning a specified period but shall always indicate definite dates. Such time limits shall be as short as the character of the case permits.[49]

---

[44] Rules Art 54.
[45] Rules Art 55.
[46] Rules Art 44.
[47] Rules Art 49.
[48] Rules Art 45.
[49] Rules Art 46.

ITLOS may at any time direct the proceedings in two or more cases to be joined. It may also direct the written or oral proceedings, including the calling of witnesses, to be in common; or ITLOS may, without effecting any formal joinder, direct common action in any of these respects.[50] The parties may jointly propose particular modifications or additions to the Rules concerning the procedure, which may be applied by ITLOS or by a chamber if ITLOS or the chamber considers them appropriate in the circumstances of the case.[51] In *Southern Bluefin Tuna*, ITLOS joined the proceedings upon the requests for provisional measures in relation to the cases between New Zealand and Japan and between Australia and Japan after New Zealand and Australia had stated that they appeared as parties in the same interest.[52] However, ITLOS did not join two prompt release proceedings instituted by Japan against Russia on the same day[53] because each case concerned a different vessel and related to a different factual ground. Instead, ITLOS conducted the hearings in these two cases immediately after one another to ensure an efficient handling of the cases and delivered the two judgments on the same day.[54]

Details of the written proceedings are as follows.

ITLOS shall make the necessary orders, after the ITLOS President ascertains the views of the parties, to determine, inter alia, the number and the order of filing of the pleadings and the time limits within which they must be filed. The time limits for each pleading shall not exceed six months, which may be extended by ITLOS at the request of a party, or ITLOS may decide that any step taken after the expiration of the time limit fixed therefore shall be considered as valid. It may not do so, however, unless it is satisfied there is adequate justification for the request. In either case the other party shall be given an opportunity to state its views within a time limit to be fixed by ITLOS.[55]

The pleadings in a case begun by means of an application shall consist, in the following order, of a memorial by the applicant and a counter-memorial by the respondent. As noted, ITLOS may authorize or direct that there shall be a reply by the applicant and a rejoinder by the respondent if the parties

---

[50] Rules Art 47.

[51] Rules Art 48.

[52] *Southern Bluefin Tuna (New Zealand v Japan; Australia v Japan)* (Provisional Measures, Order of 16 August 1999) ITLOS Reports 1999, 274.

[53] *'Hoshinmaru' (Japan v Russian Federation)* (Prompt Release) ITLOS Reports 2005–07, 18; *'Tomimaru' (Japan v Russian Federation)* (Prompt Release) ITLOS Reports 2005–07, 74.

[54] As pointed out by Rao and Gautier (n 22) 187.

[55] Rules Art 59.

are so agreed or if ITLOS decides, at the request of a party or *proprio motu*, that these pleadings are necessary.[56]

In a case begun by the notification of a special agreement, the number and order of the pleadings shall be governed by the provisions of the agreement, unless ITLOS, after ascertaining the views of the parties, decides otherwise. If the special agreement contains no such provision, and if the parties have not subsequently agreed on the number and order of pleadings, they shall each file a memorial and counter-memorial, within the same time limits. In such cases, ITLOS shall not authorize the presentation of replies and rejoinders unless it finds them to be necessary.[57]

The disputing parties shall submit any pleading or any part of a pleading in English or French, or both. A party may use a language other than English or French for its pleadings. A translation into English or French, certified as accurate by the party submitting it, must then be submitted together with the original of each pleading. When a document annexed to a pleading is not in English or French, it must similarly be accompanied by a certified translation into English or French. The translation may be confined to part of an annex, but it must then be accompanied by an explanatory note indicating what passages are translated. ITLOS may, however, require a more extensive or a complete translation to be furnished. When a language other than English or French is chosen by the parties and that language is an official language of the United Nations, the decision of ITLOS shall, at the request of any party, be translated into that official language of the United Nations at no cost for the parties.[58]

After the closure of the written proceedings and before the hearing, ITLOS holds initial deliberations in private concerning the written pleadings and the conduct of the case.[59] Where necessary, the President may hold another consultation with the agents of both parties with regard to questions of procedure.[60] Copies of the written pleadings and documents annexed thereto are made accessible to the public on the date of the opening of the hearing, or earlier if ITLOS so decides after ascertaining the views of the parties.[61]

---

[56] Rules Art 60.
[57] Rules Art 61.
[58] Rules Art 64.
[59] Rules Art 68.
[60] Rules Art 45.
[61] Rules Art 67(2).

As a general rule, the date for the opening of the hearing is fixed by ITLOS to fall within a period of six months from the closure of the written proceedings unless ITLOS is satisfied there is adequate justification for deciding otherwise. ITLOS may also decide, when necessary, that the opening or the continuance of the hearing be postponed. When fixing the date for the opening of the hearing or postponing the opening or continuance of the hearing, ITLOS must have regard to (a) the need to hold the hearing without unnecessary delay; (b) the priority required in case of requests for provisional measures or prompt release of detained vessels and crews; (c) any special circumstances, including the urgency of the case or other cases on the List of cases; and (d) the views expressed by the parties.[62]

Prior to the opening of the hearing, each party should submit to ITLOS (a) a brief note on the points which in its opinion constitute the issues that still divide the parties; (b) a brief outline of the arguments that it wishes to make in its oral statement; and (c) a list of authorities, including, where appropriate, relevant extracts from such authorities, proposed to be relied upon in its oral statement. None of these materials will be treated as documents or parts of the pleadings. The oral statements should be as succinct as possible and should not repeat the facts and arguments contained in the written pleadings.[63]

The hearing is held in public, unless ITLOS decides otherwise or unless the parties request that the public be not admitted. Such a decision or request may concern either the whole or part of the hearing, and may be made at any time.[64] At the hearing, exhibits, including photographs and extracts from documents, can be displayed by the parties on video monitors in the court room. Before the termination of the hearing, ITLOS may request the submission of additional documents by either or both of the parties as well as pose questions in the name of ITLOS or an individual judge for the parties to respond orally. Submission of additional documents not requested by ITLOS may be subject to objection by the other party, in which case ITLOS will decide whether to authorize the production of the additional documents submitted by the other party because it considers their production necessary.[65]

---

[62] Rules Art 69.
[63] The Guidelines concerning the Preparation and Presentation of Cases before ITLOS, paras 14 and 15.
[64] Rules Art 74 and Statute Art 26(2).
[65] Rules Art 71(1) and (2).

Throughout the written and oral proceedings, a modification of the submissions of a party is permissible provided it does not prejudice the right of the other party to respond.[66] It is a legal requirement that any new claim to be admitted must arise directly out of the application or special agreement or be implicit in it. This is because Article 24(1) of the ITLOS Statute requires, inter alia, that when disputes are submitted to ITLOS either by notification of a special agreement or by written application, the 'subject of the dispute' must be indicated. Similarly, by virtue of Article 54(1) of ITLOS's Rules, the application instituting the proceedings must indicate the 'subject of the dispute'. While the subsequent pleadings may elucidate the terms of the application or special agreement, they must not go beyond the limits of the claim as set out in the application or special agreement since the dispute brought before ITLOS by an application or special agreement cannot be transformed into another dispute which is different in character.[67]

At the end of the oral proceedings, each party shall make their final submissions[68] which shall form the basis of ITLOS's deliberation.

When ITLOS has completed its deliberations and adopted its judgment, the parties shall be notified of the date on which it will be read at a public sitting of ITLOS. ITLOS's judgment is final and binding on all the parties to the particular dispute on the day of the reading.[69]

In the event of dispute as to the meaning or scope of a judgment, any party may make a request to ITLOS for its interpretation.[70] A request for the interpretation of a judgment may be made either by an application or by the notification of a special agreement to that effect between the parties; the precise point or points in dispute as to the meaning or scope of the judgment shall be indicated.[71]

A request for revision of a judgment may be made only when it is based upon the discovery of some fact of such a nature as to be a decisive factor,

---

[66] *M/V 'Saiga' (No 2) (Saint Vincent and the Grenadines v Guinea)* (Provisional Measures, Order of 11 Mar 1998) ITLOS Reports 1998, 24, 38 [33].

[67] *M/V 'Louisa' (Saint Vincent and the Grenadines v Kingdom of Spain)* (Merits) ITLOS Reports 2013, 4, 44–45 [142]–[150]. Although ITLOS in that particular case specifically addresses the dispute submitted to it by an application, the same rationale applies to disputes submitted to it by special agreements as well. According to ITLOS, in interpreting Article 24(1) of its Statute and Article 54(1) and (2) of its Rules, ITLOS 'concludes that these provisions are essential from the point of view of legal security and the good administration of justice' (ibid 45 [148]).

[68] Rules Art 75(2).

[69] Statute Art 33(1) and (2); Rules Art 124.

[70] Statute Art 33(3); Rules Art 126(1).

[71] Rules Art 126(2).

which fact was, when the judgment was given, unknown to ITLOS and also to the party requesting revision, always provided that such ignorance was not due to negligence. Such request must be made by an application at the latest within six months of the discovery of the new fact and before the lapse of 10 years from the date of the judgment. The proceedings for revision is to be opened by a decision of ITLOS in the form of a judgment expressly recording the existence of the new fact, recognizing that it has such a character as to lay the case open to revision, and declaring the application admissible on this ground.[72] The other party shall be entitled to file written observations on the admissibility of the application for revision of a judgment within a time limit fixed by ITLOS, which shall be communicated to the party making the application.[73] Before giving its judgment on the admissibility of the application, ITLOS may afford the parties a further opportunity of presenting their views thereon.[74] If ITLOS decides to make the admission of the proceedings in revision conditional on previous compliance with the judgment, it shall make an order accordingly,[75] so as to ensure that the request for revision is not used as a subterfuge by the applicant not to comply with the judgment already rendered by ITLOS. If ITLOS finds that the application is admissible it shall fix time limits for such further proceedings on the merits of the application as, after ascertaining the views of the parties, it considers necessary.[76]

If the judgment to be revised or to be interpreted was given by a chamber, the request for its revision or interpretation shall, if possible, be dealt with by that chamber. If that is not possible, the request shall be dealt with by a chamber composed in conformity with the relevant provisions of the Statute and the Rules of ITLOS. If, according to the Statute and these Rules, the composition of the chamber requires the approval of the parties which cannot be obtained within time limits fixed by ITLOS, the request shall be dealt with by ITLOS itself.[77]

The decision on a request for interpretation or revision of a judgment shall be given in the form of a judgment.[78]

---

[72] Rules Arts 127 and 128(1).
[73] Rules Art 128(2).
[74] Rules Art 128(3).
[75] Rules Art 128(4).
[76] Rules Art 128(5).
[77] Rules Art 129(2).
[78] Rules Art 129(3).

In exceptional circumstances such as the COVID-19 pandemic in 2020, ITLOS may decide, as an exceptional measure, for public health, security, or other compelling reasons, to hold hearings and meetings entirely or in part by video link. . The virtual attendance of a judge shall be taken into account when it is being decided whether the meeting is quorate—a judge participating by means of a video link is considered 'present'. Where secret ballot is required, as in elections of the President and the Vice-President of ITLOS as well as of the Presidents of the Chambers, secured technical arrangements are used for secret voting.[79]

9. Jurisdiction and admissibility

ITLOS follows the settled jurisprudence in international adjudication that a tribunal must at all times be satisfied it has jurisdiction to entertain the case submitted to it and, for this purpose, it has the power to examine *proprio motu* the basis of its jurisdiction.[80] Therefore, it possesses the right to deal with all aspects of the question of jurisdiction, whether or not they have been expressly raised by the parties.[81]

For ITLOS to be seized of contentious jurisdiction over a particular dispute, several preconditions must be fulfilled. By virtue of Articles 21 and 22 of the ITLOS Statute, jurisdiction may be founded on the basis of jurisdictional clauses in an agreement or an international agreement binding on the disputing parties and that confers jurisdiction on ITLOS or a special chamber of ITLOS with respect to any dispute between the parties. Otherwise, the following preconditions are applicable. First, the disputing parties must be party to UNCLOS at the time of submission of their dispute to ITLOS. Second, they must have chosen ITLOS as their preferred dispute settlement mechanism or agreed to submit their dispute to ITLOS by means of a special agreement. Where a dispute is not submitted

---

[79] Rules Arts 41(7), 74(2), 112(5), 124(3), and 135(1 bis), as amended on 25 September 2020. cf the two amendments to the Rules of the ICJ that entered into force on 25 June 2020. ICJ Rules Art 59(2) allows the ICJ to decide, for health, security or other compelling reasons, to hold a hearing entirely or in part by video link in consultation with the parties on the organization of such a hearing. The ICJ Rules Art 94(2) provides that although, in general, the ICJ's judgment shall be read at a public sitting, the ICJ may decide, for health, security, or other compelling reasons, that the judgment shall be read at a sitting of the ICJ accessible to the parties and the public by video link.

[80] *'Grand Prince' (Belize v France)* (Prompt Release) ITLOS Reports 2001, 17, 41 [77].

[81] ibid 41 [79].

pursuant to a special agreement, it may be submitted by an application of one disputing party (the applicant) against another disputing party (the respondent) on the basis of their respective declarations made under Article 287 of UNCLOS accepting ITLOS's jurisdiction, or on the basis of ITLOS's compulsory jurisdiction as stipulated in UNCLOS; namely, the prompt release of detained vessels and their crews under Article 292, the prescription of provisional measures pending the establishment and functioning of an Annex VII arbitral tribunal under Article 290(5), and the jurisdiction of the Seabed Disputes Chamber over disputes concerning the activities in the Area under Article 187. Third, the dispute must be one concerning the interpretation or application of UNCLOS. Fourth, the dispute must not fall within the limitations or exceptions stipulated in section 3 of Part XV of UNCLOS declared by one or both of the disputing parties not to be subject to the dispute settlement regime of UNCLOS, unless the parties otherwise agree.[82] Where States Parties to UNCLOS have made declarations of differing scope under Article 287, ITLOS's jurisdiction exists only to the extent to which the substance of the declarations of the two parties to a dispute coincides. For example, where a State Party's declaration is of general purport but another State Party's declaration is limited to the settlement of a specific dispute or category of disputes, ITLOS's jurisdiction is confined to the terms of the narrower of the two declarations.[83] UNCLOS itself does not preclude the possibility of a disputing party making a declaration immediately before filing a case.[84]

Even where ITLOS has jurisdiction, the application may not be admissible on certain grounds. For example, the applicant has not exhausted local remedies, where this is required, or the applicant is prevented from pursuing its application due to the applicability of the principle of acquiescence, estoppel, or extinctive prescription, as will be explained in Chapter 3.

By virtue of Article 97 of the Rules of ITLOS, any objection to its jurisdiction or to the admissibility of the application, or other objection the decision upon which is requested before any further proceedings on the merits, shall be made in writing within 90 days from the institution of

---

[82] See also James Harrison, 'Defining Disputes and Characterizing Claims: Subject-Matter Jurisdiction in Law of the Sea Convention Litigation' (2017) 48 ODIL 269; Rao and Gautier(n 22) 176–81.

[83] *M/V 'Louisa'* (Merits) (n 67) 29–30 [74]–[82]; *M/V 'Norstar'* (Preliminary Objections) (n 35) para 58. For a detailed analysis of Art 287, see Miguel García García-Revillo, *The Contentious and Advisory Jurisdiction of the International Tribunal for the Law of the Sea* (Brill/Nijhoff 2015) 155–73.

[84] *M/V 'Louisa'* (Merits) (n 67) 30 [79].

proceedings. The preliminary objection shall set out the facts and the law on which the objection is based, as well as the submissions. Upon receipt by the ITLOS Registry of a preliminary objection, the proceedings on the merits shall be suspended and ITLOS shall fix a time limit not exceeding 60 days within which the other party may present its written observations and submissions and a further time limit not exceeding 60 days from the receipt of such observations and submissions within which the objecting party may present its written observations and submissions in reply. Copies of documents in support shall be annexed to such statements and evidence which it is proposed to produce shall be mentioned. Unless ITLOS decides otherwise, the further proceedings shall be oral. The written observations and submissions and the statements and evidence presented at the hearings shall be confined to those matters which are relevant to the objection. Whenever necessary, however, ITLOS may request the parties to argue all questions of law and fact and to adduce all evidence bearing on the issue. ITLOS shall give its decision in the form of a judgment, by which it shall uphold the objection or reject it or declare that the objection does not possess, in the circumstances of the case, an exclusively preliminary character. If ITLOS rejects the objection or declares that it does not possess an exclusively preliminary character, it shall fix time limits for the further proceedings. However, ITLOS shall give effect to any agreement between the parties that an objection submitted under paragraph 1 be heard and determined within the framework of the merits. ITLOS clarifies that this provision gives the disputing parties the right to raise objections to admissibility, subject to any restrictions clearly established under the terms of the special agreement and the Rules of ITLOS.[85]

In 'Saiga' (No 2), ITLOS considered the contention of Saint Vincent and the Grenadines that the objections of Guinea were not receivable because they were raised after the expiry of the 90-day time limit specified in Article 97 of the Rules. ITLOS explained that Article 97 deals with objections to jurisdiction or admissibility raised as preliminary questions to be dealt with in incidental proceedings, and that the article applies to an objection 'the decision upon which is requested before any further proceedings on the merits'. Accordingly, the time limit in the article does not apply to objections to jurisdiction or admissibility only raised in proceedings on

---

[85] M/V 'Virginia G' (Panama/Guinea-Bissau) ITLOS Reports 2014, 4, 39–40 [97]–[98], citing M/V 'Saiga' (No 2) (Saint Vincent and the Grenadines v Guinea) (Merits) ITLOS Reports 1999, 10, 32 [51].

the merits. In *'Saiga' (No 2)*, this was confirmed by the parties agreeing to have the proceedings before ITLOS 'comprise a single phase dealing with all aspects of the merits (including damages and costs) and the objection as to jurisdiction …'. ITLOS, therefore, concluded that Article 97 did not preclude the raising of objections to admissibility in that case, and the objections to admissibility raised by Guinea could be considered.[86]

10. Applicable law

According to Article 293 of UNCLOS, a court or tribunal having jurisdiction in compulsory proceedings entailing binding decisions under section 2 of Part XV shall apply UNCLOS and other rules of international law not incompatible with UNCLOS.[87] This is without prejudice to the power of the court or tribunal having jurisdiction under this section to decide a case *ex aequo et bono*, if the parties so agree (though there is no case to date in which this has happened). Article 23 of the ITLOS Statute, unsurprisingly, provides that ITLOS shall decide all disputes and applications in accordance with Article 293 of UNCLOS.

As regards the Seabed Disputes Chamber, Article 38 of the ITLOS Statute stipulates that in addition to the provisions of Article 293 of UNCLOS, the Chamber shall apply the rules, regulations, and procedures of the Authority adopted in accordance with UNCLOS and the terms of contracts concerning activities in the Area in matters relating to those contracts.

A slight complication is created by the 1994 Agreement relating to the Implementation of Part XI of UNCLOS ('the Implementing Agreement').[88] The Implementing Agreement was concluded to modify the application of certain parts of the seabed mining regime originally set out in Part XI of UNCLOS in order to induce industrialized States to become parties to UNCLOS.[89] Pursuant to Article 2(1) of the Implementing Agreement, the provisions of the Implementing Agreement and Part XI of UNCLOS shall be interpreted and applied together as a single instrument, but the provisions

---

[86] *M/V 'Saiga' (No 2)* (Merits) (n 85) 32–33 [52]–[54]; followed in *M/V 'Virginia G'* (n 85) 40 [100]–[101].

[87] The meaning of 'other rules of international law not incompatible with UNCLOS' will be explained in Chapter 3, Part 1, section (b).

[88] (1994) 33 ILM 1309.

[89] RR Churchill and AV Lowe, *The Law of the Sea* (3rd edn, Manchester University Press 1987) 20–21.

of the Implementing Agreement shall prevail in the event of any inconsistency. Besides, section 6 of the Annex to the Implementing Agreement
regarding production policy provides, inter alia, that the provisions of the
General Agreement on Tariffs and Trade,[90] its relevant codes, and successor
or superseding agreement shall apply with respect to the activities in the
Area.[91] In this connection, the following shall apply to the settlement of disputes concerning the provisions of these agreements: (i) where the States
Parties concerned are parties to such agreements, they shall have recourse
to the dispute settlement procedures of those agreements; but (ii) where
one or more of the States Parties concerned are not parties to such agreements, they shall have recourse to the dispute settlement procedures set out
in UNCLOS.[92]

11. Counter-claims

Article 98 of the ITLOS Rules regulates counter-claims. A party to the dispute may present a counter-claim provided it is directly connected with the
subject matter of the claim of the other party and it comes within ITLOS's
jurisdiction. A counter-claim shall be made in the counter-memorial of
the party presenting it and appear as part of its submissions. In the event
of doubt as to the connection between the question presented by way of
counter-claim and the subject matter of the original claim, ITLOS shall,
after hearing the parties, decide whether or not the question thus presented
shall be joined to the original proceedings.

The issue of a counter-claim has arisen in, for example, *M/V 'Virginia G'
(Panama/Guinea-Bissau)*. The dispute in that case relates to the Panamanian
flagged oil tanker 'Virginia G', which, according to Panama's statement of
claim, was arrested by the authorities of Guinea-Bissau in the latter's exclusive economic zone while carrying out refuelling activities. Panama alleged that Guinea-Bissau had breached its international obligations under
UNCLOS, thereby leading to 'a prejudice being caused to the Panamanian
flag and to severe damages and losses being incurred by the vessel and other
interested persons and entities because of the detention and the length of
the period of detention'. In its counter-memorial, Guinea-Bissau presented

---

[90]   1867 UNTS 187.
[91]   Annex to the Implementing Agreement, s 6, para 1(b).
[92]   ibid para 1(f).

a counter-claim stating that Panama had violated Article 91 of UNCLOS by granting its nationality to a ship without any genuine link to Panama, which had facilitated the practice of illegal actions of bunkering without permission in Guinea-Bissau's exclusive economic zone, and that Guinea-Bissau was entitled to claim from Panama all damages and costs caused by the ship to Guinea-Bissau resulting from Panama's granting of the flag of convenience to the ship. ITLOS noted that the agreement concluded between the parties referred to 'the dispute between them concerning the Virginia G' and stated that the proceedings before ITLOS were to deal with 'all aspects of the merits (including damages and costs)', and that ITLOS was to 'address all claims for damages and costs'. ITLOS, therefore, found that the counter-claim presented by Guinea-Bissau met the jurisdictional requirement of Article 98 of the ITLOS Rules. On the requirement of the direct connection of Guinea-Bissau's counter-claim with the subject matter of Panama's claim, ITLOS found the counter-claim related to an alleged breach of UNCLOS by Panama in the granting of its nationality to the 'Virginia G', and was therefore directly connected with the subject matter of Panama's claims. ITLOS thus granted Panama's request to file an additional pleading in response to Guinea-Bissau's counter-claim, in order to ensure equality between the parties.[93]

12. Intervention

As Article 31 of the ITLOS Statute makes clear, only a State Party to UNCLOS has a right to intervene in a dispute before ITLOS.

Should a State Party to UNCLOS consider it has an interest of a legal nature which may be affected by the decision in any dispute, it may submit a request to ITLOS to be permitted to intervene. If a request to intervene is granted, ITLOS's decision in respect of the dispute shall be binding upon the intervening State Party insofar as it relates to matters in respect of which that State Party intervened.[94]

Whenever the interpretation or application of UNCLOS is in question, the ITLOS Registrar shall notify all States Parties to UNCLOS forthwith. Whenever pursuant to Article 21 or 22 of the ITLOS Statute the

---

[93] *M/V 'Virginia G' (Panama/Guinea-Bissau)*, Order of 2 Nov 2012, ITLOS Reports 2012, 309.
[94] Statute Art 31.

interpretation or application of an international agreement is in question, the Registrar shall notify all the parties to the agreement. Every party referred to above has the right to intervene in the proceedings; if it uses this right, the interpretation given by the judgment will be equally binding upon it.[95]

13. Amicus curiae

As of this writing, ITLOS has received a request for permission by a third party to file submissions as amicus curiae in one contentious case, *'Arctic Sunrise' (Kingdom of the Netherlands v Russian Federation)*, by Greenpeace International. After the ITLOS Registrar invited the parties to provide comments on the request submitted by Greenpeace International, the Netherlands informed ITLOS it had informally informed Greenpeace International that the Netherlands did not have any objection to such petition. However, ITLOS declined the request by Greenpeace International as well as deciding not to include its submissions in the case file. One day later, Russia informed ITLOS, inter alia, that taking into account the non-governmental character of Greenpeace International, the Russian side saw no reason for granting to this organization the possibility to furnish information to ITLOS in that particular case.[96] ITLOS did not explain the reason for declining to accede to Greenpeace International's request. This is probably because contentious proceedings concern a dispute between two parties and a view expressed by a third party, even labelled as 'amicus curiae', could undermine the principle of strict equality between the parties.[97]

In advisory proceedings, ITLOS has limited the participation to States Parties to UNCLOS and intergovernmental organizations likely to be able to furnish information on the questions raised in the request for the advisory opinion. This results from ITLOS's interpretation of Article 133 of its Rules, which requires it to invite States Parties and the aforesaid organizations to present written statements on the questions.

---

[95] Statute Art 32. The Rules of ITLOS Arts 99–104 cover procedures for such intervention in detail.

[96] *'Arctic Sunrise' (Kingdom of the Netherlands v Russian Federation)* (Provisional Measures, Order of 25 Oct 2013) ITLOS Rep 2013, 230, 234 [15]–[18].

[97] Rao and Gautier (n 22) 284–85.

In *Responsibilities and obligations of States with respect to activities in the Area*[98] the Seabed Disputes Chamber received a statement submitted jointly by Stichting Greenpeace Council (Greenpeace International) and the World Wildlife Fund for Nature ('WWF'), accompanied by a petition requesting permission to participate in the advisory proceedings as amici curiae. At the request of the President of the Chamber, the Registrar informed those organizations in writing that their statement would not be included in the case file since it had not been submitted under Article 133 of the Rules; it would, however, be transmitted to the States Parties, the Authority, and the intergovernmental organizations that had submitted written statements, which would also be informed that the document was not part of the case file and that it would be posted on a separate section of ITLOS's website. Subsequently, the Chamber, having considered the aforesaid petition to participate in the advisory proceedings as amici curiae, decided not to grant that request.

Likewise, in *Request for Advisory Opinion submitted by the Sub-Regional Fisheries Commission*,[99] ITLOS did not permit the WWF to participate as amicus curiae since the WWF was not identified by ITLOS, pursuant to Article 133 of its Rules, as among the intergovernmental organizations likely to be able to furnish information which could be useful to ITLOS in response to the questions seeking its advisory opinion. Nonetheless, ITLOS tried to accommodate the WWF as much as practicable. Although the WWF's written statements were not included in the case file, the statements were notified to the States Parties, the organization requesting the advisory opinion, and the intergovernmental organizations which had presented written statements, and were placed on ITLOS's website in a separate section of documents relating to the case. However, ITLOS declined to grant the WWF's request to make a statement as amicus curiae in the oral proceedings of the case. With respect to the written statement presented by the USA, a State not party to UNCLOS, submitting that ITLOS should not grant the Sub-Regional Fisheries Commission's request for an advisory opinion, ITLOS decided to consider it as part of the case file and post it on ITLOS's website, in a separate section of documents related to the case, entitled 'States Parties to the 1995 Straddling Fish Stocks Agreement', or the FSA, to which the USA is party.

---

[98] (Advisory Opinion) ITLOS Reports 2011, 10.
[99] (Advisory Opinion) ITLOS Reports 2015, 4.

14. Discontinuance

If at any time before the final judgment on the merits has been delivered the parties, either jointly or separately, notify ITLOS in writing of their agreement to discontinue the proceedings, ITLOS shall make an order recording the discontinuance and directing the ITLOS Registrar to remove the case from the List of cases. If the parties have agreed to discontinue the proceedings in consequence of having reached a settlement of the dispute and if they so desire, ITLOS shall record this fact in the order for the removal of the case from the List, or indicate in, or annex to, the order the terms of the settlement.[100] Any intervening State Party/intervenor in the case shall not be entitled to object to an agreement to discontinue the proceedings.[101]

If, in the course of proceedings instituted by means of an application, the applicant informs ITLOS in writing it is not continuing with the proceedings, and if, at the date on which this communication is received by the ITLOS Registry, the respondent has not yet taken any step in the proceedings, ITLOS shall make an order officially recording the discontinuance of the proceedings and directing the removal of the case from the List of cases. A copy of this order shall be sent by the ITLOS Registrar to the respondent. If, at the time when the notice of discontinuance is received, the respondent has already taken some step in the proceedings, ITLOS shall fix a time limit within which the respondent may state whether it opposes the discontinuance of the proceedings. If no objection is made to the discontinuance before the expiration of the time limit, acquiescence will be presumed and ITLOS shall make an order recording the discontinuance of the proceedings and directing the Registrar to remove the case from the List of cases. However, if objection is made, the proceedings shall continue.[102]

15. Competence to examine national law

ITLOS has competence to examine the applicability and scope of national law to ascertain whether the application of the national law in a dispute before ITLOS by a party to the dispute is in conformity with its obligations towards the other disputing party under UNCLOS. For example, the rights

---

[100] Rules Art 105.
[101] Rules Arts 103(4) and 104(3).
[102] Rules Art 106.

and duties of coastal and other States in the exclusive economic zone under Article 58(3) of UNCLOS arise not only from the provisions of UNCLOS but also from national laws and regulations 'adopted by the coastal State in accordance with the provisions of [UNCLOS]'. Thus, ITLOS is competent to determine the compatibility of such laws and regulations with UNCLOS.[103]

16. Judges ad hoc

ITLOS judges of the nationality of any of the parties to a dispute shall retain their right to participate as judges in the case. If ITLOS, when hearing a dispute, includes upon the bench a member of the nationality of one of the parties, any other party to the case may choose a person to participate as a judge ad hoc.[104] If ITLOS, when hearing a dispute, does not include upon the bench a member of the nationality of the parties, each of those parties may choose a person to participate as a judge ad hoc. This rule also applies to the Seabed Disputes Chamber and special chambers of ITLOS—in which cases, the ITLOS President, in consultation with the parties, shall request specified ITLOS judges forming the chamber, as many as necessary, to give place to the ITLOS judges of the nationality of the parties concerned, and, failing such, or if they are unable to be present, to the members specially chosen by the parties. Should there be several parties in the same interest, they shall, for the purpose of the foregoing, be considered as one party only—any doubt on this point shall be settled by ITLOS.[105]

If an ITLOS judge having the nationality of one of the parties is or becomes unable to sit in any phase of a case, that party is entitled to choose a judge ad hoc within a time limit to be fixed by ITLOS, or by the ITLOS President if ITLOS is not sitting. Parties in the same interest shall be deemed not to have an ITLOS judge of one of their nationalities upon the bench if every ITLOS judge having one of their nationalities is or becomes unable to sit in any phase of the case. If an ITLOS judge having the nationality of one of the parties becomes able to sit not later than the closure of the written proceedings in that phase of the case, that judge shall resume the seat on the bench in the case.[106]

---

[103] *M/V 'Saiga' (No 2)* (Merits) 52–53 [121]; *M/V 'Virginia G'* (n 85) 71 [227].
[104] See also Zimmermann (n 11) 256–61.
[105] Statute Art 17. See also Rules Art 20.
[106] Rules Art 21.

A judge ad hoc may be of a nationality other than that of the party which chooses him or her.[107] Judges ad hoc shall take precedence after the elected ITLOS judges and in order of seniority of age.[108] They shall participate in the decision on terms of complete equality with the other judges[109] although they shall not be taken into account for the calculation of the quorum.[110]

An entity other than a State (most usually a 'sponsored' commercial entity engaged in deep seabed mining) may choose a judge ad hoc only if (a) one of the other parties is a State Party to UNCLOS and there is upon the bench a judge of its nationality or, where such party is an international organization, there is upon the bench a judge of the nationality of one of its Member States or the State Party has itself chosen a judge ad hoc, or (b) there is upon the bench a judge of the nationality of the sponsoring State of one of the other parties. However, an international organization or a natural or juridical person or State enterprise is not entitled to choose a judge ad hoc if there is upon the bench a judge of the nationality of one of the Member States of the international organization or a judge of the nationality of the sponsoring State of such natural or juridical person or State enterprise. Where an international organization is a party to a case and there is upon the bench a judge of the nationality of a Member State of the organization, the other party may choose a judge ad hoc. Where two or more judges on the bench are nationals of Member States of the international organization concerned or of the sponsoring States of a party, the President may, after consulting the parties, request one or more of such judges to withdraw from the bench.[111]

If no objection to the parties' choice of judges ad hoc is raised by the respective other party and no objection appears to ITLOS itself, the nominated judges ad hoc will be admitted to participate in the proceedings, after making the solemn declaration required under Article 9 of ITLOS's Rules at a public sitting in the case in which the judges ad hoc are participating.

Provisions in the ITLOS Statute and Rules on appointment of judges ad hoc do not extend to the Seabed Disputes Chamber's ad hoc chambers, each of which is composed of three of its members as determined by the Chamber with the approval of the parties, set up to deal with a dispute

---

[107] Rules Art 19(1).
[108] Rules Art 8(2).
[109] Statute Art 17(6); Rules Art 8(1).
[110] Rules Art 41(3).
[111] Rules Art 22.

submitted under Article 188(1)(b) of UNCLOS.[112] They do, however, extend to the Chamber's advisory proceedings when the request for its advisory opinion relates to a legal question pending between two or more parties.[113]

Any intervening State Party/intervenor is not entitled to appoint a judge ad hoc.[114]

17. Incompatible activities

According to Article 7 of the ITLOS Statute, ITLOS judges may not exercise any political or administrative function, or associate actively with or be financially interested in any of the operations of any enterprise concerned with the exploration for or exploitation of the resources of the sea or the seabed or other commercial use of the sea or the seabed.[115] Nor may an ITLOS judge act as agent, counsel, or advocate in any case. Any doubt on these points shall be resolved by decision of the majority of the other ITLOS judges present. This provision applies only to elected judges of ITLOS.[116]

In practice, the objective of this regulation against incompatible activities is to ensure the impartiality of judges by insulating them from any activity or position which could influence them in their performance of duties or give the impression that such influence exists, as well as to protect the dignity of individual judges and the reputation of ITLOS as a whole. Determination of whether any particular function or activity is compatible with his or her judicial function will normally be made first by the judge concerned and, if necessary, by the President or ITLOS itself taking into consideration information, ideas, and conclusions applicable to other international judicial bodies such as the International Court of Justice.[117] Unlike the situation in the ICJ, engagement of a member of ITLOS in an occupation of professional nature will not necessarily be incompatible with his or her office, depending on the nature of the functions involved. An occupation or

---

[112] See also Statute Art 36; Gudmundur Eiriksson, *The International Tribunal for the Law of the Sea* (Martinus Nijhoff 2000) 48–49, 74–76.

[113] Rules Art 130(2).

[114] Rules Art 103(4) and Art 104(3).

[115] See also Zimmermann (n 11) 277–80.

[116] Virginia Commentary (n 25) 351.

[117] eg, Resolution of the Institut de Droit International on 'The Position of the International Judge' (9 September 2011); Robert Kolb, *The Elgar Companion to the International Court of Justice* (Edward Elgar 2014) 114–21.

activity in academia is generally not considered incompatible regardless of whether the host institution is State-owned or private. Members of ITLOS may serve as arbitrators in general or as special arbitrators under Annex VII of UNCLOS. They may also be included in the list of conciliators or arbitrators under Annexes V and VII of UNCLOS. However, they should decline to serve in cases where the dispute, or some related aspect of it, will possibly come before ITLOS. While certain functions or activities may not in themselves be incompatible, engaging in them may give rise to a situation in which the member concerned would be required to refrain from participating in the decision of particular cases.[118]

Article 7 of the Statute is not among the provisions of the Statute stipulating conditions for judges ad hoc to fulfil,[119] but they, like elected ITLOS judges, could be barred from participating in a case 'for some special reason'.[120]

18. Privileges and immunities

Article 10 of the ITLOS Statute reads: 'The members of the Tribunal, when engaged on the business of the Tribunal, shall enjoy diplomatic privileges and immunities.' This provision corresponds to Article 19 of the Statute of the ICJ, and it is to be assumed that it will be applied in a similar way.[121] The expression 'member of the Tribunal' encompasses not only elected ITLOS judges but also judges ad hoc of ITLOS. The privileges and immunities granted are those generally granted to members of the diplomatic corps, and are available to ITLOS judges only when they are engaged on ITLOS's business; that is, when they are acting in their official capacity.[122]

The Statute of ITLOS binds all States Parties to UNCLOS. In addition, the 1997 Agreement on the Privileges and Immunities of ITLOS,[123] in

---

[118] See Statute Art 8 (Conditions relating to participation of members in a particular case). cf Philippe Couvreur, 'Article 17' in Andreas Zimmermann and others (eds) *The Statute of the International Court of Justice: A Commentary* (2nd edn, OUP 2012) 372; Chiara Giorgetti (ed), *Challenges and Recusals of Judges and Arbitrators in International Courts and Tribunals* (Brill 2015).

[119] See Statute Art 17(6).

[120] Statute Art 8(2) and (3). This provision does not elaborate what such special reason may be, though. See Eiriksson (n 112) 40.

[121] See also Zimmermann (n 11) 275–77.

[122] Virginia Commentary (n 25) 355.

[123] 2167 UNTS 271.

force as of 30 December 2001 with 41 parties[124] as of this writing, elaborates in more detail the privileges and immunities accorded under Article 10 of the ITLOS Statute as well as accords to persons participating in proceedings and officials of ITLOS such privileges and immunities as are necessary for the independent exercise of their functions in connection with ITLOS. The 1997 Agreement recognizes, inter alia, the inviolability of ITLOS's premises and archives; the immunity of ITLOS's property, assets, and funds—wherever located and by whomsoever held—from search, requisition, confiscation, seizure, expropriation, or any other form of interference, whether by executive, administrative, judicial, or legislative action.

In particular, Article 13 of the 1997 Agreement provides, inter alia, that ITLOS judges shall, when engaged on ITLOS business, enjoy the privileges, immunities, facilities, and prerogatives accorded to heads of diplomatic missions. They and members of their families forming part of their households shall be accorded every facility for leaving the country where they may happen to be and for entering and leaving the country where ITLOS is sitting. On journeys in connection with the exercise of their functions, they shall in all countries through which they may have to pass enjoy all the privileges, immunities, and facilities granted by these countries to diplomatic agents in similar circumstances. If ITLOS judges, for the purpose of holding themselves at ITLOS's disposal, reside in any country other than that of which they are nationals or permanent residents, they shall, together with the members of their families forming part of their households, be accorded diplomatic privileges, immunities, and facilities during the period of their residence there. The foregoing shall apply to ITLOS judges even after they have been replaced if they continue to exercise their functions in any unfinished proceedings which they may have begun before the date of their replacement. In order to secure, for ITLOS judges, complete freedom of speech and independence in the discharge of their functions, the immunity from legal process in respect of words spoken or written and all acts done by them in discharging their functions shall continue to be accorded,

---

[124] Argentina, Australia, Austria, Belgium, Belize, Bolivia, Bulgaria, Cameroon, Chile, Croatia, Cyprus, Czech Republic, Denmark, Estonia, Finland, France, Germany, Greece, India, Ireland, Italy, Jamaica, Kuwait, Lebanon, Liberia, Lithuania, Malta, Netherlands, Norway, Panama, Poland, Portugal, Qatar, Rep of Korea, Russia, Saudi Arabia, Slovakia, Slovenia, Spain, UK, and Uruguay.

notwithstanding that the persons concerned are no longer ITLOS judges or performing those functions.

There are three declarations made upon ratification or accession to the 1997 Agreement. Argentina declares it will accord such privileges and immunities as are specified in the Agreement to members of the ITLOS Secretariat who are nationals or permanent residents in its territory to the extent necessary for the adequate fulfilment of their duties. With regard to fiscal and customs matters, those members will be subject to the national norms application in the territory of Argentina. France declares its intention to limit the exemption from taxation provided for under Article 11(1) of the Agreement[125] to the salaries and emoluments paid to ITLOS judges and officials, excluding any allowances paid to them by ITLOS. Moreover, in the case of ITLOS judges and officials residing in France, France intends to retain the option to take the exempted income into account in determining the tax rate applicable to the total income of such persons. For its part, Italy interprets Article 11(2)[126] and Article 16(4)[127] as referring exclusively to income paid by ITLOS, excluding any exemption for income from other sources.

Article 1(3) of the Statute of ITLOS allows ITLOS to sit and exercise its functions elsewhere whenever it considers this desirable. According to Article 7 of the 1997 Agreement on the Privileges and Immunities of ITLOS, when ITLOS considers it desirable to sit or otherwise exercise its functions elsewhere than at its headquarters, it may conclude with the State concerned an arrangement concerning the provision of the appropriate facilities for the exercise of its functions.

On 6 February 2008, the President of ITLOS and the Ministry of Foreign Affairs of Bahrain issued a joint declaration stating that whenever ITLOS considers it appropriate for a special chamber established in accordance with Article 15 of the ITLOS Statute to sit or otherwise exercise its functions at a place in the Middle East region, ITLOS will give due consideration to such sitting or exercise of functions of the

---

[125] Art 11(1): 'The salaries, emoluments, and allowances paid to Members and officials of the Tribunal shall be exempt from taxation.'

[126] Art 11(2): 'Where the incidence of any form of taxation depends upon residence, periods during which such Members or officials are present in a State for the discharge of their functions shall not be considered as periods of residence if such Members or officials are accorded diplomatic privileges, immunities, and facilities.'

[127] Art 16(4): 'Where the incidence of any form of taxation depends upon residence, periods during which such agents, counsel, or advocates are present in a State for the discharge of their functions shall not be considered as periods of residence.'

special chamber being held in Bahrain, provided the parties to the dispute so agree. In return, the Government of Bahrain agrees to provide necessary facilities to ITLOS subject to the terms and conditions to be determined in an arrangement between ITLOS and the Government of Bahrain which shall grant, inter alia, privileges and immunities to ITLOS consistent with the 1997 Agreement on the Privileges and Immunities of ITLOS. On 28 May 2008, ITLOS and the Ministry of Foreign Affairs of Argentina issued a press release affirming Argentina's willingness to provide the necessary facilities when ITLOS and the parties to a dispute consider it desirable for a special chamber of ITLOS to sit or otherwise exercise its functions in Buenos Aires. Any assistance given to ITLOS by the Argentine Government in such a case will be subject to an arrangement containing, inter alia, provisions consistent with the 1997 Agreement on the Privileges and Immunities of ITLOS. On 31 August 2015, ITLOS and the Ministry of Law of Singapore issued a joint declaration recording their commitment to start negotiations on a model agreement to specify the terms and conditions as well as privileges and immunities as the basis for a special arrangement to be concluded with respect to each particular case to be heard in Singapore by a special chamber of ITLOS established in accordance with Article 15 of the ITLOS Statute for which the Government of Singapore would provide appropriate facilities. Furthermore, it is also understood that if the 'States Parties to a dispute' so propose and if financial conditions on the part of ITLOS and the Government of Singapore so permit, ITLOS may sit or otherwise exercise its functions in Singapore, and that a special arrangement will then have to be concluded for this purpose. Argentina is party to the 1997 Agreement, whereas Bahrain and Singapore are not. Yet, Bahrain and Singapore are willing to grant, inter alia, privileges and immunities to ITLOS consistent with the 1997 Agreement. For its part, ITLOS considers privileges and immunities stipulated in the 1997 Agreement as the minimum to be accorded to ITLOS. On 11 June 2020, ITLOS and the Government of Singapore signed the model agreement for the provision of facilities for not only a special chamber of ITLOS, but also the full-bench ITLOS and the Seabed Disputes Chamber, to sit or otherwise exercise their respective functions in Singapore. This model agreement will form the basis of a future agreement with Singapore when ITLOS, the Seabed Disputes Chamber, or a special chamber of ITLOS considers it desirable that a case submitted to it be heard in Singapore.

19. Experts and witnesses

By virtue of Article 289 of UNCLOS, in any dispute involving scientific or technical matters, a court or tribunal exercising jurisdiction under section 2 (Compulsory Proceedings Entailing Binding Decisions) of Part XV may, at the request of a party or *proprio motu*, select in consultation with the disputing parties no fewer than two scientific or technical experts chosen preferably from the relevant list prepared in accordance with Article 2 of Annex VIII (Special Arbitration) to sit with the court or tribunal but without the right to vote.[128]

Under Article 2 of Annex VIII of UNCLOS, a list of experts shall be established and maintained in respect of each of the fields of (1) fisheries, (2) protection and preservation of the marine environment, (3) marine scientific research, and (4) navigation, including pollution from vessels and by dumping. The lists of experts shall be drawn up and maintained, in the field of fisheries by the Food and Agriculture Organization of the United Nations; in the field of protection and preservation of the marine environment by the United Nations Environment Programme; in the field of marine scientific research by the Intergovernmental Oceanographic Commission; in the field of navigation, including pollution from vessels and by dumping, by the International Maritime Organization; or in each case by the appropriate subsidiary body concerned to which such organization, programme, or commission has delegated this function. Every State Party to UNCLOS is entitled to nominate two experts in each field whose competence in the legal, scientific, or technical aspects of such field is established and generally recognized and who enjoy the highest reputation for fairness and integrity. The names of the persons so nominated in each field shall constitute the appropriate list. If at any time the experts nominated by a State Party in the list so constituted shall be fewer than two, that State Party shall be entitled to make further nominations as necessary. The name of an expert shall remain on the list until withdrawn by the State Party that made the nomination, but such expert shall continue to serve on any special arbitral tribunal to which that expert has been appointed until the completion of the proceedings before that special arbitral tribunal.

---

[128] See also Zimmermann (n 11) 261–64; Lucas Carlos Lima, 'The Use of Experts by the International Tribunal for the Law of the Sea and Annex VII Arbitral Tribunals' in Angela Del Vecchio and Roberto Virzo (eds), *Interpretation of the United Nations Convention on the Law of the Sea by International Courts and Tribunals* (Springer 2019) 412–19.

Pursuant to Article 15 of the Rules of ITLOS, a request by a party for the selection by ITLOS of scientific or technical experts under Article 289 of UNCLOS shall, as a general rule, be made not later than the closure of the written proceedings. ITLOS may consider a later request made prior to the closure of the oral proceedings, if appropriate in the circumstances of the case. When ITLOS decides to select experts, at the request of a party or *proprio motu*, it shall select such experts upon the proposal of the ITLOS President, who shall consult the parties before making such a proposal. Experts shall be independent and enjoy the highest reputation for fairness, competence, and integrity. An expert in a field mentioned in Article 2 of Annex VIII to UNCLOS shall be chosen preferably from the relevant list prepared in accordance with that annex. This Article applies *mutatis mutandis* to any ITLOS chamber and its President.

Article 82 of the Rules of ITLOS allows ITLOS, if it considers it necessary to arrange for an inquiry or an expert opinion after hearing the parties, to issue an order to this effect, defining the subject of the inquiry or expert opinion, stating the number and mode of appointment of the persons to hold the inquiry or of the experts, and laying down the procedure to be followed. Every report or record of an inquiry and every expert opinion shall be communicated to the parties, which shall be given the opportunity to comment upon it.

As of this writing, ITLOS has not made use of these experts.

The aforesaid experts must be distinguished from witnesses and experts called upon by the disputing parties at their own initiative or at ITLOS's behest to produce such evidence or to give such explanations as ITLOS may consider to be necessary for the elucidation of any aspect of the matters in issue before ITLOS.[129]

According to Article 78 of ITLOS's Rules, the parties themselves may call any witnesses or experts appearing on the list communicated to ITLOS before the opening of the oral proceedings. If at any time during the hearing a party wishes to call a witness or expert whose name was not included in that list, it shall make a request to ITLOS and inform the other party, and shall supply a list of the experts whom the party intends to call, with indications of the point or points to which their evidence will be directed. The witness or expert may be called either if the other party raises no objection or, in the event of objection, if ITLOS so authorizes. ITLOS may, at the request of a

---

[129] See Rules Arts 72 and 77.

party or *proprio motu*, decide that a witness or expert be examined otherwise than before ITLOS itself. The ITLOS President shall take the necessary steps to implement such a decision. This Article must be read in conjunction with Article 27 of the Statute of ITLOS requiring ITLOS to make orders for the conduct of the case, decide the form and time in which each party must conclude its arguments, and make all arrangements connected with the taking of evidence.

For example, experts and witnesses were called upon by both parties in the *M/V 'Norstar'* case to testify in support of their respective positions, cross-examined by the other party, and questioned by some ITLOS judges. Their testimonies included the physical conditions and monetary value of the vessel M/V 'Norstar' at specific periods, financial losses incurred as a result of the seizure of the vessel, and the duty to maintain a vessel under seizure.

20. Rules of evidence

In the *M/V 'Norstar'* case, ITLOS also addressed issues relating to the rules of evidence, including the standard of proof and the probative weight to be given to the witness and expert testimony. Although the parties did not disagree that Panama, the applicant, had the burden of proving its claims, they disagreed as to the standard of proof for Panama to meet. Panama, as part of its Memorial, filed a document entitled 'Request for Evidence', requesting ITLOS, inter alia, to order Italy, the respondent, to provide certified copies of files concerning the M/V 'Norstar' allegedly held by different authorities in Italy. ITLOS did not accept Panama's request, and instead encouraged the parties to continue their cooperation with respect to evidence, taking note of the exchange of letters between them in this regard, in particular the offer by Italy to share a list of the documents contained in Italy's files, subject to conditions of reciprocity with Panama with respect to Panama's own files. Italy would then consider a specific and qualified request from Panama and reserved the right to make a similar request to Panama. The parties subsequently exchanged, through the ITLOS Registrar, a list of documents in their respective files concerning the case. However, no further action on this matter was taken. ITLOS considered Italy's suggestion that it would consider a specific and qualified request for evidence from Panama as reasonable and would not have created an obstacle for Panama in making a request for evidence. Panama nonetheless made no attempt to make any such request. ITLOS further noted that Panama instituted the proceedings against Italy at ITLOS in 2015, some 17 years after the arrest of the M/V 'Norstar'. The lapse of time might have caused Panama difficulties in obtaining relevant evidence, but such difficulties stemmed from Panama's own decision. ITLOS was accordingly not persuaded by Panama's argument on the need to adjust the standard of proof placed upon it because of Italy's refusal of Panama's request for evidence.

Regarding witness and expert testimony, the parties called several witnesses and experts to prove their claims. ITLOS assessed the relevance and probative value of their testimonies by taking into account, inter alia, whether those testimonies concerned the existence of facts or represented only personal opinions; whether they were based on first-hand knowledge; whether they were duly tested through cross-examination; whether they were corroborated by other evidence; and whether a witness or expert might have an interest in the outcome of the proceedings.[130] ITLOS accepted the estimation of the vessel's value by a sea captain and member of the national register for experts for naval evaluation, called by the respondent as an expert in that case. He assessed the value of the M/V 'Norstar' at the time of the arrest at approximately €250,000, although he admitted it had not been possible for him to inspect the M/V 'Norstar' and he had to use normal estimates usually applicable in such circumstances.[131] In ITLOS's observation, although the estimates of the vessel's value presented by that expert and the estimate by a third party submitted by the applicant were not based on physical inspection of the vessel, the estimate by the respondent's expert, unlike the applicant's, made no assumption for the profitability of the operations of the vessel in assessing its value, and his testimony was duly tested through cross-examination. Moreover, ITLOS had no reason to believe that he had an interest in the outcome of the proceedings in that case. Since the applicant failed to establish the loss of profits to be generated by the operations of the vessel, ITLOS concluded the amount of US$285,000—the equivalent of estimate by the expert called upon by the respondent—was to be compensated to the applicant for the loss of the vessel.[132]

Therefore, ITLOS generally discounts the value of affidavits that merely represent the opinions of private individuals regarding certain facts[133] or

---

[130] *M/V 'Norstar' (Panama v Italy)* (Merits) ITLOS Judgment of 10 April 2019 para 99.
[131] ibid para 405.
[132] ibid paras 411–17.
[133] *Delimitation of the Maritime Boundary in the Bay of Bengal (Bangladesh/Myanmar)* ITLOS Reports 2012, 4, 40 [113].

affidavits from government officials who may have an interest in the outcome of the proceedings.[134]

21. Non-appearance

Pursuant to Article 28 of the ITLOS Statute, when one of the parties does
not appear before ITLOS or fails to defend its case, the other party may request ITLOS to continue the proceedings and make its decision. Absence
of a party or failure of a party to defend its case thus shall not constitute a
bar to the proceedings. Before making such a decision, ITLOS must satisfy
itself not only that it has jurisdiction over the dispute, but also that the claim
is well founded in fact and law.

ITLOS follows the well-established jurisprudence of the ICJ, according
to which the parties, including the non-appearing party, must be given an
opportunity of presenting their observations on the subject.[135] The non-
appearing State is deemed a party to the proceedings, with ensuing rights
and obligations.[136] A State which decides not to appear must accept the
consequences of its decision—despite its non-participation, the case will
continue and the non-appearing party remains a party to the case and is
bound by the eventual judgment.[137] Where one party to a dispute does
not participate in the proceedings before ITLOS, ITLOS must identify
and assess the respective rights of the parties involved on the best available evidence.[138]

---

[134] ibid 40 [114].

[135] 'Arctic Sunrise' (Provisional Measures, Order of 25 October 2013) 242 [48], citing
Fisheries Jurisdiction (United Kingdom v Iceland) (Interim Protection: Order) [1972] ICJ
Rep 12, 15 [11]; *Fisheries Jurisdiction (Federal Republic of Germany v Iceland)* (Interim
Protection: Order) [1972] ICJ Rep 30, 32–33 [11]; *Nuclear Tests (Australia v France)* (Interim
Protection: Order) [1973] ICJ Rep 99, 101 [11]; *Nuclear Tests (New Zealand v France)* (Interim
Protection: Order) [1973] ICJ Rep 135, 137 [12]; *Aegean Sea Continental Shelf Case (Greece
v Turkey)* (Interim Protection: Order) [1976] ICJ Rep 3, 6 [13]; *United States Diplomatic and
Consular Staff in Tehran (United States of America v Iran)* (Provisional Measures, Order of
15 December 1979) [1979] ICJ Rep 7, 11–12 [9], 13 [13]. See also Sotirios-Ioannis Lekkas
and Christopher Staker, 'Art 28 Annex VI' in Alexander Proelss (ed), *The United Nations
Convention on the Law of the Sea: A Commentary* (Hart 2017) 2412–22.

[136] 'Arctic Sunrise' (Provisional Measures, Order of 25 October 2013) 242 [51], quoting
Nuclear Tests (Australia v France) (Interim Protection: Order) [1973] ICJ Rep 99, 103–04 [24].

[137] 'Arctic Sunrise' (Provisional Measures, Order of 25 October 2013) (n 136) 242–43 [52],
citing *Military and Paramilitary Activities in and against Nicaragua (Nicaragua v United States
of America)* (Merits) [1986] ICJ Rep 14, 24 [28].

[138] 'Arctic Sunrise' (Provisional Measures, Order of 25 October 2013) (n 136) 243 [57].

22. End of tenure of judges

ITLOS judges who have been replaced following the expiration of their terms of office shall continue to sit in a case until the completion of any phase of the case in respect of which they have participated in initial deliberations, held after the closure of the written proceedings and prior to the opening of the oral proceedings, to exchange views concerning the written pleadings and the conduct of the case.[139]

The ITLOS judge who is presiding in a case on the date on which ITLOS meets for initial deliberations shall continue to preside in the case until completion of the current phase of the case, notwithstanding the election in the meantime of a new President or Vice-President of ITLOS. Should he or she become unable to act, the presidency for the case shall be determined in accordance with the ITLOS Rule as regards a vacancy in the presidency or the inability of the ITLOS President to exercise the functions of the presidency and on the basis of the composition of ITLOS on the date on which it met for initial deliberations.[140]

In *Request for Advisory Opinion submitted by the Sub-Regional Fisheries Commission*, Judge Yanai, whose term of office as ITLOS President expired on 30 September 2014, continued to preside over ITLOS in that case until its completion. Judges Nelson and Türk, whose respective terms of office also expired on 30 September 2014, having participated in the meeting for initial deliberations, continued to sit in the case until its completion on 2 April 2015. However, in *M/V 'Norstar'* the ITLOS judges who participated in the preliminary objections phase and who were not re-elected to serve after the end of their term of office on 30 September 2017 did not continue to sit in that case at the merits phase since their tenure had terminated prior to the initial deliberations on the merits of that case.

As regards the Seabed Disputes Chamber, if any proceedings are still pending at the end of any three-year period for which the Chamber has been selected, the Chamber shall complete the proceedings in its original composition.[141]

---

[139] Rules Arts 17 and 68.
[140] Rules Art 16(2).
[141] Statute Art 35(5).

3
Contentious Cases before ITLOS and the Seabed Disputes Chamber

1. Contentious cases before ITLOS

a) What constitutes a 'dispute'?

ITLOS has to determine whether, on the date of the institution of proceedings before it, a dispute existed between the parties.

ITLOS concurs with the International Court of Justice that a dispute is a disagreement on a point of law or fact, a conflict of legal views or interests, or the positive opposition of the claim of one party by the other, which need not necessarily be stated *expressis verbis*, and that, in the determination of the existence of a dispute, the position or the attitude of a party can be established by inference, whatever the professed view of that party.[1]

Disputing parties are not permitted to abuse the process during the course of the proceedings by introducing new claims not already included in the application or special agreement. Article 24(1) of the ITLOS Statute stipulates, inter alia, that when disputes are submitted to ITLOS by either of these two means, the 'subject of the dispute' must be indicated. Similarly, by virtue of Article 54(1) of the Rules of ITLOS, the application instituting the proceedings must indicate the 'subject of the dispute', and Article 54(2) adds that the application shall specify as far as possible the legal grounds upon which the jurisdiction of ITLOS is said to be based as well as specify the precise nature of the claim, together with a succinct statement of the

---

[1] *M/T 'San Padre Pio' (Switzerland v Nigeria)* (Provisional Measures, Order of 6 July 2019) para 57, quoting *Land and Maritime Boundary between Cameroon and Nigeria (Cameroon v Nigeria)* (Preliminary Objections) [1998] ICJ Rep 275, 315 [89]. See also *Southern Bluefin Tuna (New Zealand v Japan; Australia v Japan)* (Provisional Measures, Order of 27 August 1999) ITLOS Reports 1999, 280, 293 [44]; *M/V 'Norstar'* (Preliminary Objections) ITLOS Judgment of 4 November 2016 para 100; *Detention of three Ukrainian naval vessels (Ukraine v Russian Federation)* (Provisional Measures, Order of 25 May 2019) para 43.

facts and grounds on which the claim is based. ITLOS is consistent in ruling that while subsequent pleadings may elucidate the terms of the application, they must not go beyond the limits of the claim as set out in the application. ITLOS follows the established jurisprudence of the Permanent Court of International Justice and the ICJ in setting a legal requirement that any new claim to be admitted must arise directly out of the application or be implicit in it, and that it cannot allow a dispute brought before it by an application to be transformed in the course of proceedings into another dispute of a different character.[2] By referring also to Article 24(1) of the Statute to support its reasoning in this respect and by finding Article 24(1) of its Statute and Article 54(1) and (2) of its Rules to be 'essential from the point of view of legal security and the good administration of justice',[3] ITLOS must have intended to apply this ruling to disputes submitted to ITLOS by notification of a special agreement as well.

b) Scope of a dispute

When there is a dispute between the parties at the time of the institution of proceedings, the dispute must be one over which ITLOS has jurisdiction. When a dispute is submitted to it by the notification of a special agreement, ITLOS must construe the scope of that special agreement conferring jurisdiction upon it. When a dispute is submitted to ITLOS by means of an application, Article 288(1) of UNCLOS provides that a court or tribunal chosen by the disputing parties by declarations pursuant to Article 287 shall have jurisdiction over any dispute 'concerning the interpretation or application' of UNCLOS which is submitted to it according to Part XV of UNCLOS. Article 288(2) adds that such court or tribunal shall also have jurisdiction over any dispute 'concerning the interpretation or application' of an international agreement related to the purposes of UNCLOS, which is submitted to it according to Part XV of UNCLOS.

In *M/V 'Louisa' (Saint Vincent and the Grenadines v Kingdom of Spain)*, ITLOS had to determine the scope of Saint Vincent and the Grenadines' declaration accepting ITLOS's jurisdiction over disputes 'concerning the

---

[2] *M/V 'Louisa' (Saint Vincent and the Grenadines v Kingdom of Spain)* (Merits) ITLOS Reports 2013, 4, 44–45 [143]–[149] and the cases cited therein. See also *M/V 'Norstar' (Panama v Italy)* (Merits) ITLOS Judgment of 10 April 2019 paras 130–46.

[3] *M/V 'Louisa'* (Merits) (n 2) 44 [143], 45 [148].

arrest or detention' of vessels. ITLOS held that the use of the term 'concerning' in the declaration indicated that the declaration extended not only to the articles of UNCLOS which expressly contain the word 'arrest' or 'detention', but also to 'any provision of UNCLOS having a bearing on' the arrest or detention of vessels. This interpretation was reinforced by taking into account the intention of Saint Vincent and the Grenadines at the time it made the declaration to cover all claims connected with the arrest or detention of its vessels. ITLOS, therefore, considered that the declaration of Saint Vincent and the Grenadines covered the arrest or detention of its vessels and all matters connected therewith.[4]

To determine whether a dispute between the disputing parties in a particular case concerns the interpretation or application of UNCLOS, ITLOS must also establish a link between the facts advanced by the applicant and the provisions of UNCLOS referred to by it and show that such provisions can sustain the claims submitted by the applicant.[5] In *M/V 'Louisa'*, the applicant alleged that the respondent detained the vessel M/V 'Louisa' flying the flag of Saint Vincent and the Grenadines and its crew when the vessel was docked in a Spanish port in violation of UNCLOS's Articles 73 (enforcement of laws and regulations of a coastal State in the exercise of its sovereign rights to explore, exploit, conserve, and manage the living resources in its exclusive economic zone), 87 (freedom of the high seas), 226 and 227 (investigation of foreign vessels for violation of applicable laws and regulations or international rules and standards for the protection and preservation of the marine environment), 245 (marine scientific research in the territorial sea), and 304 (responsibility and liability for damage). ITLOS found that the vessel was detained by Spain in the context of criminal proceedings relating to the alleged violations of Spanish laws on 'the protection of the underwater cultural heritage and the possession and handling of weapons of war in Spanish territory' that were not within the scope of the UNCLOS provisions forming the legal basis of the applicant's application. Besides, the question of the application of Article 304 of UNCLOS might arise only if ITLOS were to hold that it had jurisdiction to deal with the merits of the case. ITLOS, therefore, concluded that no dispute concerning the interpretation or application of UNCLOS existed between the parties at the time of the filing of the application and that it had no jurisdiction *ratione*

---

[4] ibid 31 [83]–[84].
[5] *M/V 'Norstar' (Panama v Italy)* (Preliminary Objections) (n 1) para 110, citing *M/V 'Louisa'* (Merits) (n 2) 34 [99].

materiae to entertain the case.[6] By contrast, in *M/V 'Norstar' (Panama v Italy)*, ITLOS found Article 87 of UNCLOS, which concerns the freedom of the high seas, to be relevant because the Decree of Seizure by the Public Prosecutor at the Italian Court of Savona against the M/V 'Norstar' flying the flag of Panama with regard to activities conducted by that vessel on the high seas and the request for its execution by the Prosecutor at the Court of Savona might be viewed as an infringement of the rights of Panama under Article 87 as the flag State of the vessel.[7] In addition, ITLOS found Article 300 on good faith and abuse of rights of UNCLOS to be relevant to determining whether Italy had fulfilled in good faith the obligations assumed by it under Article 87 UNCLOS.[8] ITLOS, therefore, rejected the objection raised by Italy based on non-existence of a dispute concerning the interpretation or application of UNCLOS.[9]

The word 'concerning the interpretation or application' of UNCLOS or an international agreement related to the purposes of UNCLOS as stipulated in Article 288(1) and (2), respectively, defines the scope of jurisdiction *ratione materiae* of the court or tribunal, which must be distinguished from the provision of Article 293, under the heading 'Applicable law', that a court or tribunal having jurisdiction under this section shall apply UNCLOS and other rules of international law not incompatible with UNCLOS.[10] In *M/V 'Norstar'*, ITLOS, noting such distinction, ruled that Article 293 might not be used to extend ITLOS's jurisdiction. In the proceedings on the merits in the case at bar, ITLOS was called upon to interpret and apply Article 87 of UNCLOS regarding Panama's freedom of navigation on the high seas. In order to assess what such freedom entailed, ITLOS might have recourse to other provisions of UNCLOS pursuant to Article 293, including Article 92 as regards the principle of exclusive jurisdiction of the flag State over its vessels on the high seas, as applicable law. This was not the same thing as enlarging the scope of the dispute, the limits of which had been set by ITLOS's judgment on Preliminary Objections.[11] Similarly, in *M/V 'Saiga' (No 2)* ITLOS reasoned that although UNCLOS did not contain express

---

[6] *M/V 'Louisa'* (Merits) (n 2) 34 [98]–46 [151].

[7] *M/V 'Norstar'* (Preliminary Objections) (n 1) para 122.

[8] ibid para 132.

[9] ibid para 133.

[10] cf David H Anderson, 'Peaceful Settlement of Disputes under UNCLOS' in Jill Barrett and Richard Barnes (eds), *Law of the Sea: UNCLOS as a Living Treaty* (British Institute of Int'l & Comparative Law 2016) 399; Peter Tzeng, 'Supplemental Jurisdiction Under UNCLOS' (2016) 38 Houston JIL 499, 519–35.

[11] *M/V 'Norstar'* (Merits) (n 2) paras 136–38.

provisions on the use of force in the arrest of ships, international law, which was applicable by virtue of Article 293 of UNCLOS, required the use of force to be avoided as far as possible and, where force was unavoidable, it was not to go beyond what was reasonable and necessary in the circumstances.[12] ITLOS found the respondent in this latter case had used excessive force and endangered human life before and after boarding the M/V 'Saiga', thereby violating the rights of the applicant under international law.[13]

c) Preliminary objections

Article 294 (Preliminary proceedings) of UNCLOS seeks to accommodate the concerns expressed by certain coastal States at the Third UN Conference on the Law of the Sea that dispute settlement procedures for some disputes relating to the exercise by a coastal State of sovereign rights or jurisdiction under the provisions of UNCLOS relating to the exclusive economic zone and the continental shelf might force these States to defend too many cases before international courts or tribunals, stretching thin their financial resources and skilled manpower. In balancing the protection of these coastal States against harassment through frivolous complaints, on the one hand, and the right of other States to protect their interests or the interests of their citizens, on the other hand,[14] Article 294 requires a court or tribunal enumerated in Article 287 to which an application is made in respect of such disputes to determine at the request of a party, or *proprio motu*, whether the claim constitutes an abuse of legal process or whether prima facie it is well founded. If the court or tribunal determines the claim to be an abuse of legal process or is prima facie unfounded, it shall take no further action in the case. Upon receipt of the application, the court or tribunal shall immediately notify the other party or parties of the application, and shall fix a reasonable time limit within which they may request it to

---

[12] *M/V 'Saiga' (No 2) (Saint Vincent and the Grenadines v Guinea)* (Merits) ITLOS Reports 1999, 10, 61–62 [155].

[13] ibid 63 [159], cited, with approval, in *M/V 'Virginia G' (Panama/Guinea-Bissau)* ITLOS Reports 2014, 4, 103 [362]. See also *Dispute Concerning the Delimitation of the Maritime Boundary between Ghana and Côte d'Ivoire in the Atlantic Ocean (Ghana/Côte d'Ivoire)* (Merits) ITLOS Judgment of 23 September 2017 para 555.

[14] Myron H Nordquist, Shabtai Rosenne, and Louis B Sohn (eds), *United Nations Convention on the Law of the Sea 1982: A Commentary*, vol 5 (Brill 1989) ('Virginia Commentary') 76–78.

make such determination. Nothing in Article 294 affects the right of any party to a dispute to make preliminary objections in accordance with the applicable rules of procedure.

As explained in Chapter 2, Article 97 of the Rules of ITLOS requires any objection to the jurisdiction of ITLOS or to the admissibility of the application, or other objection the decision upon which is requested before any further proceedings on the merits, to be made in writing within 90 days from the institution of proceedings.

In *M/V 'Norstar' (Panama v Italy)* Italy filed with ITLOS written preliminary objections under Article 294 challenging ITLOS's jurisdiction as well as the admissibility of Panama's claim. In response, Panama submitted a request to ITLOS for a ruling concerning the scope of the subject matter based on the preliminary objections filed by Italy, but Italy objected to this request by Panama. Italy submitted that its preliminary objections to ITLOS's jurisdiction were grounded on the following alleged facts: no dispute existed between Panama and Italy; Italy was the wrong respondent and, in any event, adjudication over the claim advanced by Panama would require ITLOS to ascertain rights and obligations pertaining to Spain, a third party, in Spain's absence; and Panama had failed to appropriately pursue the settlement of the dispute by negotiation or other peaceful means under Article 283(1) of UNCLOS.[15] Having thoroughly examined the facts and applicable law, ITLOS rejected Italy's aforesaid preliminary objections to ITLOS's jurisdiction.[16]

Italy's legal arguments in the preliminary objections maintained that the application was preponderantly, if not exclusively, one of a diplomatic protection character, while the alleged victims of the seizure were not Panamanian nationals and, anyhow, they had failed to exhaust the local remedies available in Italy with regard to the claim for damages for the allegedly unlawful arrest of the vessel M/V 'Norstar'. Besides, argued Italy, Panama was time-barred and estopped from validly bringing this case before ITLOS due to the lapse of 18 years since the seizure of the vessel and to Panama's contradictory attitude throughout that time. With respect to the latter, ITLOS considered the question of the admissibility of an application might be assessed in the light of the well-established principles of international law governing acquiescence, estoppel, and extinctive

---

[15] *M/V 'Norstar'* (Preliminary Objections) (n 1) para 61.
[16] ibid paras 220, 316(1).

prescription as such principles might be invoked by virtue of Article 293 of UNCLOS which allows reference to such principles to the extent they are not incompatible with UNCLOS.[17] While the concepts of acquiescence and estoppel both follow from the fundamental principles of good faith and equity, they are based on different legal reasoning. Acquiescence is equivalent to tacit recognition manifested by unilateral conduct which the other party may interpret as consent, whereas estoppel is linked to the idea of preclusion in which lapse of time may have the effect of rendering an application inadmissible.[18] A situation of estoppel in international law exists when a State, by its conduct, has created the appearance of a particular situation and another State, relying on such conduct in good faith, has acted or abstained from an action to its detriment, with the effect that a State is precluded, by its conduct, from asserting it did not agree to, or recognize, a certain situation.[19] On the facts of M/V 'Norstar', ITLOS found the conditions of acquiescence, estoppel, and extinctive prescription were not met.[20] In particular, since neither UNCLOS nor general international law provides a time limit regarding the institution of proceedings before it, it is for ITLOS to determine in the light of the circumstances of each case whether the passage of time renders an application inadmissible.[21] In ITLOS's view, Panama did not fail to pursue its claim since the time when it first made it, so as to render the application inadmissible.[22] The other legal grounds raised by Italy in its preliminary objections to the admissibility of Panama's claim are analysed in sections (d) and (e) below. In the end, ITLOS rejected Italy's preliminary objections to the admissibility of Panama's claim.[23]

Even when disputing parties have agreed to submit their dispute to ITLOS by a special agreement, the respondent may still raise preliminary objections to ITLOS's jurisdiction. For example, the dispute in 'Saiga' (No

---

[17] ibid para 301.

[18] ibid para 303, quoting *Delimitation of the Maritime Boundary in the Gulf of Maine Area* [1984] ICJ Rep 246, 305 [130]; *Certain Phosphate Lands in Nauru (Nauru v Australia)* (Preliminary Objections) [1992] ICJ Rep 240, 253–54 [32]; *Ambatielos Claim (Greece, United Kingdom of Great Britain and Northern Ireland)* Award of the Commission of Arbitration of 6 March 1956, RIAA, vol XII, 83, 103.

[19] *M/V 'Norstar'* (Preliminary Objections) (n 1) para 306, quoting *Case concerning the Delimitation of the Maritime Boundary in the Bay of Bengal (Bangladesh/Myanmar)* ITLOS Reports 2012, 4, 45 [124].

[20] *M/V 'Norstar'* (Preliminary Objections) (n 1) paras 305, 308, 314.

[21] ibid para 311.

[22] ibid para 313.

[23] ibid para 316(2).

2) (Saint Vincent and the Grenadines v Guinea) originally submitted by the applicant to an Annex VII arbitral tribunal was subsequently transferred to ITLOS by the disputing parties' special agreement dated 20 February 1998. Paragraph 2 of the 1998 agreement reads:

> The written and oral proceedings before [ITLOS] shall comprise a single phase dealing with all aspects of the merits (including damages and costs) and the objection as to jurisdiction raised in the Government of Guinea's Statement of Response dated 30 January 1998.

That objection, based on Article 297(3) of UNCLOS on the limitation of ITLOS's jurisdiction in disputes concerning the interpretation or application of the provisions of UNCLOS with regard to fisheries, was raised in the phase of the proceedings relating to the applicant's request for the prescription of provisional measures. In its Order of 11 March 1998, ITLOS held that another provision of UNCLOS invoked by the applicant appeared prima facie to afford a basis for the jurisdiction of ITLOS. In the merits phase of the proceedings, Guinea did not reiterate its objection based on Article 297(3) of UNCLOS. On the contrary, it confirmed that, in its view, the basis for ITLOS's jurisdiction on the merits of the dispute was the 1998 agreement of the parties. ITLOS, therefore, ruled that the reference, in the 1998 agreement, to the 'objection as to jurisdiction' did not affect its jurisdiction to deal with the dispute, and that, accordingly, ITLOS had jurisdiction over the dispute as submitted to it.[24]

Dispute Concerning Delimitation of the Maritime Boundary between Mauritius and Maldives in the Indian Ocean (Mauritius/Maldives) was submitted to a special chamber of ITLOS by means of a special agreement and notification addressed to ITLOS on 24 September 2019 whereby the Mauritius and Maldives jointly transferred the dispute instituted by the former against the latter in an Annex VII arbitral tribunal. Subsequently, on 18 December 2019, Maldives filed preliminary objections to the jurisdiction of the special chamber and to the admissibility of the claims submitted by Mauritius. Pursuant to Article 97(3) of the Rules, the proceedings on the merits were suspended upon receipt of the preliminary objections by the ITLOS Registry.

---

[24] *M/V 'Saiga' (No 2)* (Merits) (n 12) 30–31 [41]–[45].

d) Exhaustion of local remedies

According to Article 295 of UNCLOS, any dispute between States Parties concerning the interpretation or application of UNCLOS may be submitted to the procedures provided for in section 2 of Part XV on compulsory procedures entailing binding decisions 'only after local remedies have been exhausted where this is required by international law'. It is a well-established principle of customary international law that exhaustion of local remedies is a prerequisite for the exercise of diplomatic protection (ie, when a State brings a claim on behalf of one or more of its nationals), but the exhaustion of local remedies rule does not apply where the claimant State brings a claim on its own behalf as a State 'directly injured' by the wrongful act of another State.[25]

In ITLOS's case law, the question of whether local remedies must be exhausted is answered by international law.[26] Where all the rights claimed by the applicant to have been violated by the respondent are those belonging to the applicant under UNCLOS, such as the freedom of navigation, and not an international obligation concerning the treatment to be accorded to aliens, the claim is not subject to the rule requiring local remedies to be exhausted.[27]

In 'Saiga' (No 2), the respondent Guinea's application of its customs laws to a customs radius extending to 250 nautical miles from its coast, which included parts of the exclusive economic zone, was held by ITLOS to be contrary to UNCLOS. Accordingly, the arrest of the ship 'Saiga' flying the flag of Saint Vincent and the Grenadines at a point approximately 22 nautical miles from Guinea's island of Alcatraz, the detention of the ship, the prosecution and conviction of its Master, the confiscation of the cargo, and the seizure of the ship were contrary to UNCLOS. None of these violations of rights claimed by the applicant could be described as breaches of obligations concerning the treatment to be accorded to aliens. They were all direct violations of the rights of Saint Vincent and the Grenadines, and the damage to the persons involved in the operation of the ship arose from

---

[25] M/V 'Virginia G' (n 13) 53–54 [153]. See also *Application of the International Convention for the Suppression of the Financing of Terrorism and of the International Convention on the Elimination of All Forms of Racial Discrimination (Ukraine v Russian Federation)* (Preliminary Objections) ICJ's Judgment of 8 November 2019 paras 129–30.

[26] M/V 'Saiga' (No 2) (Merits) (n 12) 45 [96].

[27] ibid 45–46 [97]–[98]. See also 'Enrica Lexie' (Italy v India) (Provisional Measures, Order of 24 August 2015) ITLOS Reports 2015, 182, 194 [67].

those violations. The claims in respect of such damage were, therefore, held by ITLOS not to be subject to the rule of exhaustion of local remedies.[28]

When the claim contains elements of both injury to a State and injury to an individual, for the purpose of deciding the applicability of the exhaustion of local remedies rule ITLOS has to determine which element is 'preponderant'.[29] In *M/V 'Virginia G'*, for example, ITLOS considered 'the principal rights' alleged by Panama to have been violated by Guinea-Bissau to include the right of Panama to enjoy freedom of navigation and other internationally lawful uses of the seas in the exclusive economic zone of the coastal State and its right to have the coastal State enforce its laws and regulations in conformity with Article 73 of UNCLOS. These were rights belonging to Panama under UNCLOS and their alleged violations thus amounted to 'direct injury' to Panama.[30] The claim for damages to the persons and entities with an interest in the ship or its cargo arising from such alleged violations was, therefore, not subject to the rule of exhaustion of local remedies.[31]

In *M/V 'Norstar' (Panama v Italy)*, Italy contended, inter alia, that Panama's claim predominantly, if not exclusively, pertained to alleged 'indirect violations' relating to the rights of the owner of the vessel M/V 'Norstar' especially since the remedy sought by Panama concerned preponderantly, if not exclusively, the monetary interests of the owner of the M/V 'Norstar', and, consequently, the local remedies rule applied. This submission was rejected by ITLOS. After examining the nature of the rights under UNCLOS alleged by Panama to have been violated by Italy, ITLOS concluded that the right at issue was the right of Panama to enjoy freedom of navigation on the high seas, a violation of which would amount to direct injury to Panama. Since the claim for the damage caused to the persons and entities with an interest in the ship or its cargo arose from the alleged injury to Panama, it was not subject to the rule of exhaustion of local remedies.[32]

---

[28] *M/V 'Saiga' (No 2)* (Merits) (n 12) 45–56 [97]–[136].

[29] *M/V 'Virginia G'* (n 13) 54 [157].

[30] ibid.

[31] ibid 55 [158]. For criticisms of the preponderant test, see José Luis Jesus, 'The Exhaustion of Local Remedies and the Nationality of Claims in the Jurisprudence of the International Tribunal for the Law of the Sea' in Tafsir Malick Ndiaye and Rodrigo Fernandes More (eds), *Prospects of Evolution of the Law of the Sea, Environmental Law and the Practice of ITLOS* (SAG Editoração 2018) 100.

[32] *M/V 'Norstar'* (Preliminary Objections) (n 1) paras 269–71.

e) Legal standing (*locus standi*) and nationality of claims

Article 286 of UNCLOS stipulates in a very broad manner that, subject to the limitations and exceptions to the applicability of the compulsory dispute settlement regime as provided in section 3 of Part XV of UNCLOS, 'any dispute concerning the interpretation or application of [UNCLOS]' shall be submitted 'at the request of any party to the dispute' to the court or tribunal having compulsory jurisdiction under section 2 of Part XV. There seems to be no explicit requirement for such a party to have a special interest before it can have a legal standing (*locus standi*) to bring a claim concerning the interpretation or application of UNCLOS in the court or tribunal with jurisdiction over the dispute.[33]

The issue of legal standing based on the nationality of claims has arisen before ITLOS in the context where the legal interests of a ship are at stake. The State of nationality of a ship is the flag State or the State whose flag the ship is entitled to fly.[34]

ITLOS alludes to the fact that UNCLOS contains detailed provisions concerning the duties of flag States regarding ships flying their flag. In particular, Articles 94 and 217 set out the obligations of the flag State which can be discharged only through the exercise of appropriate jurisdiction and control over natural and juridical persons such as the Master and other members of the crew, the owners or operators, and other persons involved in the activities of the ship. No distinction is made in these provisions between nationals and non-nationals of a flag State. Additionally, Articles 106, 110(3), and 111(8) contain provisions applicable to cases in which measures have been taken by a State against a foreign ship. These measures are, respectively, seizure of a ship on suspicion of piracy, exercise of the right of visit on board a ship, and arrest of a ship in exercise of the right of hot pursuit. In these cases, UNCLOS provides that, if the measures are found not to be justified, the State taking the measures shall be obliged to pay compensation 'for any loss or damage' sustained, without linking the right to compensation to the nationality of persons suffering loss or damage. Besides, in relation to proceedings for prompt release under Article 292, no significance

---

[33] See also P Chandrasekhara Rao and Philippe Gautier, *The International Tribunal for the Law of the Sea: Law, Practice and Procedure* (Edward Elgar 2018) 138–41.

[34] '*Tomimaru*' *(Japan v Russian Federation)* (Prompt Release) ITLOS Reports 2007, 74, 95 [70].

is attached to the nationalities of persons involved in the operations of an arrested ship. ITLOS concludes that UNCLOS considers a ship as a unit as regards the obligations of the flag State with respect to the ship and the right of the flag State to seek reparation for loss or damage caused to the ship by acts of other States as well as the right to institute proceedings under Article 292 of UNCLOS. Therefore, the ship, everything on it, and every person involved or interested in its operations are treated as an entity linked to the flag State. The nationalities of these persons are not relevant. ITLOS also bears in mind two basic characteristics of modern maritime transport: the transient and multinational composition of ships' crews and the multiplicity of interests involved in the cargo on board a single ship. According to international law, the exercise of diplomatic protection by a State in respect of its nationals is to be distinguished from claims made by a flag State for damages in respect of natural and juridical persons involved in the operation of a ship who are not nationals of that State. Since any ship may have a crew comprising persons of several nationalities, undue hardship would ensue if each person sustaining damage were obliged to look for protection from the State of which such person is a national.[35]

In *M/V 'Norstar'*, Italy maintained that since the vessel M/V 'Norstar' flying the flag of Panama was neither owned, fitted out, nor rented, by a natural or legal person of Panamanian nationality, nor were the accused in the Italian criminal proceedings Panamanian nationals, ITLOS should declare the claim by Panama inadmissible. ITLOS, citing its earlier judgments in *M/V 'Saiga' (No 2)* and *M/V 'Virginia G'*, rejected Italy's submission, considering the ship flying the flag of Panama to be a single unit; hence, the M/V 'Norstar', its crew, and cargo on board as well as its owner and every person involved or interested in its operations were to be treated as an entity linked to the flag State, irrespective of their nationalities.[36]

Nationality of ships is governed by Article 91(1) of UNCLOS, according to which every State shall fix the conditions for the grant of its nationality to ships, for the registration of ships in its territory, and for the right to fly its flag, and ships shall have the nationality of the State whose flag they are entitled to fly. Article 91(1) also requires the existence of a 'genuine link' between the State and the ship. ITLOS has held that this genuine link requirement 'should not be read as establishing prerequisites or conditions to be satisfied for the exercise of the right of the flag State to grant its nationality

---

[35] *M/V 'Saiga' (No 2)* (Merits) (n 12) 47–48 [105]–[107]; *M/V 'Virginia G'* (n 13) 48 [128].
[36] *M/V 'Norstar'* (Preliminary Objections) (n 1) paras 230–31.

to ships'.[37] ITLOS observes that Article 94 of UNCLOS obligates the flag State to 'effectively exercise its jurisdiction and control in administrative, technical, and social matters over ships flying its flag' through different measures, including such measures as are necessary to ensure safety at sea, which must conform to generally accepted international regulations, procedures, and practices. Article 94(6) outlines the procedure to be followed where another State 'has clear grounds to believe that proper jurisdiction and control with respect to a ship have not been exercised', but there is nothing in Article 94 to permit a State which discovers evidence indicating the absence of proper jurisdiction and control by a flag State over a ship to refuse to recognize the right of the ship to fly the flag of the flag State. In ITLOS's view, the purpose of UNCLOS's requirement on the need for a genuine link between a ship and its flag State is to secure more effective implementation of the duties of the flag State, and not to establish criteria by reference to which the validity of the registration of ships in a flag State may be challenged by other States. Once a ship is registered, the flag State is required, under Article 94, to exercise effective jurisdiction and control over the ship in order to ensure that it operate in accordance with generally accepted international regulations, procedures, and practices. This meaning of 'genuine link' cannot be challenged by the respondent if the applicant exercises effective jurisdiction and control over the vessel in question at the time of the incident giving rise to the applicant's claim.[38]

However, the conduct of a flag State at all times material to the dispute is an important consideration in determining the nationality or registration of a ship.[39] The nationality of a ship is a question of fact to be determined, like other facts in dispute before ITLOS, on the basis of evidence adduced by the parties.[40] The initial burden of establishing the identity of the flag State when the application is made is on the applicant.[41]

Where a provisional registration of a ship has expired at the time of bringing a claim before ITLOS, the State provisionally registering the ship

---

[37] *M/V 'Virginia G'* (n 13) 44 [110].

[38] ibid 44–45 [111]–[114], citing *M/V 'Saiga' (No 2)* (Merits) (n 12) 41–42 [82]–[83]. For some criticisms of ITLOS's reasoning regarding the nationality of claims for in relation to ships and their crews, see Tullio Scovazzi, 'ITLOS and Jurisdiction over Ships' in Henrik Ringbom (ed), *Jurisdiction over Ships: Post-UNCLOS Developments in the Law of the Sea* (Brill/Nijhoff 2015) 385–90; James L Kateka, 'The International Tribunal for the Law of the Sea and Africa' (2016) 22 African YBIL 155, 167–69.

[39] *M/V 'Saiga' (No 2)* (Merits) (n 12) 37 [68]; *'Grand Prince' (Belize v France)* (Prompt Release) ITLOS Reports 2001, 17, 43 [89].

[40] *'Grand Prince'* (Prompt Release) (n 39) 41 [81].

[41] ibid 38 [67].

cannot be considered the flag State of the ship that is entitled to bring the claim before ITLOS.[42]

In *M/V 'Louisa'*, Saint Vincent and the Grenadines submitted that although the 'Gemini III' was not flying the flag of Saint Vincent and the Grenadines, it served as a tender for the M/V 'Louisa' registered in Saint Vincent and the Grenadines and was thus 'inextricably linked' to the latter vessel and was not required to have a flag of its own. In ITLOS's opinion, even if this view were to be accepted, the 'Gemini III' worked independently of the M/V 'Louisa' and enjoyed 'an identity of its own'. Consequently, it was not covered by the declaration of Saint Vincent and the Grenadines accepting ITLOS's jurisdiction to settle disputes concerning the arrest or detention of Saint Vincent and the Grenadines' vessels. ITLOS, therefore, concluded it lacked jurisdiction in respect of the 'Gemini III'.[43]

f) The obligation for the parties to exchange views before resorting to ITLOS

Before ITLOS may exercise jurisdiction over a case, the parties to the dispute must also fulfil the requirements under Article 283 of UNCLOS.[44] According to Article 283(1), when a dispute arises between States Parties concerning the interpretation or application of UNCLOS the parties to the dispute 'shall proceed expeditiously to an exchange of views regarding its settlement by negotiation or other peaceful means'. Pursuant to Article 283(2), the parties shall also proceed expeditiously to an exchange of views where a procedure for the settlement of such a dispute has been terminated without a settlement or where a settlement has been reached and the circumstances require consultation regarding the manner of implementing the settlement. This obligation to proceed expeditiously to an exchange of views applies equally to both parties to the dispute.[45]

---

[42] ibid 44 [93].

[43] *M/V 'Louisa'* (Merits) (n 2) 31–32 [86]–[87].

[44] See also David Anderson, 'Article 283 of the United Nations Convention on the Law of the Sea' in Tafsir Malick Ndiaye and Rüdiger Wolfrum (eds), *Law of the Sea, Environmental Law and Settlement of Disputes* (Martinus Nijhoff 2007) 848–54, 860; Nigel Bankes, 'Precluding the Applicability of Section 2 of Part XV of the Law of the Sea Convention' (2017) 48 ODIL 239, 253–59; Deyi Ma, 'Obligation to Exchange Views under Article 283 of the United Nations Convention on the Law of the Sea: An Empirical Approach for Improvement' (2019) 12 J East Asia & Int'l L 305.

[45] *M/T 'San Padre Pio'* (n 1) para 74, quoting *M/V 'Norstar'* (Preliminary Objections) (n 1) 91 [213] and *Detention of three Ukrainian naval vessels* (n 1) para 88. Also, *Land Reclamation*

ITLOS is consistent in holding that 'a State Party is not obliged to continue with an exchange of views when the possibilities of reaching agreement have been exhausted'.[46] This happens, for example, when one of the parties to the dispute receives no response from the other party to its various communications relating to the alleged breach of UNCLOS and, where applicable, other rules of international law, and that other party therefore does not engage in an exchange of views with it.[47] Under these circumstances, the former party can reasonably conclude that the possibility of reaching agreement is exhausted, and it is not relevant whether the former party refers to any specific claim or rights under a particular international agreement in its communications with the latter party regarding the settlement of the dispute.[48] The requirements under Article 283 are also satisfied where one of the parties can reasonably conclude, in good faith, that continuing to exchange of views cannot yield a positive result.[49]

According to ITLOS's jurisprudence, under international law it is for each State to determine the persons, including private persons, who represent the State or are authorized to act on its behalf in its relations with other States, international organizations, and international institutions, including international courts and tribunals. This is without prejudice to the specific treaty regimes or other applicable rules on State representation. For communications sent by a lawyer in private practice on behalf of a State to be opposable to another State, the latter needs to be duly informed of the authority conferred on the lawyer to represent the former State, and the mere reference in a letter by a private person to the authorization given to that person by the State may not be sufficient. Once the latter State is duly informed by the former State of such authority conferred on the private person, it cannot validly question that the private person is duly

---

in and around the Straits of Johor (Provisional Measures, Order of 8 October 2003) ITLOS Reports 2003, 10, 19 [38].

[46] *M/T 'San Padre Pio'* (Provisional Measures, Order of 29 May 2019) para 73, quoting *MOX Plant (Ireland v United Kingdom)* (Provisional Measures, Order of 3 December 2001) ITLOS Reports 2001, 95, 107 [60]; *'ARA Libertad' (Argentina v Ghana)* (Provisional Measures, Order of 20 November 2012) ITLOS Reports 2012, 332, 345 [71]; *'Arctic Sunrise' (Kingdom of the Netherlands v Russian Federation)* (Provisional Measures, Order of 25 October 2013) ITLOS Reports 2013, 230, 247 [76]; *Detention of three Ukrainian naval vessels* (n 1) para 87.

[47] *M/T 'San Padre Pio'* (n 1) para 72.

[48] ibid para 71.

[49] *Land Reclamation in and around the Straits of Johor* (Provisional Measures, Order of 8 October 2003) 20 [48].

authorized to represent the former State in all exchanges of views relating to the dispute.[50]

g) Indispensable third party

ITLOS acknowledges the notion of indispensable party as a well-established procedural rule in international judicial proceedings developed mainly through the decisions of the ICJ. According to this notion, where the vital issue to be settled concerns the international responsibility of a third State or where the legal interests of a third State would form the very subject matter of the dispute, a court or tribunal cannot exercise jurisdiction over the dispute without the consent of that third State.[51]

In *M/V 'Norstar'* between Panama and Italy, the detention of the vessel M/V 'Norstar' flying the flag of Panama was carried out by Spain as part of the criminal investigation and proceedings conducted by Italy against the vessel. It was Italy that adopted legal positions and pursued legal interests with respect to the detention of the vessel through the investigation and proceedings. Spain merely provided assistance in accordance with its obligations under a treaty binding on Spain and Italy. It was also Italy that had held legal control over the vessel during its detention. Accordingly, concluded ITLOS, the dispute before it concerned the rights and obligations of Italy and ITLOS's decision would affect the legal interests of Italy. ITLOS did not consider Spain to be an indispensable party in the case—it was the legal interests of Italy, not those of Spain, that formed the subject matter of the decision to be rendered by ITLOS on the merits of Panama's application, and ITLOS's decision on jurisdiction and admissibility did not require the prior determination of Spain's rights and obligations. Thus, it was not necessary, let alone indispensable, for Spain to be a party to the proceedings for ITLOS to determine whether Italy violated the provisions of UNCLOS. In the light of the foregoing, ITLOS rejected the objection raised by Italy based on lack of jurisdiction *ratione personae*.[52]

---

[50] *M/V 'Norstar'* (Preliminary Objections) (n 1) paras 94–97.
[51] ibid para 172.
[52] ibid paras 167–68, 173–75.

h) Limitations and exceptions to compulsory dispute settlement under UNCLOS

Article 297 of UNCLOS provides certain automatic limitations on the applicability of the compulsory dispute settlement regime established under section 2 of Part XV so as to accommodate the range of views on the desirable scope of compulsory dispute settlement expressed during the Third Conference.[53] Some States wanted to insulate the exercise of sovereign rights in the newly established exclusive economic zone from judicial review. They thus advocated excluding particular classes of disputes arising out of the exercise by coastal States of their sovereign rights or jurisdiction conferred by UNCLOS in the exclusive economic zone from Part XV dispute settlement. Other States wanted to have certain categories of dispute concerning the aforesaid sovereign rights or jurisdiction subject to the dispute settlement system, lest States Parties to UNCLOS, especially relatively small and weak States, would be left at the mercy of arbitrary interpretations and unilateral measures by other States Parties strong enough to impose their will.[54]

The eventually adopted Article 297 aims at balancing the interests of the coastal States, on the one hand, and those of the States with major navigational interests as well as the landlocked and geographically disadvantaged States, on the other hand, both of the latter groups desiring to ensure, in particular, that the few rights they had would be protected by the availability of recourse to third-party dispute settlement procedures. The basic freedoms and rights of the sea as well as other internationally lawful uses of the sea related to these freedoms enjoy the complete protection of the compulsory dispute settlement procedures entailing binding decisions. Such protection also covers cases involving violation of international rules and standards established for the protection and preservation of the marine environment. Under a parallel provision, non-coastal States acting in breach of UNCLOS, or of the laws or regulations enacted by a coastal State, were made subject to adjudication under section 2 of Part XV, as long as those laws and regulations were adopted in conformity with both UNCLOS itself and with other rules of international law not incompatible with UNCLOS.

---

[53] See also Gudmundur Eiriksson, *The International Tribunal for the Law of the Sea* (Martinus Nijhoff 2000) 136–42.

[54] Andrew Serdy, 'Art 297' in Alexander Proelss (ed), *United Nations Convention on the Law of the Sea: A Commentary* (Hart 2017) 1908–12; Virginia Commentary (n 14) 85, 87–94.

Disputes relating to marine scientific research and fisheries fell into three categories: those which would remain subject to adjudication, those which would be completely excluded from adjudication, and those which would be subject to compulsory resort to conciliation. The second group primarily encompasses disputes relating to the exercise by a coastal State of those powers with respect to which UNCLOS granted coastal States complete discretion. The third group covers disputes involving blatant abuses of discretion, where a State manifestly or arbitrarily has failed to comply with some basic obligations under UNCLOS, in which case the conciliation commission shall, in accordance with Annex V, section 2, examine the claims and objections of the parties and make recommendations to the parties for an amicable settlement. However, the conciliation commission shall not substitute its discretion for that of the coastal State. The report of the conciliation commission is to be communicated to the appropriate international organization.

Having recourse to conciliation originated from the concerns among some States that they might not be able to effectively exercise their sovereign rights and discretions if they were to be harassed by an abuse of legal process and by a proliferation of applications to dispute settlement procedures. These States were, therefore, not willing to accept compulsory recourse to adjudication, whereas other States wanted to ensure the effective protection of all their rights through compulsory recourse to adjudication. The concept of compulsory recourse to conciliation in certain cases, but without an obligation to accept as binding the report of the conciliation commission, then emerged, and the negotiating group on this issue reached a consensus on the categories of issues to be subject to compulsory conciliation.[55]

Finally, coastal States also accepted a provision requiring their agreements with the landlocked and geographically disadvantaged States with respect to the latter's access to coastal fisheries to include a clause on measures which they shall take to minimize the possibility of a disagreement concerning the interpretation or application of the agreements, and on how they should proceed if a disagreement nevertheless arises.[56]

By virtue of Article 297(1), disputes concerning the interpretation or application of UNCLOS with regard to the exercise by a coastal State of its sovereign rights or jurisdiction shall be subject to the procedures provided for in section 2 in the following cases: (a) when it is alleged that a coastal

---

[55] Virginia Commentary (n 14) 101, 105–06.
[56] ibid 105–06 and UNCLOS Art 297(3)(e).

State has acted in contravention of the provisions of UNCLOS in regard to the freedoms and rights of navigation, overflight, or the laying of submarine cables and pipelines, or in regard to other internationally lawful uses of the sea specified in Article 58; (b) when it is alleged that a State in exercising the aforementioned freedoms, rights, or uses has acted in contravention of UNCLOS or of laws or regulations adopted by the coastal State in conformity with UNCLOS and other rules of international law not incompatible with UNCLOS; or (c) when it is alleged that a coastal State has acted in contravention of specified international rules and standards for the protection and preservation of the marine environment which are applicable to the coastal State and which have been established by UNCLOS or through a competent international organization or diplomatic conference in accordance with UNCLOS.

According to Article 297(2)(a), disputes concerning the interpretation or application of the provisions of UNCLOS with regard to marine scientific research shall be settled in accordance with section 2, except that the coastal State shall not be obliged to accept the submission to such settlement of any dispute arising out of (i) the exercise by the coastal State of a right or discretion to withhold its consent to the conduct of a marine scientific research project of another State or competent international organization in its exclusive economic zone or on its continental shelf in accordance with Article 246; or (ii) a decision by the coastal State to order suspension or cessation of a research project in accordance with Article 253. Under Article 297(2)(b), a dispute arising from an allegation by the researching State that with respect to a specific project the coastal State is not exercising its rights under Articles 246 and 253 in a manner compatible with UNCLOS shall be submitted, at the request of either party, to compulsory submission to conciliation procedure.

Pursuant to Article 297(3)(a), disputes concerning the interpretation or application of the provisions of UNCLOS with regard to fisheries shall be settled in accordance with the Part XV compulsory dispute settlement regime, except that the coastal State shall not be obliged to accept the submission to such settlement of any dispute relating to its sovereign rights with respect to the living resources in the exclusive economic zone or their exercise, including its discretionary powers for determining the allowable catch, its harvesting capacity, the allocation of surpluses to other States, and the terms and conditions established in its conservation and management laws and regulations.[57] By virtue of Article 297(3)(b), where no settlement has been reached by recourse

---

[57] It has been argued that such discretionary powers also encompass the coastal State's power to determine the terms and regulations for fisheries conservation and management and

to any peaceful means of dispute settlement, a dispute concerning an abuse of discretion by the coastal State shall be submitted to conciliation, at the request of any party to the dispute, when it is alleged that (i) a coastal State has manifestly failed to comply with its obligations to ensure through proper conservation and management measures that the maintenance of the living resources in the exclusive economic zone is not seriously endangered; (ii) a coastal State has arbitrarily refused to determine, at the request of another State, the allowable catch and its capacity to harvest living resources with respect to stocks which that other State is interested in fishing; or (iii) a coastal State has arbitrarily refused to allocate catch to any State from the whole or part of the surplus it has declared to exist under Articles 62, 69, and 70.

Article 297 is also linked to Article 294 (on preliminary proceedings) discussed above and Article 300—requiring States Parties to fulfil in good faith the obligations assumed under UNCLOS and to exercise the rights, jurisdiction, and freedoms recognized in UNCLOS in a manner which would not constitute an abuse of right—in the sense that the coastal State should not be harassed by submission of disputes that were frivolous, vexatious, or without any prima facie basis.[58]

aa) Automatic and optional limitations upon the scope of UNCLOS dispute settlement

The Third Conference found it necessary to avoid confusion between limitations on international adjudication that would apply automatically and those which would be optional and would require a special declaration. Thus, they were put in separate articles, with Article 297 covering the former and Article 298 the latter.[59]

Article 298 stipulates the optional exceptions to the applicability of section 2 of Part XV.[60] These exceptions are optional because unless a State

---

their consequential conditions vis-à-vis other States. See AO Adede, *The System for Settlement of Disputes under the United Nations Convention on the Law of the Sea: A Drafting History and a Commentary* (Martinus Nijhoff 1987) 254; Natalie Klein, *Dispute Settlement in the UN Convention on the Law of the Sea* (Cambridge University Press 2005) 179, 389. cf Erietta Scalieri, 'Discretionary Power of the Coastal State and the Control of Its Compliance with International Law by International Tribunals' in Angela Del Vecchio and Roberto Virzo (eds), *Interpretation of the United Nations Convention on the Law of the Sea by International Courts and Tribunals* (Springer 2019) 349–81.

[58] Virginia Commentary (n 14) 99, 103–04.
[59] ibid 96.
[60] See also Miguel García García-Revillo, *The Contentious and Advisory Jurisdiction of the International Tribunal for the Law of the Sea* (Brill/Nijhoff 2015) 87–94.

Party to UNCLOS makes an express declaration under Article 298 to exclude the disputes enumerated in that Article the default compulsory dispute settlement provisions under section 2 of Part XV would apply to the categories of disputes listed in Article 298.[61]

Article 298 responds to the concerns of many States during the Third Conference reluctant to see politically sensitive disputes being subjected to the principle of compulsory settlement of disputes in Part XV, but Article 298 does not affect the operation of section 1 of Part XV (concerning the settlement of disputes by peaceful means agreed by the parties), which applies to all disputes under UNCLOS.[62]

According to Article 298(1), when signing, ratifying, or acceding to UNCLOS or at any time thereafter, a State may, without prejudice to the obligations for peaceful dispute settlement, declare in writing it does not accept any one or more of the procedures provided for in section 2 with respect to one or more of the following categories of disputes.

The first category is listed in Article 298(1)(a)(i); namely, disputes concerning the interpretation or application of Articles 15, 74, and 83 relating to sea boundary delimitations, or those involving historic bays or titles. However, a State having made such a declaration shall, when such a dispute arises subsequent to the entry into force of UNCLOS and where no agreement is reached within a reasonable period of time in negotiations between the parties, accept submission of the matter to conciliation. Such conciliation is subject to the further limitation that any dispute which necessarily involves the concurrent consideration of any unsettled dispute concerning sovereignty or other rights over continental or insular land territory shall be excluded from a conciliation. Pursuant to Article 298(1)(a)(ii),

> after the conciliation commission has presented its report ... the parties shall negotiate an agreement on the basis of that report; if these negotiations do not result in an agreement, the parties shall, by mutual consent, submit the question to one of the procedures provided for in section 2, unless the parties otherwise agree.

---

[61] S Jayakumar, 'Compulsory Dispute Settlement and Conciliation Under UNCLOS' in Hao Duy Phan, Tara Davenport, and Robert Beckman (eds), *The Timor-Leste/Australia Conciliation: A Victory for UNCLOS and Peaceful Settlement of Disputes* (World Scientific 2019) 11.

[62] Virginia Commentary (n 14) 109–10.

Such a process was successfully used between Australia and Timor Leste to settle their maritime boundary dispute in the Timor Sea.[63] It remains an open question whether the said parties failing to reach the agreement based on the conciliation commission's report must revert to the compulsory dispute settlement system in section 2 of Par XV.[64] Article 298(1)(a)(iii) clarifies that Article 298(1)(a) does not apply to any sea boundary dispute finally settled by an arrangement between the parties, or to any such dispute which is to be settled in accordance with a bilateral or multilateral agreement binding upon those parties.

The second category as elaborated in Article 298(1)(b) encompasses disputes concerning military activities, including military activities by government vessels and aircraft engaged in non-commercial service, and disputes concerning law enforcement activities in regard to the exercise of sovereign rights or jurisdiction excluded from the jurisdiction of a court or tribunal under Article 297(2) or (3).

The third category of disputes as stipulated in Article 298(1)(c) covers disputes in respect of which the UN Security Council is exercising the functions assigned to it by the UN Charter, unless the Security Council decides to remove the matter from its agenda or calls upon the parties to settle it by the means provided for in UNCLOS. This provision reflects the need to avoid a conflict between any dispute settlement procedure commenced under UNCLOS and any action the Security Council might be taking under the UN Charter to maintain international peace and security.[65]

The exceptions in subparagraphs (b) and (c) of Article 298 differ from the exception in subparagraph (a) in one important aspect—they are more absolute, at least since in no case are they subject to compulsory recourse to conciliation.[66]

A State Party which has made a declaration under Article 298(1) may at any time withdraw it, or agree to submit a dispute excluded by such declaration to any procedure specified in UNCLOS.[67] A State Party which has

---

[63] See *Timor Sea Conciliation (Timor-Leste v Australia)* <https://pca-cpa.org/en/cases/132/>; Anais Kedgley Laidlaw and Hao Duy Phan, 'Inter-State Compulsory Conciliation Procedures and the Maritime Boundary Dispute Between Timor-Leste and Australia' (2019) 10 J Int'l Dispute Settlement 126; Duy Phan, Davenport, and Beckman (n 61); Jianjun Gao, 'The Timor Sea Conciliation (Timor-Leste v Australia): A Note on the Commission's Decision on Competence' (2018) 49 ODIL 208.

[64] Jayakumar (n 61) 25–26.

[65] Virginia Commentary (n 14) 138.

[66] ibid 134.

[67] UNCLOS Art 298(2).

made a declaration under Article 298(1) shall not be entitled to submit any dispute falling within the excepted category of disputes to any procedure in UNCLOS as against another State Party, without the consent of that party.[68] If one of the States Parties has made a declaration under Article 298(1)(a), any other State Party may submit any dispute falling within an excepted category against the declarant party to the procedure specified in such declaration.[69] This is to ensure that where an alternative procedure is chosen for sea boundary disputes, the other party must also have access to that procedure.[70] A new declaration, or the withdrawal of a declaration, does not in any way affect proceedings pending before a court or tribunal in accordance with Article 298, unless the parties otherwise agree.[71]

To be effective, declarations and notices of withdrawal of declarations under Article 298 must be deposited with the UN Secretary-General, who shall transmit copies thereof to States Parties to UNCLOS.[72]

Article 298 is ambiguous as to whether a declaration has to apply to all disputes within a particular category, or can exclude only certain specific disputes such as a particular dispute with one of its neighbours or in a particular maritime area. Since the basic idea of the Third Conference was to limit to the maximum extent possible the available exceptions, Article 298 should be narrowly construed, as also implicit in paragraph 1(a)(i), where disputes relating to sea boundary delimitations are separated by a disjunctive 'or' from disputes involving historic bays or titles, thus enabling a State to select only one of these subcategories for an exclusion through its declaration.[73]

As of this writing, 42 States Parties to UNCLOS have made a declaration under Article 298.

The following States Parties have declared they do not accept compulsory dispute settlement procedures with respect to any disputes referred to in Article 298(1)(a), (b), and (c)—Algeria, Argentina, Belarus, Canada, Chile, China, Ecuador, Egypt, France, Portugal, Republic of Korea, Russia, Thailand, and Tunisia. Nicaragua accepts only the jurisdiction of the ICJ with respect to the categories of disputes referred to in Article 298(1)(a), (b), and (c).

---

[68] UNCLOS Art 298(3).
[69] UNCLOS Art 298(4).
[70] Virginia Commentary (n 14) 117–18; Andrew Serdy, 'Art 298' in Proelss (n 54) 1922.
[71] UNCLOS Art 298(5).
[72] UNCLOS Art 298(6).
[73] Virginia Commentary (n 14) 115.

Australia, Equatorial Guinea, Gabon, Italy, Montenegro, Palau, and Spain, as well as Trinidad and Tobago do not accept compulsory dispute settlement procedures regarding the categories of disputes listed in Article 298(1)(a) (concerning sea boundaries and historic bays and titles). Angola does not accept Annex VII arbitral tribunal proceedings for the categories of disputes referred to in Article 298(1)(a). Similarly, DR Congo, Greece, Kenya, Malaysia, and Singapore do not accept compulsory dispute settlement procedures regarding the interpretation or application of Articles 15, 74, and 83 relating to sea boundary delimitations, or those involving historic bays or titles. In addition, Greece does not accept compulsory dispute settlement procedures regarding disputes concerning military activities; disputes concerning law enforcement activities in regard to the exercise of sovereign rights or jurisdiction 'excluded from the jurisdiction of a court or tribunal under [Article 297(2) or (3)]'; and disputes in respect of which the UN Security Council is exercising its functions, unless the Security Council decides to remove the matter from its agenda or calls upon the parties to settle it by the means provided for in UNCLOS.

Capo Verde and Uruguay do not accept compulsory dispute settlement procedures regarding the categories of disputes listed in Article 298(1)(b) (regarding military activities).

Mexico and Saudi Arabia do not accept compulsory dispute settlement procedures regarding the categories of disputes listed in Article 298(1)(a) and (b). Ukraine does not accept compulsory dispute settlement procedures regarding the categories of disputes listed in Article 298(1)(a) and (b), unless otherwise provided by specific international treaties between Ukraine and relevant States.

Neither Togo nor the UK accepts compulsory dispute settlement procedures regarding the disputes referred to in Article 298(1)(b) and (c) concerning, respectively, military activities and disputes in respect of which the UN Security Council is exercising its functions.

Denmark, Norway, and Slovenia do not accept an Annex VII arbitral tribunal proceeding for any of the categories of disputes mentioned in Article 298.

Iceland declares that any interpretation of Article 83 relating to the delimitation of the continental shelf shall be submitted to conciliation under Annex V, section 2, of UNCLOS.

Cuba and Guinea-Bissau declare their non-acceptance of the ICJ's jurisdiction and, consequently, they will not accept the ICJ's jurisdiction 'with respect to the provisions of either Article 297 or 298' of UNCLOS.

The following analysis will focus on topical and salient aspects of the exclusions and exceptions under Articles 297 and 298. In particular it shall touch on disputes regarding fisheries, territorial disputes, historic titles, law enforcement activities, and military activities.

bb) Fisheries disputes

Of the 29 cases submitted to ITLOS as of this writing, 15 of them were fisheries-related disputes. Of the 15 fisheries-related disputes, 9 were for prompt release of fishing vessels and their crews. This must be seen in the context that international judicial bodies have only dealt with three international fisheries disputes over the 100-year period prior to the establishment of ITLOS.[74] A frequently asked question is why the entry into force of UNCLOS in 1994 and the establishment of ITLOS have not led to more fisheries-related disputes being brought before ITLOS. Another question is whether the dispute settlement regime under UNCLOS itself hinders bringing fisheries-related disputes before ITLOS.[75]

An example of fisheries agreements allowing their States Parties to resort to ITLOS, with the consent of all the disputing parties, is the 1993 FAO Agreement to Promote Compliance with International Conservation and Management Measures by Fishing Vessels on the High Seas.[76]

Another example is the 1995 UN Agreement for the Implementation of the Provisions of the UN Convention on the Law of the Sea of 10 December 1982 relating to the Conservation and Management of Straddling Fish Stocks and Highly Migratory Species Fish Stocks ('FSA').[77] As already explained in Chapter 1, Part VIII of the FSA applies the dispute settlement

---

[74] Ted L McDorman, 'An Overview of International Fisheries Disputes and the International Tribunal for the Law of the Sea' (2002) 40 Canadian YBIL 119, 120–22, citing the 1893 *Bering Sea Fur-Seals* arbitration (*Bering Sea Fur-Seals (Great Britain v US)* 1 Int'l Environmental L Rep 43, 67); *Filleting within the Gulf of St Lawrence between Canada and France* (1986) 19 RIAA 225; *Fisheries Jurisdiction (United Kingdom v Iceland)* (Merits) [1974] ICJ Rep 3; *Fisheries Jurisdiction (Federal Republic of Germany v Iceland)* [1974] ICJ Rep 175.

[75] See, eg, Gurdip Singh, *United Nations Convention on the Law of the Sea Dispute Settlement Mechanisms* (Academic Publications 1985) 138; William T Burke, *The New International Law of Fisheries: UNCLOS 1982 and Beyond* (OUP 1994) 63–64; Francisco Vicuña Orrego, *The Changing International Law of High Seas Fisheries* (Cambridge University Press 1999) 284; Alan E Boyle, 'Problems of Compulsory Jurisdiction and the Settlement of Disputes Relating to Straddling Fish Stocks' (1999) 14 Int'l J Marine & Coastal L 1; Robin Churchill, 'The Jurisprudence of the International Tribunal for the Law of the Sea Relating to Fisheries: Is There Much in the Net?' (2007) 22 Int'l J Marine & Coastal L 383, 389.

[76] (1994) 33 ILM 968. Art IX lists ITLOS among the three choices of forum, the other two being the ICJ and arbitration.

[77] 2167 UNTS 88.

regime under UNCLOS *mutatis mutandis* to any disputes between States Parties to the FSA concerning the interpretation or application of the FSA, *whether or not they are also Parties to UNCLOS.* In addition, the dispute settlement regime under UNCLOS applies *mutatis mutandis* to any dispute between States Parties to the FSA concerning the interpretation or application of a subregional, regional, or global fisheries agreement relating to straddling fish stocks or highly migratory fish stocks to which they are parties, including any dispute concerning the conservation and management of such stocks, *whether or not they are also Parties to UNCLOS.* However, a State Party to the FSA which is not party to UNCLOS, shall be free to choose, by means of a written declaration, one or more of the means set out in Article 287(1) of UNCLOS for the settlement of disputes.[78]

The legal literature on this subject has identified several ambiguities concerning the dispute settlement regime under the FSA. First, can disputes arising under regional fisheries management agreements be subject to compulsory third-party resolution, in particular since no exemption exists in UNCLOS to redirect this type of dispute to a non-compulsory procedure?[79] Second, by virtue of Article 3 of the FSA, the FSA applies to the conservation and management of straddling fish stocks and highly migratory fish stocks *beyond* areas under national jurisdiction, except that Articles 6 (application of the precautionary approach) and 7 (compatibility of conservation and management measures) apply also to the conservation and management of such stocks *within* areas under national jurisdiction. It has been questioned whether disputes relating to Articles 6 and 7 of the FSA are also exempt from compulsory jurisdiction through the operation of Article 297(3) of UNCLOS. Third, the duty to cooperate under Article 7(3) and (4) of the FSA requires States to make every effort to agree on compatible conservation and management measures within a reasonable period of time, failing which any of the States concerned may invoke the procedure for the compulsory dispute settlement provided for in the FSA. This may lead to a situation where recourse to compulsory settlement of disputes relating to cooperation on conservation and management measures, including in the exclusive economic zone, is

---

[78] FSA Art 30. See also McDorman (n 74) 129–31.

[79] cf Peter Örebech, Ketill Sigurjonsson, and Ted L McDorman, 'The 1995 United Nations Straddling and Highly Migratory Fish Stocks Agreement: Management, Enforcement and Dispute Settlement' (1998) 13 Int'l J Marine & Coastal Law 119, 136; Andrew Serdy, 'The Paradoxical Success of UNCLOS Part XV: A Half-Hearted Reply to Rosemary Rayfuse' (2005) 36 Victoria University Wellington L Rev 713, 718.

specifically provided for (under the FSA) while the exclusion from compulsory jurisdiction is simultaneously operational (under UNCLOS). Thus a question arises: is the dispute relating to the alleged failure of a State to comply with its duty to cooperate and not to the actual content of conservation and management measures as part of the exercise of sovereign rights in the exclusive economic zone to be subject to the compulsory dispute settlement procedure under UNCLOS?[80] Fourth, disputes concerning a State's rights and obligations on the high seas are generally not covered by the limitation contained in Article 297(3) of UNCLOS, but there are conflicting views as to whether the limitations under UNCLOS on fisheries disputes apply *mutatis mutandis* to fisheries disputes in the high seas when the species in question are the ones covered by the FSA. In the view of the majority of the commentators such disputes are subject to the compulsory dispute settlement jurisdiction under UNCLOS.[81] Probably, as disputes regarding the use of the high seas are not exempted from the compulsory dispute settlement obligations entailing binding decisions under UNCLOS, disputes related to fisheries on the high seas are not so exempted, either.[82] However, the Annex VII arbitral tribunal in *Chagos Marine Protected Area Arbitration (Mauritius v United Kingdom)* rejects the view, 'advanced in certain academic settings', that the limitations to compulsory dispute settlement entailing binding decisions under Article 297(3) of UNCLOS should be construed narrowly in its application to the FSA. The arbitral tribunal sees no textual basis for such a construction in either UNCLOS or the FSA. In its view, the latter agreement afforded ample opportunity to remedy any ambiguity of drafting in

---

[80] See the conflicting views on this issue in Tullio Treves, 'The Settlement of Disputes According to the Straddling Stocks Agreement of 1995' in Alan Boyle and David Freestone (eds), *International Law and Sustainable Development: Past Achievements and Future Challenges* (OUP 1999) 260; Vicuña Orrego (n 75) 286; Boyle, 'Problems of Compulsory Jurisdiction' (n 75) 21; Bjorn Kunoy, 'The Ambit of *Pactum de Negotiatum* in the Management of Shared Fish Stocks: A Rumble in the Jungle' (2012) 11 Chinese JIL 689, 705 [36].

[81] Klein, *Dispute Settlement* (n 57) 201–02 and the different views cited therein. However, the late ITLOS Judge Dolliver Nelson wrote: 'Arguably, the role of tribunals in settling disputes with regard to living resources of the high seas may be limited': Dolliver Nelson, 'The Development of the Legal Regime of High Seas Fisheries' in Boyle and Freestone (n 80) 132.

[82] See *Southern Bluefin Tuna (New Zealand v Japan, Australia v Japan)* concerning a dispute over catch allowances for highly migratory species applicable 'principally in the high seas' (Award on Jurisdiction and Admissibility, 4 August 2000, RIAA, vol XXIII, 1, 8 [21]). The Award did not indicate that the jurisdictional exclusion in the exclusive economic zone pursuant to Article 297(3) of UNCLOS was potentially applicable, and Japan did not raise any jurisdictional objection on this basis.

UNCLOS, but nevertheless expressly provides, in Article 32, that Article 297(3) of UNCLOS applies also to the FSA.[83]

Regional Fisheries Management Organizations ('RFMOs') utilize different dispute settlement procedures.[84] Several RFMOs resort to nonbinding ad hoc expert panel proceedings to settle disputes among their respective members,[85] while others use conciliation[86] or ad hoc arbitration,[87] and/or Part XV of UNCLOS.[88] Under Article 34 of the 2012 Convention on the definition of the minimum access conditions and exploitation of fisheries resources within the maritime zones under the jurisdiction of the Member States of the Sub-Regional Fisheries Commission ('SRFC'),[89] any dispute among the SFRC Member States on the interpretation or implementation of the Convention not resolved through amicable procedures shall, at the request of one of the disputing parties, be brought before ITLOS.

Although the dispute settlement regime of some RFMOs provides for the submission of disputes for binding decision in accordance with Part XV of UNCLOS, where the disputes concern one or more straddling stocks the provisions in Part VIII of the FSA and the relevant part of UNCLOS and the

[83] *In re the Chagos Marine Protected Area Arbitration (Mauritius v UK)*, Award of 18 March 2015, ICGJ 486 (PCA 2015) para 301.

[84] See Jean-François Pulvenis de Séligny-Maurel, 'Regional Fisheries Bodies and Regional Fisheries Management Organizations and the Settlement of Disputes Concerning Marine Living Resources' in Lilian Del Castillo (ed), *Law of the Sea, From Grotius to the International Tribunal for the Law of the Sea: Liber Amicorum Judge Hugo Caminos* (Brill/Nijhoff 2015) 698–712.

[85] eg, 1978 Northwest Atlantic Fisheries Organization (NAFO) Convention on Cooperation in the Northwest Atlantic Fisheries (<www.nafo.int/Portals/0/PDFs/key-publications/NAFOConvention-2017.pdf> accessed 23 November 2019), Art XIV(7)–(12); 2001 Convention on the Conservation and Management of Fishery Resources in the South East Atlantic Ocean (2002) 41 ILM 257 Art 24(3); 2003 Antigua Convention for the Strengthening of the Inter-American Tropical Tuna Commission (<www.iattc.org/PDFFiles/IATTC-Instruments/_English/IATTC_Antigua_Convention%20Jun%202003.pdf> accessed 19 October) Art XXV(3).

[86] eg, 1982 Agreement Instituting the Latin American Organization for Fisheries Development (1427 UNTS 132) Art 38.

[87] eg, 2003 Agreement on the Institutionalization of the Bay of Bengal Programme as an Inter-Governmental Organization Art 19 (reprinted in M Habibur Rahman, *Legal Regime of Marine Environment in the Bay of Bengal* (Atlantic 2007) 328); the review panel referred to in Art 20(6) of the 2000 Convention on the Conservation and Management of Highly Migratory Fish Stocks in the Western and Central Pacific Ocean (2001) 40 ILM 278.

[88] eg, 2001 Convention on the Conservation and Management of Fishery Resources in the South East Atlantic Ocean Art 24; 2006 Southern Indian Ocean Fisheries Agreement (OJ L 196/15) Art 20(1); 1978 NAFO Convention on Cooperation in the Northwest Atlantic Fisheries Art XV(6) and (8).

[89] <www.itlos.org/fileadmin/itlos/documents/cases/case_no.21/Convention_CMA_ENG.pdf> accessed 23 March 2020.

FSA shall apply, whether or not the parties to the dispute are also parties to these instruments.[90] As of this writing, the FSA has only 90 States Parties; hence, several Member States of the RFMOs are not party to the FSA.

Although a few Annex VII arbitral tribunals have dealt with the scope of the types and spatial limitation of disputes excluded under Article 297 of UNCLOS,[91] ITLOS has not yet had an occasion to rule on this matter, including pertaining to fisheries disputes. As already pointed out above in the context of preliminary objections, the respondent in *M/V 'Saiga' (No 2)* raised its objection to ITLOS's jurisdiction based on Article 297(3) of UNCLOS in the phase of the proceedings relating to the applicant's request for the prescription of provisional measures pending the constitution of an Annex VII arbitral tribunal pursuant to Article 290(5) of UNCLOS. However, the respondent did not reiterate its objection based on Article 297(3) during the merits phase of the proceedings after the parties had transferred their dispute to ITLOS in lieu of the Annex VII arbitral tribunal.

Some current and former ITLOS judges have expressed their view on this matter.

In Judge Paik's Separate Opinion in *Request for Advisory Opinion submitted by the Sub-Regional Fisheries Commission*, any dispute arising from an alleged failure to comply with the obligation under Article 63(1) of UNCLOS concerning conservation and management of transboundary fish stocks can be submitted to the compulsory procedure under Part XV, section 2, of UNCLOS, unlike those disputes arising from the exercise of sovereign rights of the coastal State with respect to the living resources in its exclusive economic zone.[92]

Are there other circumstances in which fisheries disputes are arguably not excluded from the scope of compulsory dispute settlement under UNCLOS? In *Chagos Marine Protected Area Arbitration (Mauritius v United Kingdom)* concerning the UK's declaration of a marine protected area ('MPA') in the waters surrounding the Chagos Archipelago in which all

---

[90] eg, 2001 Convention on the Conservation and Management of Fishery Resources in the South East Atlantic Ocean Art 24(4); 2006 Southern Indian Ocean Fisheries Agreement Art 20(1).

[91] See, eg, *Barbados v Trinidad and Tobago, Award*, ICGJ 371 (PCA 2006) paras 279–83; Stephen Allen, 'Article 297 of the United Nations Convention on the Law of the Sea and the Scope of Mandatory Jurisdiction' (2017) 48 ODIL 313; Natalie Klein, 'The Vicissitudes of Dispute Settlement under the Law of the Sea Convention' (2017) 32 Int'l J Marine & Coastal L 332.

[92] *Request for Advisory Opinion submitted by the Sub-Regional Fisheries Commission* (Advisory Opinion) ITLOS Reports 2015, 4, 117 [37].

fishing would be prohibited, ITLOS Judges Kateka and Wolfrum concurred with the majority of the Annex VII arbitral tribunal in that case that since this was a decision on an MPA, rather than a decision on fishing, Article 297(3)(a) of UNCLOS did not apply. They opined, obiter, that if that provision were considered to be applicable, one would have to bear in mind that Article 297(3)(a) contains two parts. The first part—stating the general principle—requires disputes concerning fisheries to be settled in accordance with section 2 of Part XV of UNCLOS concerning the compulsory settlement of disputes. This is a confirmation of jurisdiction and not a limitation. Any limitation starts with the word 'except', introducing the second part. If the first part of this clause—the confirmation of jurisdiction—is to retain some meaning, not all disputes on fisheries can be interpreted as 'any dispute relating to its sovereign rights with respect to living resources'. The second part of the clause must be narrower in scope than the scope of the first part. Thus, some categories of fisheries disputes must remain within jurisdiction. This was not taken into account by the UK, according to whose submission all disputes on fisheries would be excluded from the jurisdiction of the tribunal. This interpretation, however, would deprive the first part of Article 297(3)(a) of its meaning. The fact that the MPA proclaimed around the Chagos Archipelago proclaimed by the UK included a prohibition of fishing did not turn this zone in its entirety into a measure concerning fishing, and it was doubtful whether a total ban on fishing was covered by the exception clause under Article 297(3)(a). The second part of Article 297(3)(a) focuses on utilizing living resources, including their proper management and conservation, but does not obviously contemplate banning fishing completely. That fishing and management of living resources are to be seen from the perspective of their utilization is confirmed by the object and purpose of UNCLOS, one of whose goals, as stated in its preamble, is to establish

> ... a legal order for the seas and the oceans which ... will promote ... the equitable and efficient utilization of their resources, the conservation of their living resources ... and preservation of the marine environment.

As provided in Article 31(1) of the 1969 Vienna Convention on the Law of Treaties,[93] treaties are to be interpreted in the light of their object and

---

[93] 1155 UNTS 331.

purpose. To sum up, the two judges shared the conclusion of the tribunal that it had jurisdiction pursuant to Article 288(1) and Article 297(1)(c) of UNCLOS to consider Mauritius's Fourth Submission concerning the compatibility of the MPA with the relevant provisions of UNCLOS.[94] The tribunal itself ruled unanimously that since the UK repeatedly justified the MPA on broad environmental grounds, in particular in relation to the protection of coral, it was not open to the UK to limit the tribunal's jurisdiction with the argument that the MPA was merely a fisheries measure. The tribunal also ruled that Mauritius's rights in the waters of the Chagos Archipelago were not limited to fishing, noting in particular that the UK's undertaking to eventually return the Archipelago to Mauritius gave Mauritius the types of management, conservation, and environmental protection measures taken in respect of the archipelago.

In the opinion of former ITLOS President Rao, the effect of Article 297(2) and (3) of UNCLOS is not to exclude all disputes relating to fisheries or marine scientific activities in the exclusive economic zone from the compulsory mechanism under Part XV of UNCLOS. Since the limitations in Article 297 relate to disputes concerning rights or discretion granted by UNCLOS to coastal States, 'the provision would logically not apply to measures which are not in conformity with [UNCLOS]', for example, a dispute concerning the legality of imprisonment penalty for violations of fisheries laws proscribed by Article 73(3) of UNCLOS.[95]

In any event, as Judge Treves has pointed out, while the limitations and exceptions to jurisdiction set out in Articles 297 and 298 of UNCLOS undoubtedly apply to disputes submitted to adjudication under section 2 of Part XV as they are included in section 3, entitled 'Limitations and Exceptions to Applicability of Section 2', these two Articles do not apply to cases submitted by the agreement of the parties on the basis of section 1 of Part XV.[96]

cc) Territorial disputes

Maritime rights derive from the coastal State's sovereignty over the land, a principle which can be summarized as 'the land dominates the sea'—it is

---

[94] *Chagos Marine Protected Area Arbitration* (n 83), Final Award, paras 57–61 of the joint dissenting and concurring opinion of Judges Kateka and Wolfrum.

[95] Rao and Gautier (n 33) 95.

[96] Declaration of Judge Treves in *Case concerning the Delimitation of the Maritime Boundary in the Bay of Bengal* (n 19) 146 [12].

the terrestrial territorial situation that must be taken as starting point for the determination of the maritime rights of a coastal State.[97]

At the Third UN Conference on the Law of the Sea, some States feared that under the guise of a dispute relating to a sea boundary delimitation, a party to a dispute might bring up a dispute involving claims to land territory or an island. This concern was found to be reasonable, culminating in Article 298(1)(a)(i) to exclude from compulsory conciliation 'any dispute that necessarily involves the concurrent consideration of any unsettled dispute concerning sovereignty or other rights over continental or insular land territory'.[98] Article 298(1)(a)(iii) clarifies that this subparagraph 1(a) of Article 298 does not apply to any sea boundary dispute 'which is to be settled in accordance with a bilateral or multilateral agreement binding upon those parties'. Beyond that, Article 298 does not clarify whether concurrent land sovereignty issues, so-called 'mixed disputes', are also excluded in the absence of such declarations under Article 298(1). It can also be argued that the express exclusion of consideration of territorial disputes *only* in the case of compulsory conciliation may imply that concurrent consideration of such disputes is otherwise possible under those dispute settlement options entailing binding decisions. It thus has been argued that the drafting history of this provision seems to indicate that mixed disputes will, in the absence a declaration excluding it pursuant to Article 298(1), fall under the scope of Part XV.[99] Similarly, in *Chagos Marine Protected Area Arbitration (Mauritius v United Kingdom)* Mauritius suggested that if it were necessary for Article 298(1)(a)(i) to expressly stipulate that disputes concerning sovereignty over continental or insular land territory were to be excluded from compulsory conciliation when a declaration pursuant to the Article was made, then a fortiori such disputes would fall within the ambit of compulsory settlement when no such declaration was made. Mauritius presented this argument to support its submission that the UK was not entitled to declare a marine protected area or other maritime zones around the Chagos Archipelago because the UK was not the 'coastal State' of the Chagos Archipelago within the meaning of, inter alia, Articles 2, 55, 56, and 76 of UNCLOS.

---

[97] *Maritime Delimitation and Territorial Questions between Qatar and Bahrain* (Merits) [2001] ICJ Rep 40, 97 [185].

[98] Virginia Commentary (n 14) 117–21.

[99] Irina Buga, 'Territorial Sovereignty Issues in Maritime Disputes: A Jurisdictional Dilemma for Law of the Sea Tribunals' (2012) 27 Int'l J Marine & Coastal Law 59, 69–72, 91; similarly, Alan E Boyle, 'Dispute Settlement and the Law of the Sea Convention: Problems of Fragmentation and Jurisdiction' (1997) 46 ICLQ 37, 49. cf Tzeng (n 10) 563, 568–69.

Mauritius's aforesaid contention was rejected by the majority of the Annex VII arbitral tribunal in that case on the grounds that Article 298(1)(a)(i) relates only to the application of UNCLOS to disputes involving maritime boundaries and historic titles, and that,

> [a]t most, an *a contrario* reading of the provision supports the proposition that an issue of land sovereignty might be within the jurisdiction of a Part XV court or tribunal if it were genuinely ancillary to a dispute over a maritime boundary or a claim of historic title.[100]

The case at bar, however, was not such a dispute. To read Article 298(1)(a)(i) as a warrant to assume jurisdiction over matters of land sovereignty on the pretext that UNCLOS uses the term 'coastal State' would do violence to the intent of the drafters of UNCLOS to craft a balanced text and to respect the manifest sensitivity of States to the compulsory settlement of disputes relating to sovereign rights and maritime territory—such sensitivities arise to an even greater degree in relation to land territory.[101] The tribunal added that, as a general matter,

> where a dispute concerns the interpretation or application of UNCLOS, the jurisdiction of a court or tribunal pursuant to Article 288(1) extends to making such findings of fact or ancillary determinations of law as are necessary to resolve the dispute presented to it (see *Certain German Interests in Polish Upper Silesia, Preliminary Objections, Judgment of 25 August 1925, PCIJ Series A, No 6, p 4 at p 18*)

but where the 'real issue in the case' and the 'object of the claim' do not relate to the interpretation or application of UNCLOS, an incidental connection between the dispute and some matter regulated by UNCLOS is insufficient to bring the dispute, as a whole, within the ambit of Article 288(1).[102] The tribunal clarified that it did not categorically exclude that in some instances a minor issue of territorial sovereignty could indeed be ancillary to a dispute concerning the interpretation or application of UNCLOS, but Mauritius's first submission concerned the parties' dispute regarding sovereignty over the Chagos Archipelago, and not the interpretation or

---

[100] *Chagos Marine Protected Area Arbitration* (n 83) para 218.
[101] ibid para 219.
[102] ibid para 220.

application of UNCLOS; hence, the tribunal had no jurisdiction to address Mauritius's aforesaid submission.[103]

Therefore, some commentators now maintain that a court or tribunal referred to in Article 287 of UNCLOS has jurisdiction over any dispute concerning the interpretation or application of 'an international agreement related to the purposes of [UNCLOS], which is submitted to it in accordance with the agreement', including mixed disputes, provided the territorial dispute is necessary for the resolution of the UNCLOS dispute and is merely ancillary to the UNCLOS dispute,[104] unless, of course, the agreement expressly excludes such ancillary territorial dispute.

It is for the court for tribunal in a particular case to determine whether the territorial dispute is necessary for the resolution of, and is merely ancillary to, the law of the sea dispute. One example may be the ICJ's judgment in *Territorial and Maritime Dispute between Nicaragua and Honduras in the Caribbean Sea (Nicaragua v Honduras)*. In order to draw a single maritime boundary line in an area of the Caribbean Sea where a number of islands and rocks were located, the ICJ would have to consider what influence these maritime features might have on the course of that line, including determining which State had sovereignty over the islands and rocks in the disputed area. The ICJ found the claim relating to sovereignty implicit in and arising directly out of the question of delimitation of the disputed areas of the territorial sea, continental shelf, and exclusive economic zone. The ICJ concluded that the Nicaraguan claim relating to sovereignty over the islands in the maritime area in dispute was admissible as it was inherent in the original claim relating to the maritime delimitation between Nicaragua and Honduras in the Caribbean Sea.[105]

It is still uncertain how ITLOS will interpret its jurisdiction as regards 'mixed' disputes before it. Anyway, there is nothing to prevent disputing parties from expressly submitting a 'mixed' dispute to ITLOS, if they so decide.[106] In the past, States have agreed to confer jurisdiction on an

---

[103] ibid para 221.

[104] Tzeng (n 10) 573–74; Rao and Gautier (n 33) 92. cf Serdy, 'Art 298' (n 70) 1925–30.

[105] *Territorial and Maritime Dispute between Nicaragua and Honduras in the Caribbean Sea (Nicaragua v Honduras)* [2007] ICJ Rep 659, 697 [114]–[115]. This reasoning is applicable to what is discussed here despite the fact that UNCLOS was not yet in force between Nicaragua and Honduras at the time of the institution of the proceedings in the ICJ in that case.

[106] According to one commentator, ITLOS is not properly 'a treaty tribunal' since both UNCLOS Art 288(2) and ITLOS Statute Art 21 assume that ITLOS's jurisdiction surpasses the limits of UNCLOS itself without clarifying how far ITLOS's jurisdiction goes beyond these limits: García-Revillo (n 60) 18.

international court or tribunal to settle the sovereignty over a disputed land territory as well as delimit their maritime zones generated from that territory.[107] In *Territorial and Maritime Dispute between Nicaragua and Honduras in the Caribbean Sea* the ICJ noted that Honduras had contested neither the ICJ's jurisdiction to entertain the Nicaraguan new claim regarding the islands, nor its admissibility. Honduras even observed that the new Nicaraguan claim made the nature of the task facing the ICJ clearer so that the ICJ was 'asked to decide both on title to the islands and on the maritime delimitation'. Honduras further added that as the ICJ was faced with a dispute over land and maritime spaces, it had to resolve the question of sovereignty over the land before it could turn to the maritime boundary. In its final submissions Honduras asked the ICJ to adjudge and declare that:

> The islands Bobel Cay, South Cay, Savanna Cay, and Port Royal Cay, together with all other islands, cays, rocks, banks and reefs claimed by Nicaragua which lie north of the 15th parallel are under the sovereignty of the Republic of Honduras.

The ICJ therefore had to rule on the claims of the two parties with respect to the islands in dispute.[108]

Nevertheless, international courts and tribunals must be careful not to overstep the jurisdiction conferred upon them by disputing parties. For example, the Annex VII arbitral tribunal in *South China Sea Arbitration, Philippines v China* would have no jurisdiction over any disputes excluded by China's declaration under Article 298(1)(a), (b), and (c). However, the Philippines' submission No 12 reflected a dispute concerning 'China's activities on Mischief Reef and their effects on the marine environment', which was not a dispute concerning sovereignty or maritime boundary delimitation. The tribunal warned, however, that its jurisdiction to address the questions raised in submission No 12 was dependent on the status of Mischief Reef as an 'island', 'rock', or 'low-tide elevation'. Had the tribunal found Mischief Reef to be a fully entitled island or rock and thus constituting land

---

[107] As in, eg, the following cases submitted to the ICJ: *Maritime Delimitation and Territorial Questions between Qatar and Bahrain* (Jurisdiction and Admissibility) [1995] ICJ Rep 6; *Land and Maritime Boundary between Cameroon and Nigeria* (Preliminary Objections) [1998] ICJ Rep 275; *Territorial and Maritime Dispute (Nicaragua v Colombia)* (Preliminary Objections) [2007] ICJ Rep 838.

[108] *Territorial and Maritime Dispute between Nicaragua and Honduras in the Caribbean Sea* (n 105) 697 [116].

territory, it would necessarily lack jurisdiction to consider the lawfulness of China's construction activities on Mischief Reef (at least in terms of the provisions of UNCLOS concerning artificial islands) or the appropriation of the feature. That is, if Mischief Reef had been found to be a rock or island capable of sovereign appropriation, the lawfulness of activities on such a feature could not be assessed without resolving the question of which State had sovereign title over the land in question. In the end, the tribunal found Mischief Reef to be a low-tide elevation (and thus not land territory) within an area where only the Philippines possessed possible entitlements to maritime zones under UNCLOS. Mischief Reef, therefore, could only constitute part of the exclusive economic zone and continental shelf of the Philippines, lying beyond any entitlement that could be generated by any feature claimed by China (or another State). UNCLOS provisions endow the coastal State with exclusive decision-making and regulatory power over the construction and operation of artificial islands, and of installations and structures covered by Article 60(1), on Mischief Reef. Within its exclusive economic zone and continental shelf, only the Philippines, or another authorized State, might construct or operate such artificial islands, installations, or structures. The tribunal, thus, considered China's initial structures on Mischief Reef from 1995 onwards to constitute installations or structures for the purposes of Article 60(1), built in an area in which only the Philippines might construct or authorize such structures. With regard to the Philippines' submission that China, through its occupation and construction activities, had, unlawfully attempted to appropriate Mischief Reef, the tribunal recalled that Mischief Reef as a low-tide elevation could not form part of the land territory of a State in the legal sense and was incapable of appropriation, by occupation or otherwise. As a low-tide elevation within the Philippines' exclusive economic zone and continental shelf, the legal relevance of Mischief Reef was that it lied within an area in which sovereign rights were vested exclusively in the Philippines and where only the Philippines could construct or authorize artificial islands. Therefore, the tribunal found that China had, through its construction of installations and artificial islands at Mischief Reef without the authorisation of the Philippines, breached Articles 60 and 80 of UNCLOS with respect to the Philippines' sovereign rights in its exclusive economic zone and continental shelf, respectively.[109]

---

[109] PCA Case No 2013–19, Award of 12 July 2016 paras 1029–43. See also 'Special Issue on Jurisdiction and Admissibility in the South China Sea Arbitration' (2016) 15(2) Chinese

dd) Historic titles

Article 288(4) of UNCLOS provides that in the event of a dispute as to whether a court or tribunal has jurisdiction, the matter shall be settled by decision of that court or tribunal. In this respect, characterization of the dispute by an international court or tribunal is decisive.[110]

According to the Annex VII arbitral tribunal in *South China Sea Arbitration, Philippines v China* the reference to 'historic titles' in Article 298(1)(a)(i) of UNCLOS is 'a reference to claims of sovereignty over maritime areas derived from historical circumstances'. In its view, this accords with the only other direct usage of the term, in Article 15 of UNCLOS, where historical sovereignty would understandably bear on the delimitation of the territorial sea. Since other 'historic rights' are nowhere mentioned in UNCLOS, nothing suggests that Article 298(1)(a)(i) was intended to also exclude jurisdiction over a broad and unspecified category of possible claims to historic rights falling short of sovereignty.[111] This is particularly the case where the rights asserted are coextensive with rights allocated by UNCLOS to, for example, coastal States in their exclusive economic zone. The latter must be taken to have extinguished claims of historic rights in the same waters, at least to the extent of any conflict.

ee) Law enforcement activities

The drafting history of Articles 297 and 298 of UNCLOS reveals that law enforcement activities under Article 297(1) (ie, those related to navigation, overflight, or the laying of submarine cables and pipelines, as well as those related to the protection and preservation of the marine environment) are subject to the jurisdiction of a court or tribunal. Only disputes concerning law enforcement activities in regard to the exercise of sovereign rights or jurisdiction expressly excluded from the jurisdiction of a court or tribunal

---

JIL 217; Chinese Society of International Law, 'The South China Sea Arbitration Awards: A Critical Study' (2018) 17(2) Chinese JIL 207.

[110] See, eg, how ITLOS has treated acts of 'bunkering' at sea in its different decisions in *M/V 'Virginia G'* (n 13) 68–70 (where ITLOS held that bunkering of foreign vessels fishing in the exclusive economic zone was subject to regulation by the coastal State concerned), and *M/T 'San Padre Pio'* (Provisional Measures, Order of 6 July 2019) paras 107–08 (where bunkering activities were held to be part of the freedom of navigation). Characterization of a dispute was the main reason for disagreement among some ITLOS judges in *M/V 'Saiga' (Saint Vincent and the Grenadines v Guinea)* (Prompt Release) ITLOS Reports 1997, 16, as evident from the dissenting opinions of several ITLOS judges in that case. cf also the characterization of the dispute in *Chagos Marine Protected Area Arbitration*, Final Award paras 283–304.

[111] PCA Case No 2013–19, Award of 12 July 2016 para 226.

under paragraph 2 (marine scientific research) or paragraph 3 (fisheries) of Article 297 can be excepted by a declaration under Article 298. Thus, other law enforcement activities, including those relating to marine scientific research or fisheries not expressly excluded under Article 297(2) or (3) may not be excepted under article 298(1)(b).[112]

In 'Arctic Sunrise' (Kingdom of the Netherlands v Russian Federation), the applicant requested ITLOS to prescribe provisional measures pending the constitution of an Annex VII arbitral tribunal. The case concerns the arrest and detention of the vessel 'Arctic Sunrise' and its crew by Russian authorities. The 'Arctic Sunrise', flying the flag of the Netherlands, is an icebreaker operated by Greenpeace International and was engaged in protesting against Russian oil exploration in the Arctic at the time of apprehension. The icebreaker's crew were initially charged with piracy, which was subsequently replaced by a charge of aggravated hooliganism. Russia referred to its declaration excluding procedures provided for in section 2 of Part XV of UNCLOS 'with respect to disputes ... concerning law enforcement activities in regard to the exercise of sovereign rights or jurisdiction'.[113] The Netherlands rebutted that the disputes excluded by virtue of Russia's aforesaid declaration concerned marine scientific research and fisheries, respectively, neither of which was at issue in the case before ITLOS.[114] ITLOS held that Russia's declaration with respect to law enforcement activities under Article 298(1)(b) prima facie applied only to disputes in regard to sovereign rights or jurisdiction excluded from the jurisdiction of a court or tribunal under Article 297(2) and (3) of UNCLOS.[115] ITLOS found a difference of opinions between the parties as to the applicability of the provisions of UNCLOS as regards the rights and obligations of a flag State and a coastal State, notably, its Articles 56 (rights, jurisdiction, and duties of the coastal State in the exclusive economic zone), 58 (rights and duties of other States in the exclusive economic zone), 60 (artificial islands, installations, and structures in the exclusive economic zone), 87 (freedom of the high seas), and 110 (right of visit), and that these provisions appeared to afford a basis on which the prima facie jurisdiction of the arbitral tribunal might be founded over the dispute.[116]

---

[112] Virginia Commentary (n 14) 137.
[113] 'Arctic Sunrise' (Provisional Measures, Order of 22 November 2013) ITLOS Reports 2013, 230, 240 [42].
[114] ibid 241 [43].
[115] ibid 241 [45].
[116] ibid 246 [68]–[71].

The Annex VII arbitral tribunal in *Arctic Sunrise* subsequently affirmed its jurisdiction over the dispute. Russia's impugned actions were held not to be 'law enforcement activities in regard to the exercise of sovereign rights or jurisdiction' within the scope of Article 298(1)(b). They did not relate to marine scientific research or fisheries, which are the only areas in which the jurisdiction of a court or tribunal can validly be excluded pursuant to Article 297(2) and (3) read with 298(1)(b) of UNCLOS. In particular, the dispute did not 'arise out of the exercise [by Russia] of a right or discretion [regarding marine scientific research] in accordance with Article 246' of UNCLOS or 'a decision [of Russia] to order suspension or cessation of a research project in accordance with Article 253' of UNCLOS; nor did it relate to the 'interpretation or application of the provisions of [UNCLOS] relating to [Russia's] sovereign rights with respect to the living resources in the exclusive economic zone or their exercise, including the discretionary powers [of Russia] for determining the allowable catch, [Russia's] harvesting capacity, the allocation of surpluses to other States, and the terms and conditions established in [Russia's] conservation and management laws or regulations'.[117]

ff) Military activities

Article 298(1)(b) of UNCLOS on the optional exception to disputes concerning military activities owes its origin to the preoccupation of the naval advisors to certain delegations to the Third UN Conference on the Law of the Sea that activities by naval vessels should not be subject to judicial proceedings in which some military secrets might have to be disclosed. They pointed out that several maritime conventions contained provisions making it clear these conventions (including their provisions for the settlement of disputes) did not apply to 'any warship, naval auxiliary, or other ship owned or operated by a State and used, for the time being, only on government non-commercial service'. Doubts were raised, however, as to whether any vessels were entitled to sovereign immunity in a case brought before an international tribunal, as that doctrine applied only to domestic courts which were not allowed to bring before them a foreign sovereign whereas the very purpose of international tribunals was to deal with

---

[117] *Arctic Sunrise Arbitration (Netherlands v Russian Federation)*, PCA Case No 2014-02, Award on Jurisdiction of 26 November 2014 paras 65–78. See also Keyuan Zou and Qiang Ye, 'Interpretation and Application of Article 298 of the Law of the Sea Convention in Recent Annex VII Arbitrations: An Appraisal' (2017) 48 ODIL 331.

disputes between sovereign States. The final compromise appears in Article 298(1)(b).[118]

In *Detention of three Ukrainian naval vessels (Ukraine v Russian Federation)*, Russia submitted that ITLOS had no jurisdiction to prescribe provisional measures pursuant to Article 290(5) of UNCLOS pending the constitution of an Annex VII arbitral tribunal since the latter lacked prima facie jurisdiction due to both disputing parties' declaration made under Article 298(1)(b) to exclude disputes concerning military activities from compulsory procedures entailing binding decisions. ITLOS noted that the dispute submitted to the Annex VII arbitral tribunal concerned the alleged violation of Ukraine's rights under UNCLOS's Articles 32 (immunities of warships and other government ships operated for non-commercial purposes), 58 (rights and duties of other States in the exclusive economic zone), 95 (immunity of warships on the high seas), and 96 (immunity of ships used only on government non-commercial service) arising from the arrest and detention of its naval vessels and their servicemen and the subsequent exercise of criminal jurisdiction over them by Russia.

For the purposes of determining whether the dispute concerned military activities under Article 298(1)(b), it was necessary for ITLOS to examine a series of events preceding the arrest and detention as these events might shed light on whether the arrest and detention took place in the context of a military operation or a law enforcement operation. ITLOS considered the following three circumstances as particularly relevant in that case. First, it appeared from the information and evidence presented by the parties to ITLOS that the underlying dispute leading to the arrest concerned the passage of the Ukrainian naval vessels through the Kerch Strait. In ITLOS's view, it was difficult to state in general that the passage of naval ships per se amounted to a military activity. Under UNCLOS, passage regimes, such as innocent or transit passage, apply to all ships. The particular passage at issue was attempted under circumstances of continuing tension between the parties, and Ukraine's naval vessels had previously passed through the Strait in question. Second, the specific cause of the incident giving rise to Ukraine's application in that case was Russia's denial of the passage of the Ukrainian naval vessels through the Strait and the attempt by those vessels to proceed nonetheless. The aforementioned facts indicated that at the core of the dispute was the parties' differing interpretation of the regime

---

[118] Virginia Commentary (n 14) 135–37.

of passage through the Strait, and that such a dispute was not military in nature. Third, the context in which force was used by Russia in the process of arrest was of particular relevance. After being held for about eight hours, the Ukrainian naval vessels apparently gave up their mission to pass through the Strait and turned around and sailed away from it. The Russian Coast Guard then ordered them to stop and, when the vessels ignored the order and continued their navigation, started chasing them. It was at this moment and in this context that the Russian Coast Guard used force, first firing warning shots and then targeted shots. One vessel was damaged, certain servicemen were injured, and the vessels were stopped and arrested. What occurred appeared to be the use of force in the context of a law enforcement operation rather than a military operation.

In ITLOS's view, the distinction between military and law enforcement activities cannot be based solely on whether naval vessels or law enforcement vessels are employed in the activities in question. Although this may be a relevant factor, the traditional distinction between naval vessels and law enforcement vessels in terms of their roles has become considerably blurred, since it is not uncommon today for States to employ the two types of vessels collaboratively for diverse maritime tasks. Nor can the distinction between military and law enforcement activities be based solely on the characterization of the activities in question by the parties to a dispute although this may be a relevant factor, especially in case of the party invoking the military activities exception. However, such characterization may be subjective and at variance with the actual conduct. The distinction between military and law enforcement activities must be based primarily on an objective evaluation of the nature of the activities in question, taking into account the relevant circumstances in each case.[119]

The aforementioned circumstances of the incident suggested that the arrest and detention of the Ukrainian naval vessels by Russia took place in the context of a law enforcement operation unrelated to Russia's exercise of sovereign rights or jurisdiction within the scope of Russia's declaration with respect to law enforcement activities under Article 298(1)(b). The subsequent proceedings and charges against the servicemen further supported such law enforcement nature of the activities of Russia. The servicemen were charged with unlawfully crossing the Russian State border and Russia invoked Article 30 of UNCLOS, entitled 'Noncompliance by warships with

---

[119] *Detention of three Ukrainian naval vessels* (n 1) paras 64–66.

the laws and regulations of the coastal State', to justify its detention of the vessels. Based on the information and evidence available to it, ITLOS accordingly considered that prima facie Article 298(1)(b) of UNCLOS did not apply in the case at bar.[120]

2. Contentious cases before the Seabed Disputes Chamber

In contentious cases, the Seabed Disputes Chamber shall be open to States Parties to UNCLOS, the Authority, the Enterprise, State enterprises, and State-sponsored natural legal persons carrying out activities in the Area.[121]

By virtue of Article 187 of UNCLOS, the Seabed Disputes Chamber shall have jurisdiction over disputes with respect to activities in the Area falling within the following six categories. The first one encompasses disputes between States Parties concerning the interpretation or application of Part XI (The Area) of UNCLOS and the Annexes relating thereto. The second category relates to disputes between a State Party and the International Seabed Authority concerning (i) acts or omissions of the Authority or of a State Party alleged to be in violation of Part XI or the Annexes relating thereto or of rules, regulations, and procedures of the Authority adopted in accordance therewith; or (ii) acts of the Authority alleged to be in excess of jurisdiction or a misuse of power. The third category concerns disputes between parties to a contract, being States Parties, the Authority or the Enterprise, State enterprises, and natural or juridical persons referred to in Article 153(2)(b),[122] concerning (i) the interpretation or application of a relevant contract or a plan of work; or (ii) acts or omissions of a party to the contract relating to activities in the Area and directed to the other party or directly affecting its legitimate interests. The fourth category encompasses disputes between the Authority and a prospective contractor who has been sponsored by a State as provided in Article 153(2)(b) and has duly fulfilled the conditions of qualification standards and paid a fee for the administrative

---

[120] ibid paras 67–77.

[121] Statute Art 37 and UNCLOS Art 187.

[122] According to Art 153(2)(b), activities in the Area shall be carried out in association with the International Seabed Authority by States Parties, or State enterprises, or natural or juridical persons which possess the nationality of States Parties or are effectively controlled by them or their nationals, when sponsored by such States, or any group of the foregoing which meets the requirements provided in Part XI and in Annex III governing the basic conditions of prospecting, exploration, and exploitation of the resources in the Area.

cost of processing an application for approval of a plan of work referred to in Article 4(6) and Article 13(2) of Annex III (Basic conditions of prospecting, exploration, and exploitation) concerning the refusal of a contract or a legal issue arising in the negotiation of the contract. The fifth category covers disputes between the Authority and a State Party, a State enterprise, or a natural or juridical person sponsored by a State Party as provided for in Article 153(2)(b), where it is alleged that the Authority has incurred liability for any damage arising out of wrongful acts in the exercise of its powers and functions as provided in Article 22 of Annex III. The sixth category covers any other disputes for which the jurisdiction of the Chamber is specifically provided in UNCLOS, as in the case where a commercial arbitral tribunal to which the dispute concerning the interpretation or application of a contract regarding the Area is submitted refers a question of the interpretation of Part XI and the Annexes relating thereto, with respect to activities in the Area, to the Chamber for a ruling.[123] In addition, when the Assembly of the Authority upon the recommendation of the Council of the Authority intends to suspend a State Party which has grossly and persistently violated the provisions of Part XI from the exercise of rights and privileges of membership, no such suspension may be taken until the Chamber has found a State Party to have grossly and persistently violated the said provisions.[124]

A declaration on the choice of procedure made by a State Party pursuant to Article 287(1) of UNCLOS shall not affect or be affected by the obligation of the State Party to accept the jurisdiction of the Seabed Disputes Chamber to the extent and in the manner provided for in Part XI, section 5 of UNCLOS governing dispute settlement and advisory opinions by the Seabed Disputes Chamber.[125]

The decisions of the Seabed Disputes Chamber shall be enforceable in the territories of the States Parties to UNCLOS in the same manner as judgments or orders of the highest court of the State Party in whose territory the enforcement is sought.[126]

In its advisory opinion in *Responsibilities and obligations of States with respect to activities in the Area*, the Seabed Disputes Chamber refers to the

---

[123] UNCLOS Art 188(2).

[124] UNCLOS Art 185 and Rules Art 122. For more detail, see Rao and Gautier (n 33) 122–25.

[125] UNCLOS Art 287(2).

[126] Statute Art 39. In addition, Article 21(2) of UNCLOS's Annex III (concerning basic conditions of prospecting, exploration, and exploitation in the Area) provides that any final decision rendered by a court or tribunal having jurisdiction under UNCLOS relating to the rights and obligations of the Authority and of the contractor shall be enforceable in the territory of any State Party to UNCLOS affected thereby.

meaning of 'activities in the Area' as defined in Article 1(1)(3) of UNCLOS as 'all activities of exploration for, and exploitation of, the resources of the Area'. According to Article 133(a) of UNCLOS, for the purposes of Part XI (The Area), the term 'resources' means 'all solid, liquid, or gaseous mineral resources *in situ* in the Area at or beneath the seabed, including polymetallic nodules'. The two definitions, however, do not indicate what is meant by 'exploration' and 'exploitation', and it is important to note that according to Article 133(b), 'resources, when recovered from the Area, are referred to as "minerals"'.[127] Article 145 of UNCLOS, which prescribes the taking of '[n]ecessary measures ... with respect to activities in the Area to ensure effective protection for the marine environment from harmful effects which may arise from such activities', indicates the activities in respect of which the Authority should adopt rules, regulations, and procedures. These activities include 'drilling, dredging, excavation, disposal of waste, construction, and operation or maintenance of installations, pipelines, and other devices related to such activities'. In the Chamber's opinion, these activities are included in the notion of 'activities in the Area'.[128] Activities directly connected with exploration and exploitation, including the recovery of minerals from the seabed and their lifting to the water surface, such as the evacuation of water from the minerals and the preliminary separation of materials of no commercial interest, including their disposal at sea, are also deemed to be covered by the expression 'activities in the Area'.[129]

However, 'processing', namely, the process through which metals are extracted from the minerals and which is normally conducted at a plant situated on land, is excluded from the expression 'activities in the Area'.[130] According to Annex IV, Article 1(1) of UNCLOS, the Enterprise is the organ of the Authority which shall carry out activities in the Area directly, pursuant to Article 153(2)(a), as well as the transporting, processing, and marketing of minerals recovered from the Area. This provision distinguishes 'activities in the Area', which the Enterprise carries out directly pursuant to Article 153(2)(a) of UNCLOS, from other activities with which the Enterprise is entrusted, namely, the transporting, processing and marketing

---

[127] *Responsibilities and obligations of States with respect to activities in the Area* (Advisory Opinion) ITLOS Reports 2011, 10, 34 [82].

[128] ibid 34–35 [85]. The Chamber adds, in para 87, that 'activities in the Area' include drilling, dredging, coring, and excavation; disposal, dumping, and discharge into the marine environment of sediment, wastes, or other effluents; and construction and operation or maintenance of installations, pipelines, and other devices related to such activities.

[129] ibid 37 [95].

[130] ibid.

of minerals recovered from the Area. Consequently, the latter activities are not included in the notion of 'activities in the Area' referred to in Annex IV, Article 1(1) of UNCLOS.[131] Transportation to points on land from the part of the high seas superjacent to the part of the Area in which the contractor operates cannot be included in the notion of 'activities in the Area', although transportation within that part of the high seas, when directly connected with extraction and lifting, should be included in activities in the Area. In the case of polymetallic nodules, this applies, for instance, to transportation between the ship or installation where the lifting process ends and another ship or installation where the evacuation of water and the preliminary separation and disposal of material to be discarded take place. The inclusion of transportation to points on land could create an unnecessary conflict with provisions of UNCLOS such as those concerning navigation on the high seas.[132] 'Prospecting', although mentioned in Annex III, Article 2, of UNCLOS and in the Nodules Regulations and the Sulphides Regulations, is not included in UNCLOS's definition of 'activities in the Area' because UNCLOS and the two Regulations distinguish it from 'exploration' and from 'exploitation'. Moreover, under UNCLOS and related instruments, prospecting does not require sponsorship.[133]

According to Article 189 of UNCLOS, the Seabed Disputes Chamber shall have no jurisdiction with regard to the exercise by the Authority of its discretionary powers in accordance with Part XI of UNCLOS, and in no case shall it substitute its discretion for that of the Authority. Without prejudice to Article 191 on the Seabed Disputes Chamber's advisory jurisdiction, in exercising its jurisdiction pursuant to Article 187, the Chamber shall not pronounce itself on the question of whether any rules, regulations, and procedures of the Authority are in conformity with UNCLOS, nor declare invalid any such rules, regulations, and procedures. Its jurisdiction in this regard shall be confined to deciding claims that the application of any rules, regulations, and procedures of the Authority in individual cases would be in conflict with the contractual obligations of the parties to the dispute or their obligations under UNCLOS, claims concerning excess of jurisdiction or misuse of power, and claims for damages to be paid or other remedy to

---

[131] ibid 34 [83]–[84].

[132] ibid 37 [96].

[133] ibid 38 [98]. However, considering that prospecting is often treated as the preliminary phase of exploration in mining practice and legislation, the Chamber considers it appropriate to observe that some aspects of this advisory opinion may also apply to prospecting (ibid).

be given to the party concerned for the failure of the other party to comply with its contractual obligations or its obligations under UNCLOS.[134]

Pursuant to Article 115 of the ITLOS Rules, proceedings in contentious cases before the Seabed Disputes Chamber and its ad hoc chambers shall, subject to the provisions of UNCLOS, the ITLOS Statute, and these Rules relating specifically to the Seabed Disputes Chamber and its ad hoc chambers, be governed by the Rules applicable in contentious cases before ITLOS. Therefore, the Chamber shall, inter alia, follow the Rules' Article 49 requiring the proceedings before ITLOS to be conducted without unnecessary delay or expense, Article 59(1) setting the time limits for each written pleading not to exceed six months, and Article 69(1)(2) requiring fixing the date for the opening of the oral proceedings to fall within a period of six months from the closure of the written proceedings unless there is adequate justification for deciding otherwise.

Contentious proceedings may be instituted before the Seabed Disputes Chamber either by unilateral written application or by notification of a special agreement.[135]

Upon receipt of the unilateral application, the Registrar must transmit forthwith a certified copy of application to the respondent.[136]

Like proceedings brought before ITLOS by the notification of a special agreement, the notification may be effected by the parties jointly or by any one or more of them. If the notification is not a joint one, a certified copy of it shall forthwith be communicated by the Registrar to any other party. In each case the notification shall be accompanied by an original or certified copy of the special agreement. The notification shall also, insofar as this is not already apparent from the agreement, indicate the precise subject of the dispute and identify the parties to it.[137]

Written proceedings in the case of disputes instituted by application consist of a memorial by applicant and a counter-memorial by respondent.[138] The Chamber may authorize a reply by the applicant and a rejoinder by the respondent if parties are so agreed or if Chamber decides *proprio motu* that these pleadings are necessary.[139] In the case of disputes

---

[134] cf Linlin Sun, 'Dispute Settlement Relating to Deep Seabed Mining: A Participant's Perspective' (2017) 18 Melbourne JIL 71, 79–80.

[135] The present author is grateful to the ITLOS Registry for its detailed explanation of these proceedings before the Seabed Disputes Chamber.

[136] Rules Arts 54(4) and 118(1).

[137] Rules Art 55.

[138] Rules Art 60(1).

[139] Rules Art 60(2).

instituted by notification of a special agreement, the number and order of pleadings are governed by the agreement, unless otherwise decided by the Chamber after ascertaining the parties' views.[140] If the special agreement contains no such provision, and if the parties have not subsequently agreed on the number and order of pleadings, they shall each file a memorial and counter-memorial, within the same time limits.[141] The presentation of replies and rejoinders is not authorized by the Chamber unless it finds them necessary.[142] The maximum time limit is not more than six months for each pleading, taking in account the parties' views.[143]

Upon the closure of the written proceedings, the date for the opening of the oral proceedings shall be fixed by the Chamber. Such date shall fall within a period of six months from the closure of the written proceedings unless the Chamber is satisfied that there is adequate justification for deciding otherwise.[144]

With regard to proceedings in all disputes before the Chamber other than disputes exclusively between States Parties and between States Parties and the Authority,[145] proceedings may be instituted before the Seabed Disputes Chamber either by unilateral written application or by notification of a special agreement. When proceedings before the Chamber are instituted by means of an application the application is the only written pleading of the applicant.[146] The application shall be served on the respondent and the sponsoring State in any case where the applicant or the respondent is a natural or juridical person or a State enterprise.[147] Within two months after service of the application, the respondent shall lodge a defence against the application although it may request the President of the Chamber to extend the time limit, provided it can convince the President that there is adequate justification for the request.[148] The Chamber may authorize or direct the filing of further pleadings if the parties so agree or the Chamber decides, *proprio motu* or at the request of a party, that these pleadings are

---

[140] Rules Art 61(1).
[141] Rules Art 61(2).
[142] Rules Art 61(3).
[143] Rules Art 59(1).
[144] Rules Art 69(1).
[145] Rules Art 116: Arts 117 to 121 apply to proceedings in all disputes before the Chamber with the exception of disputes exclusively between States Parties and between States Parties and the Authority.
[146] Rules Art 117(f)–(h).
[147] Rules Art 118(1).
[148] Rules Art 118(2) and (3).

necessary.[149] The President of the Chamber shall fix the time limits within which these pleadings are to be filed.[150] The date for the opening of oral proceedings shall be fixed by the Chamber within six months from the closure of written proceedings,[151] having regard, inter alia, to the need to hold the hearing without unnecessary delay and any special circumstances, including the urgency of the case or other cases on the List of cases.[152]

The Authority has entered into contracts with States, publicly funded companies or institutions, and private companies.[153] By virtue of Article 285 of UNCLOS, if an entity other than a State Party is a party to any dispute which pursuant to Part XI, section 5 (settlement of disputes and advisory opinions by the Seabed Disputes Chamber), is to be settled in accordance with procedures provided for in Part XV, section 1 (general provisions) of Part XV applies *mutatis mutandis*.

If a natural or juridical person is a party to a dispute referred to in Article 187 of UNCLOS, the sponsoring State shall be given notice thereof and shall have the right to participate in the proceedings by submitting written or oral statements.[154]

If an action is brought against a State Party by a natural or juridical person sponsored by another State Party in a dispute falling under the aforesaid third category of disputes, the respondent State may request the State sponsoring that person to appear in the proceedings on behalf of that person and, failing such appearance, the respondent State may arrange to be represented by a juridical person of its nationality.[155] Within two months after service of the application, the respondent State may make an application for the sponsoring State of the applicant to appear in the proceedings on behalf of the applicant,[156] with notice of the latter application communicated to the applicant and its sponsoring State.[157] If, within a time limit fixed by the President of the Chamber, the sponsoring State does not indicate it will appear in the proceedings on behalf of the applicant, the respondent State may designate a juridical person of its nationality to represent it.[158] Within two

---

[149] Rules Art 121(1).
[150] Rules Art 121(2).
[151] Rules Art 69(1).
[152] Rules Art 69(2)(a) and (c).
[153] Sun (n 134) 72–73.
[154] UNCLOS Art 190(1).
[155] UNCLOS Art 190(2).
[156] Rules Art 119(1).
[157] Rules Art 119(2).
[158] ibid.

months after service of the application on the sponsoring State of a party, such State may give written notice of its intention to submit written or oral statements.[159] Upon receipt of such a notice, the President of the Chamber shall fix the time limit within which the sponsoring State may submit its written statements. The sponsoring State shall be notified of such time limit and the date of the hearing. The written statements shall be communicated to the parties and to any other sponsoring State of a party.[160]

When proceedings are brought before the Chamber by the notification of a special agreement, the notification shall also provide information regarding participation and appearance in the proceedings by sponsoring States Parties.[161]

When a commercial arbitral tribunal refers to the Chamber a question of interpretation of Part XI of UNCLOS and the annexes relating thereto upon which its decision depends, the document submitting the question to the Chamber shall contain a precise statement of the question and be accompanied by all relevant information and documents. Upon receipt of the document, the President of the Chamber shall fix a time limit not exceeding three months within which the parties to the proceedings before the arbitral tribunal and the States Parties may submit their written observations on the question. The parties to the proceedings and the States Parties shall be notified of the time limit. The latter shall also be informed of the contents of the submission. The President of the Chamber shall fix a date for a hearing if, within one month from the expiration of the time limit for submitting written observations, a party to the proceedings before the arbitral tribunal or a State Party gives written notice of its intention to submit oral observations.[162]

---

159 Rules Art 119(3).
160 Rules Art 119(4).
161 Rules Art 120(2).
162 Rules Art 123.

4

Advisory Opinions by ITLOS

Like the International Court of Justice, ITLOS may render and has rendered advisory opinions on legal questions within its areas of competence. UNCLOS expressly provides for the advisory jurisdiction of the Seabed Disputes Chamber of ITLOS, but not the full bench of ITLOS itself.

1. Advisory jurisdiction of ITLOS's Seabed Disputes Chamber

According to Article 191 of UNCLOS, the Seabed Disputes Chamber shall give advisory opinions at the request of the Assembly or the Council of the International Seabed Authority on legal questions arising within the scope of their activities, and such opinions shall be given as a matter of urgency. In addition, pursuant to Article 159(10), upon a written request addressed to the President and sponsored by at least one-fourth of the members of the Authority for an advisory opinion on the conformity with UNCLOS of a proposal before the Assembly on any matter, the Assembly shall request the Seabed Disputes Chamber to give an advisory opinion thereon and shall defer voting on that proposal pending receipt of the advisory opinion by the Chamber. If the advisory opinion is not received before the final week of the session in which it is requested, the Assembly shall decide when it will meet to vote upon the deferred proposal.

The ITLOS Rules elaborate the procedure in this respect.[1] In addition, the Seabed Disputes Chamber shall be guided, to the extent to which it recognizes them to be applicable, by the provisions of ITLOS's Statute and Rules applicable in contentious cases.[2] The Chamber shall consider whether the request for an advisory opinion relates to a legal question pending

---

[1] Section H (Advisory Proceedings) of Part III (Procedure) of the Rules.
[2] Rules Art 130.

between two or more parties. When the Chamber so determines, judges ad hoc may be appointed as already explained in part 16 of Chapter 2.

If the request for an advisory opinion states that the question necessitates an urgent answer the Chamber shall take all appropriate steps to accelerate the procedure.[3]

ITLOS's Seabed Disputes Chamber rendered its first advisory opinion in February 2011, in *Responsibilities and obligations of States with respect to activities in the Area*.[4] The way in which the Chamber dealt with this request for its advisory opinion should provide useful guidance on how it exercises advisory jurisdiction.

By letter dated 11 May 2010, transmitted electronically to the ITLOS Registry on 14 May 2010, the Secretary-General of the International Seabed Authority officially communicated to the Seabed Disputes Chamber a decision adopted by the Council of the International Seabed Authority on 6 May 2010, which decided[5] to request the Seabed Disputes Chamber[6] to render an advisory opinion on the following three legal questions. First, what are the legal responsibilities and obligations of States Parties to UNCLOS with respect to the sponsorship of activities in the Area in accordance with UNCLOS?[7] Second, what is the extent of liability of a State Party for any failure to comply with the provisions of UNCLOS by an entity whom it has sponsored under Article 153(2)(b) of UNCLOS? Third, what are the necessary and appropriate measures that a sponsoring State must take in order to fulfil its responsibility under UNCLOS?[8]

Pursuant to Article 133(1) of the Rules of ITLOS, the ITLOS Registrar notified all States Parties to UNCLOS and notified the UN Secretary-General

---

[3] Rules Art 132.

[4] *Responsibilities and obligations of States with respect to activities in the Area* (Advisory Opinion) ITLOS Reports 2011, 10.

[5] In accordance with UNCLOS Art 191.

[6] Pursuant to Rules Art 131:

> 1. A request for an advisory opinion on a legal question arising within the scope of the activities of the Assembly or the Council of the Authority shall contain a precise statement of the question. It shall be accompanied by all documents likely to throw light upon the question.
>
> 2. The documents shall be transmitted to the Chamber at the same time as the request or as soon as possible thereafter in the number of copies required by the Registry.

[7] In particular Part XI, and the 1994 Agreement relating to the Implementation of Part XI of UNCLOS [(1994) 33 ILM 1309].

[8] In particular Art 139 and Annex III (basic conditions for prospecting, exploration, and exploitation), and the 1994 Agreement.

of the request for an advisory opinion.[9] By Order dated 18 May 2010, the President of the Chamber, after deciding that the Authority and the intergovernmental organizations participating as observers in the Assembly of the Authority were likely to be able to furnish information on the questions submitted to the Chamber, invited them and UNCLOS States Parties to present written statements on those questions.[10] By the same Order, the President fixed a date as the time limit within which written statements on those questions might be submitted to the Chamber.[11] In the Order, the President further decided that oral proceedings would be held, and fixed 14 September 2010 as the date for the opening of the hearing.[12] States Parties, the Authority, and the aforementioned intergovernmental organizations were invited to participate in the hearing and to indicate to the Registrar, not later than 3 September 2010, their intention to make oral statements. Since Article 191 of UNCLOS requires the Chamber to give advisory opinions 'as a matter of urgency', the time limits for the submission of written statements and the date of the opening of the hearing, as set out in the Orders of the President, were fixed with a view to meeting this requirement. Upon receipt of those statements, in accordance with Article 133(3) of the Rules, the Registrar transmitted copies thereof to the States Parties, the Authority, and the organizations that had submitted written statements. On 19 August 2010, pursuant to Article 134 of the Rules, the written statements submitted to the Chamber were made accessible to the public on ITLOS's website.

Prior to the opening of the hearing, the Chamber held initial deliberations on 10, 13, and 14 September 2010. At four public sittings held on 14, 15, and 16 September 2010, the Chamber heard oral statements. By letter dated 13 September 2010, the Registrar transmitted to the Authority, prior to the hearing, a list of points the Chamber wished the Authority to address in oral statements or by a letter.[13] At the request of the President of the Chamber, by letter dated 13 October 2010, the Registrar asked the Legal Counsel of the Authority to provide the Chamber with information on the various phases of the process of exploration and exploitation of resources in the Area (collection, transportation to the surface, initial treatment, and so forth) as well as information on the technology available. The Legal Counsel

---

[9] According to 1997 Agreement on Cooperation and Relationship between the UN and ITLOS (2000 UNTS 467) Art 4.
[10] In accordance with Rules Art 133(2).
[11] In accordance with Rules Art 133(3).
[12] In accordance with Rules Art 133(4).
[13] Pursuant to Rules Art 76(1).

provided this information by letter dated 15 November 2010, which was then posted on ITLOS's website.

The Chamber has to ascertain that the preconditions in Article 191 of UNCLOS are met before it can exercise jurisdiction to render an advisory opinion in reply to a request.[14]

As regards admissibility of the request for its advisory opinion, some of the participants in the proceedings drew attention to the wording of Article 191 of UNCLOS, which states that the Chamber 'shall give' advisory opinions, and compared it to Article 65(1) of the Statute of the ICJ,[15] which states that the ICJ 'may give' an advisory opinion. In the light of this difference, they argued that, contrary to the discretionary powers of the ICJ, the Chamber, once it had established its jurisdiction, had no discretion to decline a request for an advisory opinion. While noting the said difference in the wording, the Chamber considered it unnecessary to pronounce on the consequences of that difference with respect to admissibility in the present case as the Chamber deemed it appropriate to render the advisory opinion requested by the Council.[16]

With respect to applicable law and interpretation, the Chamber held that the principal rules of the 1969 Vienna Convention on the Law of Treaties[17] reflect customary international law and apply to the interpretation of provisions of UNCLOS and the 1994 Agreement.[18] The Chamber is also required to interpret instruments that are not treaties and, in particular, the Regulations adopted by the Authority, namely, the Regulations on Prospecting and Exploration for Polymetallic Nodules in the Area of 2000, and the Regulations on Prospecting and Exploration for Polymetallic Sulphides in the Area of 2010. The fact that these instruments are binding texts negotiated by States and adopted through a procedure similar to the one used in multilateral conferences permits the Chamber to consider that the interpretation rules set out in the Vienna Convention may, by analogy, provide guidance as to their interpretation. In the specific request before the Chamber, the analogy was strengthened because of the close

---

[14] *Responsibilities and obligations of States with respect to activities in the Area* (n 4) 24–26 [31]–[45].

[15] 33 UNTS 933.

[16] *Responsibilities and obligations of States with respect to activities in the Area* (n 4) 26–27 [46]–[49].

[17] Part III, section 3 entitled 'Interpretation of treaties' and comprising 1969 Vienna Convention (1155 UNTS 331) Arts 31 to 33.

[18] *Responsibilities and obligations of States with respect to activities in the Area* (n 4) 28 [57]–[58].

connection between these texts and UNCLOS.[19] In interpreting UNCLOS provisions, the Chamber bears in mind that UNCLOS is a multilingual treaty: the Arabic, Chinese, English, French, Russian, and Spanish texts are equally authentic. These six languages are also the official languages of the Council and the Regulations of the Authority. The decision of the Council containing the questions submitted to the Chamber was adopted in those languages with the original in English. By virtue of Article 33(4) of the Vienna Convention, where no particular text prevails according to the treaty and where

> a comparison of the authentic texts discloses a difference of meaning which the application of Articles 31 [general rules of treaty interpretation] and 32 [supplementary means of treaty interpretation] does not remove, the meaning which best reconciles the texts, having regard to the object and purpose of the treaty, shall be adopted.

An examination of the relevant provisions of UNCLOS reveals that the terminology used in the different language versions corresponds to the objective stated by the Drafting Committee of the Third UN Conference on the Law of the Sea, namely, to improve linguistic concordance, to the extent possible, and to achieve juridical concordance in all cases. Although there are certain inconsistencies in the terminology used within the same language version and as between language versions, there is no difference of meaning between the authentic texts of the relevant provisions of UNCLOS. A comparison between the terms used in these provisions of UNCLOS is nonetheless useful in clarifying their meaning.[20]

The Chamber replied to the three questions posed by the Council as follows.[21]

On the *first* question, sponsoring States have two kinds of obligations under UNCLOS and related instruments.

The first kind of obligations is one of 'due diligence' to ensure compliance by sponsored contractors with the terms of the contract and the obligations set out in UNCLOS and related instruments. The sponsoring State is bound to make the best possible efforts to secure compliance by the sponsored contractors. The standard of due diligence may vary over time and depends

---

[19] ibid 29 [59]–[60].
[20] ibid 29–30 [61]–[63].
[21] ibid 74–78.

on the level of risk and on the activities involved. This 'due diligence' obligation requires the sponsoring State to take measures within its legal system. These measures must consist of laws and regulations and administrative measures. The applicable standard is that the measures must be 'reasonably appropriate'.

The second kind of obligations are direct obligations with which sponsoring States must comply independently of their obligation to ensure a certain conduct on the part of the sponsored contractors. Compliance with these obligations may also be seen as a relevant factor in meeting the 'due diligence' obligation of the sponsoring State. The five most important direct obligations of the sponsoring State are (a) the obligation to assist the Authority set out in Article 153(4) of UNCLOS; (b) the obligation to apply a precautionary approach as reflected in Principle 15 of the 1992 Rio Declaration on Environment and Development[22] and set out in the Nodules Regulations and the Sulphides Regulations; this obligation is also to be considered an integral part of the 'due diligence' obligation of the sponsoring State and applicable beyond the scope of the two Regulations; (c) the obligation to apply the 'best environmental practices' set out in the Sulphides Regulations but equally applicable in the context of the Nodules Regulations; (d) the obligation to adopt measures to ensure the provision of guarantees in the event of an emergency order by the Authority for protection of the marine environment; and (e) the obligation to provide recourse for compensation.

In addition, the sponsoring State is under a due diligence obligation to ensure compliance by the sponsored contractor with its obligation to conduct an environmental impact assessment.[23] The obligation to conduct an environmental impact assessment is also a general obligation under customary law and is set out as a direct obligation for all States in Article 206 of UNCLOS and as an aspect of the sponsoring State's obligation to assist the Authority under Article 153(4) of UNCLOS.

Obligations of both kinds apply equally to developed and developing States, unless specifically provided otherwise in the applicable provisions, such as Principle 15 of the 1992 Rio Declaration, referred to in the Nodules Regulations and the Sulphides Regulations, according to which States shall apply the precautionary approach 'according to their capabilities'.

---

[22] (1992) 31 ILM 874.
[23] Set out in Annex to the 1994 Agreement, s 1, para 7.

On the *second* question, the liability of the sponsoring State arises from its failure to fulfil its obligations under UNCLOS and related instruments. Failure of the sponsored contractor to comply with its obligations does not in itself give rise to liability on the part of the sponsoring State. The conditions for the liability of the sponsoring State to arise are failure to carry out its responsibilities under UNCLOS and occurrence of damage caused by such failure.

On the *third* question, the Chamber explained in detail how UNCLOS requires the sponsoring State to adopt, within its legal system, laws and regulations and to take administrative measures that have two distinct functions, namely, to ensure compliance by the contractor with its obligations and to exempt the sponsoring State from liability.

The Chamber's replies to the three questions occupy almost five pages of the advisory opinion, and are, therefore, detailed enough for the Council to follow.

Subsequent to this advisory opinion, the Council of the International Seabed Authority has on its agenda since 2016 the proposal from the Secretary-General of the Authority to request an advisory opinion from the Seabed Disputes Chamber on legal issues arising from the conduct of marine scientific research in exploration areas. When other more urgent priorities, including drafting the Mining Code for exploitation of mineral resources in the Area, are taken care of, the Council will take a final decision on whether to request such advisory opinion from the Chamber.[24]

2. Advisory jurisdiction of the full bench of ITLOS

Request for Advisory Opinion submitted by the Sub-Regional Fisheries Commission was the first time the full bench of ITLOS had an opportunity to reply to a request for an advisory opinion. The request was by the Sub-Regional Fisheries Commission ('SRFC'), a regional fisheries management arrangement based in Dakar, Senegal, comprising seven Member States (Capo Verde, Gambia, Guinea, Guinea-Bissau, Mauritania, Senegal, and Sierra Leone).

---

[24] ISBA Press Release SB/22/5 of 13 July 2016, p 7.

The SRFC was set up in March 1985 and plays an essential role in the harmonization of fisheries policies and legislations of the States in the SRFC. In the light of the technical and legal changes which had occurred, in particular with respect to the definition of the conditions for responsible fishing, the use of the ecosystem approach for a sustainable management of fishery resources, and the fight against illegal, unreported, and unregulated ('IUU') fishing, the SRFC asked ITLOS four questions. First, what are the obligations of the flag State in cases where IUU fishing activities are conducted within the exclusive economic zone of third-party States? Second, to what extent shall the flag State be held liable for IUU fishing activities conducted by vessels sailing under its flag? Third, where a fishing licence is issued to a vessel within the framework of an international agreement with the flag State or with an international agency, shall the State or international agency be held liable for the violation of the fisheries legislation of the coastal State by the vessel in question? Fourth, what are the rights and obligations of the coastal State in ensuring the sustainable management of shared stocks and stocks of common interest, especially the small pelagic species and tuna?[25] The fourth question derived from the concerns of the SRFC about the lack of cooperation among SRFC Members, some of whom continued to act in isolation by issuing fishing licences on the shared resources, thereby undermining the interests of neighbouring States and the SRFC's initiatives in managing sustainably the stocks of common interest or shared stocks.[26]

The procedure involved in this request for advisory opinion should enlighten readers on how the full-bench ITLOS deals with requests for such advisory opinions.[27]

After receiving the request from the SRFC, the ITLOS Registrar informed the Permanent Secretary of the SRFC by letter that the request had been filed with the Registry and entered into the List of cases as Case No 21. In the same letter, the Registrar invited the Permanent Secretary of the

---

[25] Resolution of the Conference of Ministers of the SRFC on authorizing the Permanent Secretary to seek Advisory Opinion pursuant to Article 33 of the Convention on the determination of the minimum access conditions and exploitation of fisheries resources within the maritime zones under the jurisdiction of SRFC Member States ('MCA Convention'), 14th Session of the Conference of the Ministers, 27–28 March 2013, Dakar, Senegal, reproduced in *Request for Advisory Opinion submitted by the Sub-Regional Fisheries Commission* (Advisory Opinion) ITLOS Reports 2015, 4, 6–8.

[26] *Request for Advisory Opinion submitted by the Sub-Regional Fisheries Commission* (n 25) 52 [177].

[27] See also P Chandrasekhara Rao and Philippe Gautier, *The International Tribunal for the Law of the Sea: Law, Practice and Procedure* (Edward Elgar 2018) 156–65.

SRFC to transmit to ITLOS all documents referred to in the request and those likely to shed light upon the questions contained in the request.[28] The Registrar also notified the UN Secretary-General of the request.[29] By note verbale dated 8 April 2013, the Registrar notified all UNCLOS States Parties of the request.[30] All of the documents received from the SRFC were posted on ITLOS's website. By Order dated 24 May 2013, ITLOS decided[31] that the SRFC and the intergovernmental organizations listed in the annex to the Order[32] were considered likely to be able to furnish information on the questions submitted to ITLOS for an advisory opinion. Accordingly, ITLOS invited the States Parties, the SRFC, and the aforementioned intergovernmental organizations to present written statements on those questions, and fixed a time limit within which written statements could be presented to ITLOS.[33] In the same Order, ITLOS decided to hold oral proceedings, and the Order was notified to the States Parties, the SRFC, and the intergovernmental organizations listed in its annex.[34]

By Order dated 3 December 2013, in the light of a request submitted to ITLOS pursuant to Article 133(3) of the Rules, the ITLOS President extended the time limit within which written statements could be presented to ITLOS up to 19 December 2013. The Order was notified to States Parties, the SRFC, and the intergovernmental organizations concerned. Within the time limit fixed by the President, written statements were submitted by 24 States Parties, copies of which were transmitted by the Registrar to the States Parties, the SRFC, and the intergovernmental organizations that had submitted written statements. The written statements were made accessible to the public on ITLOS's website.[35] By Order dated 20 December 2013, the

---

[28] In accordance with Rules Art 131.

[29] Pursuant to the 1997 Agreement on Cooperation and Relationship between the UN and ITLOS.

[30] In accordance with Rules Art 133(1).

[31] Pursuant to Rules Art 133(2).

[32] They fell into four categories. The first comprised the relevant UN agencies; namely, the UN itself, the Food and Agriculture Organization, and the UN Environment Programme. The second category comprised regional fishery bodies invited to attend the 30th meeting of the Committee on Fisheries. Those in the third category were other intergovernmental organizations invited to attend the 30th meeting of the Committee on Fisheries. Those in the fourth category were the three observers at the 14th Extraordinary session of the Conference of Ministers of the SRFC, held on 27–28 March 2013; namely, Agence de Gestion et de Coopération Entre le Sénégal et la Guinée Bissau; the Intergovernmental Organization for Marketing, Information, and Cooperation Service for Fishery Products in Africa; and the International Union for the Conservation of Nature.

[33] By virtue of Rules Art 133(3).

[34] In accordance with Rules Art 133(4).

[35] Pursuant to Rules Art 134.

President decided[36] that the States Parties, the SRFC, and the intergovernmental organizations having presented written statements could submit written statements on the statements made, and specified a time limit for that purpose. The Order was notified to the parties concerned, and copies of the five additional statements were transmitted by the Registrar to the States Parties, the SRFC, and the intergovernmental organizations that had submitted written statements. In addition, these statements were made accessible to the public on ITLOS's website.

By Order dated 14 April 2014, the President fixed 2 September 2014 as the date for the opening of the oral proceedings and invited the States Parties, the SRFC, and the intergovernmental organizations listed in the annex to the Order of 24 May 2013 to participate in these proceedings and to indicate to the Registrar, no later than 5 August 2014, whether they intended to make oral statements at the hearing.[37]

Within the prescribed time limit, 10 States Parties to UNCLOS and the SRFC expressed their intention to participate in the oral proceedings. The Caribbean Regional Fisheries Mechanism and the International Union for Conservation of Nature, which were among the entities listed in the annex to ITLOS's Order of 24 May 2013, also expressed their intention to participate in the oral proceedings.

Prior to the opening of the oral proceedings, ITLOS held initial deliberations on 29 August and 1 September 2014. ITLOS held four public sittings on 2, 3, 4, and 5 September 2014, at which it heard oral statements. In the course of the hearing, questions were put to the SRFC by three ITLOS judges.[38] Subsequently, the ITLOS Registrar communicated these questions in writing to the SRFC. The SRFC then transmitted its written responses to the questions put by the judges, which were placed on ITLOS's website. By letter dated 9 September 2014, the Registrar invited the States Parties and the intergovernmental organizations which had participated in the oral proceedings to submit comments on the written responses of the SRFC by 16 September 2014, and the comments subsequently received were transmitted to the participants in the oral proceedings.

Numerous provisions of UNCLOS and other multilateral instruments were referred to in the various parties' written statements and oral submissions, in particular the 1993 Agreement to Promote Compliance

---

[36] In accordance with Rules Art 133(3).
[37] In accordance with Rules Art 133(4).
[38] Pursuant to Rules Art 76(3).

with International Conservation and Management Measures by Fishing Vessels on the High Seas ('FAO Compliance Agreement');[39] the 1995 UN Agreement for the Implementation of the Provisions of the UN Convention on the Law of the Sea of 10 December 1982 relating to the Conservation and Management of Straddling Fish Stocks and Highly Migratory Species Fish Stocks ('FSA');[40] and the 2009 FAO Agreement on Port State Measures to Prevent, Deter, and Eliminate Illegal, Unreported and Unregulated Fishing ('Port State Measures Agreement').[41]

Notably, at the time of the request for ITLOS's Advisory Opinion, UNCLOS bound all SRFC Member States but the 1993 FAO Compliance Agreement had been ratified by only two Member States of the SRFC (Capo Verde and Senegal), and the FSA had been ratified by only two Member States of the SRFC (Guinea and Senegal), whereas the 2009 Port State Measures Agreement had not been ratified by any SRFC Member State although Sierra Leone was in the process of ratifying this 2009 Agreement.

ITLOS held that the legal basis of its jurisdiction to give advisory opinions unrelated to a legal question arising within the scope of the activities of the Assembly or the Council of the International Seabed Authority, which is within the purview of the Seabed Disputes Chamber, is Article 21 of its Statute, providing that ITLOS's jurisdiction 'comprises all disputes and all applications submitted to it in accordance with [UNCLOS] and all matters specifically provided for in any other agreement which confers jurisdiction on [ITLOS]'.

In this connection, ITLOS clarified the relationship between UNCLOS and the ITLOS Statute, which is Annex VI to UNCLOS. Under Article 318 of UNCLOS, Annexes form an integral part of UNCLOS. Pursuant to Article 1(1) of the ITLOS Statute, ITLOS is constituted and shall function in accordance with the provisions of UNCLOS and this Statute. The Statute, therefore, enjoys the same status as UNCLOS. Accordingly, Article 21 of the Statute stands on its own footing.[42] Although neither UNCLOS nor the Statute makes explicit reference to the advisory jurisdiction of ITLOS,[43] Article 21 of the Statute deals with the 'jurisdiction' of ITLOS that

---

[39] <www.fao.org/docrep/MEETING/003/X3130m/X3130E00.HTM> accessed 7 June 2020.

[40] 2167 UNTS 88.

[41] <www.fao.org/fileadmin/user_upload/legal/docs/037t-e.pdf> accessed 7 June 2020.

[42] *Request for Advisory Opinion submitted by the Sub-Regional Fisheries Commission* (n 25) 20 [52].

[43] ibid 21 [53].

comprises three elements: all 'disputes' submitted to ITLOS in accordance with UNCLOS; all 'applications' submitted to ITLOS in accordance with UNCLOS; and all 'matters' specifically provided for in any other agreement which confers jurisdiction on ITLOS.[44] The use of the word 'disputes' in Article 21 of the Statute is an unambiguous reference to ITLOS's contentious jurisdiction, whereas the word 'applications' refers to applications in contentious cases submitted to ITLOS in accordance with UNCLOS.[45] However, the words all 'matters' should not be interpreted as covering only 'disputes', for, if that were to be the case, Article 21 of the Statute would simply have used the word 'disputes'. Consequently, it must mean something more than only 'disputes', including advisory opinions, if specifically provided for in 'any other agreement which confers jurisdiction on [ITLOS]'.[46] To be clear, the expression 'all matters specifically provided for in any other agreement which confers jurisdiction on [ITLOS]' does not by itself establish the advisory jurisdiction of ITLOS. In terms of Article 21 of the Statute it is the 'other agreement' that confers such jurisdiction on ITLOS with regard to 'all matters' specifically provided for in the 'other agreement'. Article 21 and the 'other agreement' conferring jurisdiction on ITLOS are interconnected and constitute the substantive legal basis of the full-bench ITLOS's advisory jurisdiction.[47]

A further question is to what matters the advisory jurisdiction extends. Article 21 of the ITLOS Statute lays down that such jurisdiction extends to 'all matters specially provided for in any other agreement which confers jurisdiction on [ITLOS]'. In Case No 21 itself, ITLOS found it necessary to assess whether the questions posed by the SRFC constituted matters within the framework of the Convention on the definition of the minimum access conditions and exploitation of fisheries resources within the maritime zones under the jurisdiction of SRFC Member States ('MCA Convention').[48] ITLOS concluded that the questions related to activities within the scope of the MCA Convention,[49] whose objective as stated in its preamble is to implement UNCLOS 'especially its provisions calling for the signing of regional and sub-regional cooperation agreements in the

---

44   ibid 21 [54].
45   ibid 21 [55].
46   ibid 21 [56].
47   ibid 22 [58].
48   ibid 24 [67].
49   MCA   Convention   <www.itlos.org/fileadmin/itlos/documents/cases/case_no.21/ Convention_CMA_ENG.pdf> accessed 21 March 2020.

fisheries sector as well [as] the other relevant international treaties' and ensure the policies and legislation of its Member States 'are more effectively
harmonized with a view to a better exploitation of fisheries resources in
the maritime zones under their respective jurisdictions, for the benefit of
current and future generations'. The MCA Convention is thus closely related to the purposes of UNCLOS.[50] In ITLOS's view, the questions needed
not necessarily be limited to the interpretation or application of any specific provision of the MCA Convention—it was enough if these questions
had a 'sufficient connection' with the purposes and principles of the MCA
Convention. In this respect, there was no reason why the words 'all matters
specifically provided for in any other agreement' in Article 21 of the ITLOS
Statute should be interpreted restrictively.[51]

Under Article 138 of the ITLOS Rules, ITLOS may give an advisory
opinion on a legal question if an international agreement related to the purposes of UNCLOS specifically provides for the submission to ITLOS a request for such an opinion transmitted by whatever body is authorized by or
in accordance with the agreement to make the request to ITLOS. The procedures regulating a request for an advisory opinion of the Seabed Dispute
Chamber shall be applied *mutatis mutandis*.[52] Article 138 does *not* establish ITLOS's advisory jurisdiction—it only furnishes the prerequisites to
be satisfied before ITLOS can exercise its advisory jurisdiction; namely, an
international agreement related to the purposes of UNCLOS specifically
provides for the submission to ITLOS of a request for an advisory opinion;
the request must be transmitted to ITLOS by a body authorized by or in accordance with the aforesaid agreement; and such an opinion may be given
on 'a legal question'.[53]

---

[50] *Request for Advisory Opinion submitted by the Sub-Regional Fisheries Commission* (n
25) 23 [63].

[51] ibid 24 [68], citing *Legality of the Use by a State of Nuclear Weapons in Armed Conflict*
(Advisory Opinion) [1996] ICJ Rep 66, 77 [22], where the ICJ declined to render an advisory
opinion to the World Health Organization because none of the Organization's functions had a
'sufficient connection' with the question before the ICJ for that question to be capable of being
considered as arising 'within the scope of [the] activities' of the World Health Organization.

[52] *Request for Advisory Opinion submitted by the Sub-Regional Fisheries Commission* (n
25) 26 [80]. ITLOS also refers in this regard to Article 23 of its Statute, which reads: '[ITLOS]
shall decide all disputes and applications in accordance with Article 293' on applicable law, to
conclude that UNCLOS, the MCA Convention, and other relevant rules of international law
not incompatible with UNCLOS constitute the applicable law in this case (ibid 27 [82]).

[53] ibid 22–23 [59]–[62]. See also Miguel García García-Rivello, 'The Jurisdictional Debate
in the Request for an Advisory Opinion Submitted by the Sub-Regional Fisheries Commission
(SRFC) to the International Tribunal for the Law of the Sea' in Angela Del Vecchio and
Roberto Virzo (eds), *Interpretations of the United Nations Convention on the Law of the Sea
by International Courts and Tribunals* (Springer 2019) 127–37. For early writings contending

ITLOS considered the prerequisites for it to exercise advisory jurisdiction satisfied in this request by the SRFC, and no compelling reason existed for ITLOS to exercise its discretionary power to refuse to give the advisory opinion.[54] ITLOS clarified in this regard that in advisory proceedings the consent of States not members of the SRFC was not relevant since the advisory opinion as such had no binding force on third parties and was given only to the SRFC for guidance in respect of its own actions.[55]

On the matter of substantive law, ITLOS unanimously replied to the *first* question that the flag State has the obligation to take necessary measures, including those of enforcement, to ensure compliance by vessels flying its flag with the laws and regulations enacted by the SRFC Member States concerning marine living resources within their exclusive economic zones for purposes of conservation and management of these resources. In this regard, the flag State is under an obligation under Article 58(3) of UNCLOS to have due regard, in exercising its rights and performing its duties in the exclusive economic zone of the coastal State, to the rights and duties of the latter State as well as to comply with the laws and regulations adopted by the coastal State in accordance with applicable rules of international law. In addition, the flag State is bound by Article 62(4) of UNCLOS stipulating that nationals of other States fishing in the exclusive economic zone of another State shall comply with the conservation measures and with the other terms and conditions established in the laws and regulations of that coastal State. The flag State is also under the general obligation provided in Article 192 of UNCLOS to protect and preserve the marine environment. The combined effect of these provisions obligate the flag State to take the necessary measures to ensure vessels flying its flag are not engaged in IUU fishing activities within the exclusive economic zones of the SRFC Member States. The flag State, in fulfilment of its obligation as a flag State to effectively exercise

---

Art 138 of the Rules forms the basis for ITLOS's advisory jurisdiction, see Doo-young Kim, 'Advisory Proceedings before the International Tribunal for the Law of the Sea as an Alternative Procedure to Supplement the Dispute-Settlement Mechanism under Part XV of the United Nations Convention on the Law of the Sea' (2010) 7(1) Issues in Legal Scholarship, doi:10.2202/1539-8323.1116 (accessed 21 March 2020); Tafsir Malick Ndiaye, 'The Advisory Function of the International Tribunal for the Law of the Sea' (2010) 9 Chinese JIL 565; James L Kateka, 'Advisory Proceedings before the Seabed Disputes Chamber and before ITLOS as a Full Court' (2013) 17 Max Planck YB United Nations Law 159.

[54] *Request for Advisory Opinion submitted by the Sub-Regional Fisheries Commission* (n 25) 22–26 [61]–[79].
[55] ibid 26 [76], citing *Interpretation of Peace Treaties with Bulgaria, Hungary, and Romania, First Phase* (Advisory Opinion) [1950] ICJ Rep 65, 71.

jurisdiction and control in administrative matters over vessels flying its flag as required by Article 94 of UNCLOS, has the obligation to adopt the necessary administrative measures to ensure fishing vessels flying its flag are not involved in activities in the exclusive economic zones of the SRFC Member States which undermine the flag State's responsibility for protecting and preserving the marine environment and conserving the marine living resources which are an integral element of the marine environment.

ITLOS emphasized that the foregoing obligations are obligations of 'due diligence'—they are obligations of conduct and not of result.[56] The flag State is to deploy adequate means, to exercise best possible efforts, and to do the utmost to fulfil these obligations.[57] The flag State must meet this responsibility by taking measures defined above as well as by effectively exercising its jurisdiction and control in 'administrative, technical, and social matters' over ships flying its flag in accordance with Article 94(1) of UNCLOS.[58] The standard of due diligence has to be more severe for the riskier activities.[59] Although the nature of the laws, regulations, and measures to be adopted by the flag State is left to each flag State in accordance with its legal system, the flag State has the obligation to include in them enforcement mechanisms to monitor and secure compliance with these laws and regulations, and sanctions against IUU fishing activities must be sufficient to deter violations and to deprive offenders of the benefits accruing from their IUU fishing activities.[60] Article 94(6) of UNCLOS—that '[a] State which has clear grounds to believe that proper jurisdiction and control with respect to a ship have not been exercised may report the facts to the flag State' and 'upon receiving such a report, the flag State shall investigate the matter and, if appropriate, take any action necessary to remedy the situation'—equally applies to a flag State whose ships are alleged to have been involved in IUU fishing when such allegations have been reported to it by the coastal State concerned. The flag State is then under an obligation to investigate the matter and, if appropriate, take any action necessary to remedy the situation as well as

---

[56] An obligation of result is one that requires the State concerned to attain a specific outcome within a reasonable period of time (*Request for Interpretation of the Judgment of 31 March 2004 in the Case concerning Avena and Other Mexican Nationals (Mexico v United States of America) (Mexico v United States of America)* [2009] ICJ Rep 3, 12 [27]).

[57] *Request for Advisory Opinion submitted by the Sub-Regional Fisheries Commission* (n 25) 38–40 [125], [128], [129].

[58] ibid 39 [127].

[59] ibid 41 [132], citing *Responsibilities and obligations of States with respect to activities in the Area* (Advisory Opinion) (n 4) 43 [117].

[60] *Request for Advisory Opinion submitted by the Sub-Regional Fisheries Commission* (n 25) 42 [138].

inform the reporting State of that action. The action to be taken by the flag State is without prejudice to the rights of the coastal State to take such measures to enforce laws and regulations in its exclusive economic zone against IUU fishing vessels and crew pursuant to Article 73 of UNCLOS, including boarding, inspection, arrest, and judicial proceedings, as may be necessary to ensure compliance with the laws and regulations adopted by it in conformity with UNCLOS.[61]

Having found the duty to cooperate to be a fundamental principle in general international law, ITLOS considered this obligation extends also to cases of alleged IUU fishing activities.[62]

By 18 votes to 2, ITLOS replied to the *second* question as to the extent the flag State is to be held liable for IUU fishing activities conducted by vessels sailing under its flag as follows. The liability of the flag State does not arise from a failure of vessels flying its flag to comply with the laws and regulations of the SRFC Member States concerning IUU fishing activities in their exclusive economic zones, as the violation of such laws and regulations by vessels is not per se attributable to the flag State. The liability of the flag State arises from its failure to comply with its 'due diligence' obligations concerning IUU fishing activities conducted by vessels flying its flag in the exclusive economic zones of the SRFC Member States. Phrased differently, the SRFC Member States may hold liable the flag State of a vessel conducting IUU fishing activities in their exclusive economic zones for a breach, attributable to the flag State, of its international obligations, referred to in the reply to the first question. The flag State is *not* liable if it has taken all necessary and appropriate measures to meet its 'due diligence' obligations to ensure vessels flying its flag do not conduct IUU fishing activities in the exclusive economic zones of the SRFC Member States.[63] In this connection, the frequency of IUU fishing activities by vessels in the exclusive economic zones of the SRFC Member States is not relevant to the issue as to whether there is a breach of 'due diligence' obligations by the flag State.[64]

ITLOS's replies to the first and second questions put to rest once and for all the argument that the primary responsibility for fisheries management in the exclusive economic zone rests on the coastal State, and that flag States have no obligation under customary international law to exercise their

---

[61] ibid 42–43 [139].
[62] ibid 43 [140].
[63] ibid 44–45 [146]–[149].
[64] ibid 45 [150].

jurisdiction and control over vessels flying their flag which fish in the exclusive economic zone of other States.[65]

The *third* question posed by the SRFC only relates to those international organizations referred to in Articles 305(f) and 306 and Annex IX (participation by international organizations) of UNCLOS to which their Member States, which are parties to UNCLOS, have transferred competence over fisheries matters. At present, the only such international organization is the European Union to which its Member States, which are parties to UNCLOS, have transferred competence with regard to 'the conservation and management of sea fishing resources'.

In ITLOS's unanimous opinion, where an international organization, in the exercise of its exclusive competence in fisheries matters, concludes a fisheries access agreement with an SRFC Member State to allow vessels flying the flag of a Member State of that organization to fish in the SRFC Member State's exclusive economic zone, the obligations of the flag State become the obligations of the international organization. The international organization, as the only contracting party to the fisheries access agreement with the SRFC Member State, must therefore ensure vessels flying the flag of a Member State comply with the fisheries laws and regulations of the SRFC Member State and do not conduct IUU fishing activities within the exclusive economic zone of that State. In other words, only the international organization may be held liable for any breach of its obligations arising from the fisheries access agreement. If the international organization does not meet its 'due diligence' obligations, the SRFC Member State concerned may hold the international organization liable for the violation of its fisheries laws and regulations by a vessel flying the flag of a Member State of that organization and fishing in the exclusive economic zone of the SRFC Member State within the framework of a fisheries access agreement between that organization and that SRFC Member State. The SRFC Member State may request an international organization or its Member States which are parties to UNCLOS for information as to who has responsibility in respect of any specific matter.[66] The organization and its Member States concerned must provide this information. Failure to do so within a reasonable time or the

---

[65] eg, by Valentin J Schatz, 'Combating Illegal Fishing in the Exclusive Economic Zone: Flag State Obligations in the Context of the Primary Responsibility in the Coastal State' (2016) 7 Goettingen JIL 383, 398–99, 409.

[66] Pursuant to Art 6(2) of Annex IX to UNCLOS.

provision of contradictory information results in joint and several liability of the international organization and the Member States concerned.[67]

ITLOS, by 19 votes to 1, replied to the *fourth* question posed by the SRFC as follows. It proceeded to clarify the meaning of 'sustainable management' left undefined by UNCLOS, noting that Article 63 of UNCLOS as such does not address the issue of cooperation with respect to measures necessary to ensure the sustainable management of shared stocks—Article 63 merely deals with cooperation regarding measures necessary to coordinate and ensure the 'conservation and development of such stocks' occurring within the exclusive economic zones of two or more States, and cooperation regarding measures necessary for the 'conservation of these stocks in the adjacent area' occurring both within the exclusive economic zone and in an area beyond and adjacent to the exclusive economic zone. Article 61 of UNCLOS, on the basic framework concerning the conservation and management of the living resources in the exclusive economic zone, provides guidance as to the meaning of 'sustainable management'—the ultimate goal of sustainable management of fish stocks is to conserve and develop them as a viable and sustainable resource. Therefore, the expression 'sustainable management' as used in the fourth question posed by the SFRC means 'conservation and development', as referred to in Article 63(1) of UNCLOS.[68]

The provisions of UNCLOS governing the rights and obligations of the SRFC Member States in ensuring the sustainable management of shared stocks occurring within their exclusive economic zones and shared stocks occurring both within the exclusive economic zones of the SRFC Member States and in an area *beyond and adjacent to* these zones, especially small pelagic species are Article 63(1) on the same stocks or stocks of associated species occurring within the exclusive economic zones of two or more coastal States; Article 63(2) on the same stock or stocks of associated species occurring within the exclusive economic zone and in an area beyond and adjacent to the exclusive economic zone; and Article 64(1) on the highly migratory species listed in Annex I to UNCLOS.[69]

In the case of the same stocks or stocks of associated species occurring within the exclusive economic zones of two or more coastal States, the SRFC Member States have the right to seek to agree, either directly or

---

[67] *Request for Advisory Opinion submitted by the Sub-Regional Fisheries Commission* (n 25) 51 [172]–[174].

[68] ibid 54–55 [187]–[190].

[69] ibid 55 [192]–[193].

through appropriate subregional or regional organizations, with other SRFC Member States in whose exclusive economic zones these stocks occur upon the measures necessary to coordinate and ensure the conservation and development of such stocks. Pursuant to UNCLOS, the SRFC Member States have the obligation to ensure the sustainable management of shared stocks while these stocks occur in their exclusive economic zones. This includes the obligation to cooperate, as appropriate, with the competent international organizations, whether subregional, regional, or global, to ensure through proper conservation and management measures that the maintenance of the shared stocks in the exclusive economic zone is not endangered by over-exploitation. Besides, conservation and management measures are to be based on the best scientific evidence available to the SRFC Member States and, when such evidence is insufficient, they must apply the precautionary approach. Conservation and management measures are also to be so designed as to maintain or restore stocks at levels which can produce the maximum sustainable yield, as qualified by relevant environmental and economic factors, including the economic needs of coastal fishing communities and the special needs of the SRFC Member States, taking into account fishing patterns, the interdependence of stocks, and any generally recommended international minimum standards, whether subregional, regional, or global.[70]

In particular, such measures shall take into consideration the effects on species associated with or dependent upon harvested species with a view to maintaining or restoring populations of such associated or dependent species above levels at which their reproduction may become seriously threatened. In addition, such measures shall provide for exchange on a regular basis, through competent international organizations, of available scientific information, catch and fishing efforts statistics, and other data relevant to the conservation of shared stocks. The obligation to 'seek to agree' under Article 63(1) and the obligation to cooperate under Article 64(1) are 'due diligence' obligations requiring the States concerned to consult with one another in good faith pursuant to Article 300 of UNCLOS. In order for the consultations to be meaningful, all States concerned should make substantial effort to adopt effective measures necessary to coordinate and ensure the conservation and development of shared stocks.[71]

---

[70] ibid para 219(6).
[71] ibid.

The conservation and development of shared stocks in the exclusive economic zone of an SRFC Member State require from that State effective measures aimed at preventing over-exploitation of such stocks that could undermine their sustainable exploitation and the interests of neighbouring Member States. Therefore, an SRFC Member State fishing in its exclusive economic zone for shared stocks which also occur in the exclusive economic zone of another SRFC Member State must consult that other Member State when setting up management measures for those shared stocks to coordinate and ensure the conservation and development of such stocks. Such management measures are also required in respect of fishing for those stocks by vessels flying the flag of non-Member States in the exclusive economic zones of Member States. Cooperation between the States concerned on issues pertaining to the conservation and management of shared fishery resources, as well as the promotion of the optimum utilization of those resources, is a well-established principle as reflected in Articles 61, 63, and 64 of UNCLOS.[72]

In exercising their rights and performing their duties under UNCLOS in their respective exclusive economic zones, the SRFC Member States and other States Parties to UNCLOS must have due regard to the rights and duties of one another pursuant to Articles 56(2) and 58(3) of UNCLOS and from the States Parties' obligation to protect and preserve the marine environment, a fundamental principle underlined in Articles 192 and 193 of UNCLOS and referred to in the fourth paragraph of its preamble. ITLOS reiterated its view that living resources and marine life are part of the marine environment and 'the conservation of the living resources of the sea is an element in the protection and preservation of the marine environment'.[73]

ITLOS recognized that for fisheries conservation and management measures to be effective, they should concern the whole stock unit over its entire area of distribution or migration routes. Fish stocks, in particular the stocks of small pelagic species and tuna shared by the SRFC Member States in their exclusive economic zones are also shared by several other States bordering the Atlantic Ocean. In the case of fish stocks occurring both within the exclusive economic zones of the SRFC Member States and

---

[72] ibid.

[73] ibid. In *Southern Bluefin Tuna (New Zealand v Japan; Australia v Japan)* (Provisional Measures, Order of 27 August 1999) ITLOS Reports 1999, 280, 296 [77] and [79], ITLOS referred to the notion of 'prudence and caution' and found 'the conservation of the living resources of the sea' to be 'an element in the protection and preservation of the marine environment'.

in an area beyond and adjacent to these zones, these States and the States fishing for such stocks in the adjacent area are required, under Article 63(2) of UNCLOS, to seek to agree upon the measures necessary for the conservation of those stocks in the adjacent area. With respect to highly migratory tuna species, the SRFC Member States have the right, under Article 64(1) of UNCLOS, to require cooperation from other States Parties to UNCLOS that are not also SRFC Member States whose nationals fish for tuna in the region, 'directly or through appropriate international organizations with a view to ensuring conservation and promoting the objective of optimum utilization of such species'.[74]

Evaluation of the exercise of advisory jurisdiction by the Seabed Disputes Chamber and the full bench of ITLOS as well as its future potentials will be discussed in Chapter 7, which provides an overall assessment of ITLOS's present and future jurisdictional contributions.

[74] *Request for Advisory Opinion submitted by the Sub-Regional Fisheries Commission* (n 25) 68.

5

Applications for Prompt Release of Vessels and Crews

At the Third UN Conference on the Law of the Sea, several delegations were concerned that vessels and their crews detained after violating the regulations of a coastal State (eg, those relating to fishing or marine pollution) might be prolonged and not released promptly, thereby causing huge financial losses to the owners and human sufferings to the crews on board. However, balance needed to be struck between the interests of the persons connected with the detained vessel and of the flag State, on the one hand, and the interests of the detaining coastal State, on the other hand. The Third Conference eventually agreed on an accelerated procedure in a competent international judicial body for dealing with requests for prompt release of detained vessels and crews, with the decisions of that competent international judicial body to be promptly complied with by the authorities of the detaining State. At the same time, to protect the detaining State, the release would be subject to the requirement of presentation of an adequate bond, and the proceedings in the detaining State against the vessel or its crew on the merits would not be affected either by the proceedings before the international judicial body or the release of the vessel or its crew. To accommodate the delegations reluctant to confer exclusive jurisdiction on the to-be-established ITLOS, the Third Conference allowed flexibility regarding the choice of the international judicial fora competent to deal with requests for such prompt release. In practice, however, all prompt release cases that have arisen since UNCLOS entered into force in November 1994 have been submitted to ITLOS.[1]

---

[1] Tullio Treves, 'Article 292 Prompt Release of Vessels and Crews' in Alexander Proelss (ed), *The United Nations Convention on the Law of the Sea: A Commentary* (Hart 2017) 1883; Myron H Nordquist, Shabtai Rosenne, and Louis B Sohn (eds), *United Nations Convention on the Law of the Sea 1982: A Commentary*, vol 5 (Brill 1989) ('Virginia Commentary') 67–71.

Article 292 of UNCLOS under the heading 'Prompt release of vessels and crews' reads:

1. Where the authorities of a State Party have detained a vessel flying the flag of another State Party and it is alleged that the detaining State has not complied with the provisions of this Convention for the prompt release of the vessel or its crew upon the posting of a reasonable bond or other financial security, the question of release from detention may be submitted to any court or tribunal agreed upon by the parties or, failing such agreement within 10 days from the time of detention, to a court or tribunal accepted by the detaining State under Article 287 or to the International Tribunal for the Law of the Sea, unless the parties otherwise agree.

2. The application for release may be made only by or on behalf of the flag State of the vessel.[2]

3. The court or tribunal shall deal without delay with the application for release and shall deal only with the question of release, without prejudice to the merits of any case before the appropriate domestic forum against the vessel, its owner, or its crew. The authorities of the detaining State remain competent to release the vessel or its crew at any time.

4. Upon the posting of the bond or other financial security determined by the court or tribunal, the authorities of the detaining State shall comply promptly with the decision of the court or tribunal concerning the release of the vessel or its crew.

Pursuant to Article 292(1), ITLOS has default jurisdiction over prompt release applications, unless the parties otherwise agree. The parties must be States Parties to UNCLOS and have not agreed to submit the question of release from detention to any other court or tribunal within 10 days from the time of detention.[3]

---

[2] As ITLOS states in *'Grand Prince' (Belize v France)* (Prompt Release) ITLOS Reports 2001, 17, 38 [66]:

> In the scheme of Article 292 of the Convention, it is the flag State of the vessel that is given the *locus standi* to take up the question of release in an appropriate court or tribunal. Any other entity may make an application only on behalf of the flag State of the vessel.

See also Rules Arts 110 and 111.

[3] *'Juno Trader' (Saint Vincent and the Grenadines v Guinea-Bissau)* (Prompt Release) ITLOS Reports 2004, 17, 35 [57]; *'Hoshinmaru' (Japan v Russian Federation)* (Prompt Release) ITLOS Reports 2005–07, 18, 40 [57]. See also Miguel García García-Revillo, *The Contentious and Advisory Jurisdiction of the International Tribunal for the Law of the Sea* (Brill/Nijhoff 2015) 149–55.

Article 112 of the ITLOS Rules adds, inter alia, that ITLOS shall give priority to applications for release of vessels or crews over all other proceedings before ITLOS. If ITLOS is seized of an application for release of a vessel or its crew and of a request for the prescription of provisional measures, it shall take the necessary measures to ensure both the application and the request are dealt with without delay. In any event, if the applicant has so requested in the application, the application shall be dealt with by the Chamber of Summary Procedure, provided, within five days of the receipt of notice of the application, the detaining State notifies ITLOS that it concurs with the request. ITLOS, or the ITLOS President if ITLOS is not sitting, shall fix the earliest possible date, within a period of 15 days commencing with the first working day following the date on which the application is received, for a hearing at which each of the parties shall be accorded one day to present its evidence and arguments, unless otherwise decided. ITLOS's decision shall be in the form of a judgment, which shall be adopted as soon as possible and shall be read at a public sitting of ITLOS to be held not later than 14 days after the closure of the hearing, of which the parties shall be notified of the date.

In its judgment, ITLOS must determine in each case whether or not the allegation made by the applicant that the detaining State has not complied with a provision of UNCLOS for the prompt release of the vessel or the crew upon the posting of a reasonable bond or other financial security is well founded.[4] If ITLOS decides the allegation is well founded, it shall determine the amount, nature, and form of the bond or financial security to be posted for the release of the vessel or the crew. Unless the parties agree otherwise, ITLOS shall determine whether the bond or other financial security shall be posted with the Registrar or with the detaining State.[5]

1. Applicability

Prompt release proceedings are only available for alleged non-compliance with provisions of UNCLOS requiring the prompt release of vessels upon

---

[4] Rules Art 113.

[5] Rules Art 114 deals with the situation where the bond or other financial security is posted with the ITLOS Registrar. ITLOS has also issued the Guidelines concerning the Posting of a Bond or Other Financial Security with the Registrar, dated 17 March 2009. However, as of this writing all the bonds or other financial securities ordered by ITLOS have been posted with the detaining States.

the posting of a reasonable bond or other financial security. Three provisions of UNCLOS correspond expressly to this description: Article 73(2); Article 220(6) and (7); and Article 226(1)(b).[6]

Under Article 73(2) on enforcement of laws and regulations of the coastal State in its exclusive economic zone, arrested vessels and their crews shall be promptly released upon the posting of reasonable bond or other security. Article 73(2) thus imposes three conditions: arrested vessels and their crews shall be released upon posting of bond or other security; such release shall be done promptly; and the bond or other security must be reasonable.[7] Article 73(2) does not define how the coastal State is to comply with these obligations, leaving it to the coastal State to determine the most appropriate procedure in accordance with its national law,[8] which must be considered in the light of the principle of reasonableness that applies generally to enforcement measures under Article 73.[9]

Article 220(6) of UNCLOS deals with the situation where there is clear objective evidence that a vessel navigating in the exclusive economic zone or the territorial sea of a State has, in the exclusive economic zone, committed a violation of applicable international rules and standards for the prevention, reduction, and control of pollution from vessels; or laws and regulations of that State conforming and giving effect to such rules and standards. Such a violation must result in a discharge causing major damage or threat of major damage to the coastline or related interests of the coastal State, or to any resources of its territorial sea or exclusive economic zone. Article 220(6) allows that coastal State to institute proceedings, including detention of the vessel, in accordance with its law, subject to safeguards of the rights of the States concerned and provided that the evidence so warrants.

In such pollution cases, pursuant to Article 220(7), 'whenever appropriate procedures have been established, either through the competent international organization or as otherwise agreed, whereby compliance with requirements for bonding or other appropriate financial security has been assured, the coastal State if bound by such procedures shall allow the vessel to proceed'. As pointed out by a former ITLOS judge, Article 220(7) has never been invoked in the prompt release proceedings under Article

---

[6] 'Volga' (Russian Federation v Australia) (Prompt Release) ITLOS Reports 2002, 10, 34–35 [77]. cf M/V 'Saiga' (Saint Vincent and the Grenadines v Guinea) (Prompt Release) ITLOS Reports 1997, 16, 28 [52].

[7] M/V 'Virginia G' (Panama/Guinea-Bissau) ITLOS Reports 2014, 4, 84 [283].

[8] ibid 84 [284].

[9] ibid 81 [270].

292 although tankers are frequently arrested for pollution charges, because these tankers are routinely released under industry insurance schemes probably more expeditiously, albeit in some cases perhaps at a higher cost, than it would be possible under Article 292.[10]

Article 226(1)(b) adds a third category of cases where prompt release might be sought. This concerns the situation where an investigation indicates a violation of applicable laws and regulations or international rules and standards for the protection and preservation of the marine environment. In such cases, release shall be made promptly subject to reasonable procedures such as bonding or other appropriate financial security.

The question arises as to whether these are the only cases in which prompt release may be sought. It has been suggested that Articles 73(2), 220(6) and (7) and 226(1)(b) of UNCLOS concern situations in which the detention of vessels and crews is lawful under UNCLOS.[11] In *M/V 'Saiga' (Saint Vincent and the Grenadines v Guinea)* (Prompt Release), the applicant Saint Vincent and the Grenadines suggested a 'non-restrictive interpretation' of Article 292 of UNCLOS, according to which the applicability of Article 292 to the arrest of a vessel in contravention of international law could also be argued, without reference to a specific provision of UNCLOS for the prompt release of vessels or their crews. Contravention of Article 56(2)[12] of UNCLOS was quoted in this respect by Saint Vincent and the Grenadines, contending it would be strange if the procedure for prompt release should be available in cases in which detention was permitted by UNCLOS (Articles 73, 220, and 226) and not in cases in which it was not permitted by it. ITLOS considered it 'very arguable' that the Guinean authorities had acted from the beginning in violation of international law in apprehending the vessel, while the classification under Article 73 permitted the assumption that Guinea was convinced that in arresting the vessel it was acting within its rights under UNCLOS. In ITLOS's opinion, given the choice between a legal classification implying a violation of international law and one avoiding such implication it had to opt for the latter. Having considered Saint Vincent and the Grenadines' argument based on Article 73 of UNCLOS to be well founded, it was unnecessary

---

[10] Treves, 'Article 292' (n 1) 1886.

[11] ibid.

[12] UNCLOS Art 56(2): 'In exercising its rights and performing its duties under this Convention in the exclusive economic zone, the coastal State shall have due regard to the rights and duties of other States and shall act in a manner compatible with the provisions of this Convention.'

for ITLOS to adopt a position on the non-restrictive interpretation of Article 292.[13] Therefore, as of this writing, ITLOS has not authoritatively ruled whether detention of vessels and crews not related to Articles 73(2), 220, or 226 of UNCLOS are or are not subject to the prompt release jurisdiction of ITLOS or any other court or tribunal referred to in Article 292 of UNCLOS.

Article 30(1) of the 1995 UN Fish Stocks Agreement ('FSA')[14] integrates the entire UNCLOS dispute settlement regime to settle disputes regarding the interpretation and application of the FSA, whether or not the disputing States Parties to the FSA are also parties to UNCLOS. Although an express reference to Article 292 of UNCLOS in the FSA was deleted by its draftsmen who feared such a reference might be construed as sanctioning arrest of vessels on the high seas,[15] a view has been expressed that the procedures under Article 292 UNCLOS are available to disputing States where vessels are being detained inconsistent with the FSA.[16] Another view opines, however, that there is no basis under the FSA for a prompt release procedure of Article 292 of UNCLOS, essentially because the relevant provision of the FSA requires a vessel to be released upon the flag State's request without reference to the posting of a bond.[17] ITLOS has yet to definitively decide on this matter as of this writing.

As of this writing, ITLOS has been seized of 29 cases, 9 of which are requests for prompt release of arrested vessels and their crews and all of them concern alleged violation of Article 73(2) by the respondents. All of ITLOS's case law on Article 292 thus deals only with alleged violations of Article 73(2).

---

[13] *M/V 'Saiga'* (Prompt Release) (n 6) 28 [53], 34 [72]–[73].

[14] 1995 UN Agreement for the Implementation of the Provisions of the UN Convention on the Law of the Sea of 10 December 1982 relating to the Conservation and Management of Straddling Fish Stocks and Highly Migratory Species Fish Stocks (2167 UNTS 88).

[15] Tullio Treves, 'The Proceedings Concerning Prompt Release of Vessels and Crews before the International Tribunal for the Law of the Sea' (1996) 11 Int'l J Marine & Coastal L 179, 187.

[16] ibid 187–88; Ted L McDorman, 'An Overview of International Fisheries Disputes and the International Tribunal for the Law of the Sea' (2002) 40 Canadian YBIL 119, 136.

[17] eg, García-Revillo (n 3) 136–38, citing para 12 of the FSA Art 21 (Subregional and regional cooperation in enforcement), which reads:

> Notwithstanding the other provisions of this Article, the flag State may, at any time, take action to fulfil its obligations under Article 19 [compliance and enforcement by the flag State] with respect to an alleged violation. Where the vessel is under the direction of the inspecting State, the inspecting State shall, at the request of the flag State, release the vessel to the flag State along with full information on the progress and outcome of its investigation.

2. Rationale

According to ITLOS, Article 73 strikes a fair balance between the interest of the coastal State to take appropriate measures as may be necessary to ensure compliance with the laws and regulations adopted by it, on the one hand, and the interest of the flag State in securing prompt release of its vessels and their crews from detention, on the other hand. Article 73 provides for such release upon the posting of a bond or other security, thus protecting the interests of the flag State and of other persons affected by the detention of the vessel and its crew. The release from detention can be subject only to a 'reasonable' bond. Similarly, the object of Article 292 is to reconcile the aforesaid interest of the flag State with the interest of the detaining State to secure appearance in its court of the Master and the payment of penalties. The balance of interests provides the guiding criterion for ITLOS in its assessment of the reasonableness of the bond. When determining whether the assessment made by the detaining State in fixing the bond or other security is reasonable, ITLOS will treat the laws of the detaining State and the decisions of its courts as relevant facts. However, under Article 292 of UNCLOS, ITLOS is not an appellate forum against a decision of a national court.[18]

3. Relationship with domestic and international proceedings

ITLOS has clarified the relationship of the proceedings under Article 292 of UNCLOS to domestic proceedings. By virtue of Article 292(3), the prompt release proceedings shall be 'without prejudice to the merits of any case before the appropriate domestic forum against the vessel, its owner, or its crew'. This provision should be read together with the provision of the same paragraph according to which ITLOS 'shall deal only with the question of release' and with the provision of paragraph 4 according to which 'upon the posting of the bond or other financial security determined by the court or tribunal, the authorities of the detaining State shall comply promptly with the decision of the court or tribunal concerning the release of the vessel or its crew'. Consequently, while the States which are parties to the proceedings

---

[18] 'Monte Confurco' (Seychelles v France) (Prompt Release) ITLOS Reports 2000, 86, 108 [70]–[72].

before ITLOS are bound by the judgment adopted by it as far as the release of the vessel and the bond or other security are concerned, their domestic courts, in considering the merits of the case, are not bound by any findings of fact or law ITLOS may have made in order to reach its conclusions.[19] Phrased differently, the prompt release proceedings, as clearly provided in Article 292(3), can deal only with the question of *release*, without prejudice to the merits of any case before the appropriate domestic forum against the vessel, its owner, or its crew. That said, in its prompt release proceedings, ITLOS is not precluded from examining the facts and circumstances of the case to the extent necessary for a proper appreciation of the reasonableness of the bond, which cannot be determined in isolation from facts. ITLOS emphasizes, however, that a prompt release proceeding must be conducted and concluded 'without delay', suggesting a limitation on the extent to which ITLOS could take cognizance of the facts in dispute and seek evidence in support of the allegations made by the parties.[20]

The independence of prompt release proceedings vis-à-vis other international proceedings emerges from Article 292 itself and from the fact that the ITLOS Rules deal with such proceedings in a separate section (ie, section E of Part III). These proceedings are thus not incidental to proceedings on the merits. This stands in contrast to the proceedings for interim measures set out in Article 290 which in the Rules are dealt with in section C of Part III, on 'incidental proceedings'. Prompt releases are separate, independent proceedings. Thus, by way of example, ITLOS did not rule in the prompt release proceedings in *'Volga' (Russia Federation v Australia)* (Prompt Release) on the question of whether the hot pursuit which resulted in the arrest of the 'Volga' had been improperly commenced by Australia (Australian officials having apparently signalled the vessel to stop only after it had left the Australian exclusive economic zone). This would have been a question as to the merits of the underlying case; the only relevant question in these proceedings was the reasonableness of the bond.

It cannot, however, be ruled out that a case concerning the merits of the situation that led to the arrest of the vessel could later be submitted for a

---

[19] *M/V 'Saiga'* (Prompt Release) (n 6) 27 [49].
[20] *'Monte Confurco'* (Prompt Release) (n 18) 108–09 [74]. See also *'Tomimaru' (Japan v Russian Federation)* (Prompt Release) ITLOS Reports 2005–07, 74, 96 [74]. As ITLOS explains in *M/V 'Saiga'* (Prompt Release) (n 6) 31 [62], ITLOS is not called upon to decide whether the arrest of the vessel is legitimate. It is called upon to determine whether the detention consequent to the arrest is in violation of a provision of UNCOS 'for the prompt release of the vessel or its crew upon the posting of a reasonable bond or other financial security'.

decision on the merits to ITLOS or to another court or tribunal competent according to Article 287 of UNCLOS. This circumstance does not preclude ITLOS from considering the aspects of the merits it deems necessary in order to reach its decision on the question of prompt release, but it does require ITLOS to do so with restraint. In this regard, ITLOS considers appropriate an approach based on assessing whether the allegations made are arguable or are of a sufficiently plausible character in the sense that ITLOS may rely upon them for the present purposes. By applying such a standard, ITLOS does not foreclose that if a case were presented to it requiring full examination of the merits it could or would reach a different conclusion. The standard indicated seems particularly appropriate because, in the proceedings under Article 292, ITLOS has to evaluate 'allegations' by the applicant that given provisions of UNCLOS are involved and objections by the detaining State based upon its own characterization of the rules of law on the basis of which it has acted. Applying such standard allows ITLOS in the short time available to exercise the restraint referred to above.[21]

4. Admissibility

The scope of ITLOS's jurisdiction in proceedings under Article 292 of UNCLOS encompasses only cases in which 'it is alleged that the detaining State has not complied with the provisions of UNCLOS for the prompt release of the vessel or its crew upon the posting of a reasonable bond or other financial security'. ITLOS has held that Article 292 proceedings are not available in other cases concerning allegations a coastal State has violated obligations regarding fisheries enforcement such as the prohibition on imprisonment for fisheries offences (Article 73(3)) or the requirement to notify the flag State (Article 73(4)). This follows as paragraphs 3[22] and 4,[23] unlike paragraph 2, of Article 73 make no provision for prompt release, and so submissions concerning their alleged violation are not admissible.[24] It

---

[21] M/V 'Saiga' (Prompt Release) (n 6) 27–28 [50]–[51].

[22] Art 73(3): 'Coastal State penalties for violations of fisheries laws and regulations in the exclusive economic zone may not include imprisonment, in the absence of agreements to the contrary by the States concerned, or any other form of corporal punishment.'

[23] Art 73(4): 'In cases of arrest or detention of foreign vessels the coastal State shall promptly notify the flag State, through appropriate channels, of the action taken and of any penalties subsequently imposed.'

[24] 'Camouco' (Panama v France) (Prompt Release) ITLOS Reports 2000, 10, 29–30 [59]; 'Monte Confurco' (Prompt Release) (n 18) 106 [63].

may, however, be noted, in passing, a connection between paragraphs 2 and 4 of Article 73, since absence of prompt notification may have a bearing on the ability of the flag State to invoke Articles 73(2) and 292 in a timely and efficient manner.[25]

For the purpose of the admissibility of the application for prompt release, it is sufficient for non-compliance with the UNCLOS provision triggering prompt release proceedings, such as Article 73(2), to have been 'alleged' and the allegation to be 'arguable or sufficiently plausible'.[26] However, for the application for prompt release to succeed, the allegation that the detaining State has not complied with the provisions of UNCLOS for the prompt release of the vessel or its crew upon the posting of a reasonable bond must be well founded.[27]

In M/V 'Saiga' (Prompt Release), the M/V 'Saiga', an oil tanker flying the flag of Saint Vincent and the Grenadines, was arrested by Guinean customs patrol boats and brought into Conakry, Guinea, where the vessel and its crew were detained. No bond or other financial security was requested by Guinean authorities for the release of the vessel and its crew or offered by Saint Vincent and the Grenadines. ITLOS held that in order to invoke Article 292 the posting of the bond or other security might not have been effected in fact, and that there might be an infringement of Article 73(2) even when no bond had been posted. The underlying rationale is that the requirement of promptness has a value in itself and may prevail when the posting of the bond has not been possible, has been rejected, or is not provided for in the coastal State's laws, or when it is alleged that the required bond is unreasonable.[28]

While, in principle, the decisive date for determining the issues of admissibility is the date of the filing of an application, events subsequent to the filing of an application may render an application without object. However, in prompt release proceedings before ITLOS the setting of the bond by the respondent does not per se render the application without object, as a State may make an application under Article 292 of UNCLOS not only where no bond has been set but also where it considers the bond set by the detaining

---

[25] 'Camouco' (Prompt Release) (n 24) 29–30 [59].

[26] M/V 'Saiga' (Prompt Release) (n 6) 30 [59].

[27] 'Camouco' (Prompt Release) (n 24) 30 [61]; 'Monte Confurco' (Prompt Release) (n 18) 107 [67].

[28] M/V 'Saiga' (Prompt Release) (n 6) 34–5 [76]–[77], followed in 'Camouco' (Prompt Release) (n 24) 30–31 [63] holding that the posting of a bond or other security is not necessarily a condition precedent to filing an application under Article 292 of UNCLOS.

State to be unreasonable, and it is for ITLOS to decide whether a bond is reasonable under Article 292.[29]

In *'Camouco' (Panama v France)* (Prompt Release), ITLOS explained that Article 292 requires prompt release of the vessel or its crew once ITLOS finds an allegation made in the application to be well founded—it does not require the flag State to file an application at any particular time after the detention of a vessel or its crew. The 10-day period referred to in Article 292(1) is to enable the parties to submit the question of release from detention to an agreed court or tribunal. It does not mean an application not made to a court or tribunal within the 10-day period or to ITLOS immediately after the 10-day period will not be treated as an application for 'prompt release' within the meaning of Article 292.[30] As clarified by ITLOS in a subsequent case, given the object and purpose of Article 292, the time required for setting a bond should be reasonable. Article 292 does not require the flag State to file an application at any particular time after the detention of a vessel or its crew, and the earliest date for initiating such procedure before ITLOS is, in accordance with Article 292(1), 10 days from the time of detention.[31]

Furthermore, it is not logical to read the requirement of exhaustion of local remedies or any other analogous rule into Article 292, which is designed to free a ship and its crew from prolonged detention on account of the imposition of unreasonable bonds in municipal jurisdictions, or the failure of local law to provide for release on posting of a reasonable bond, thereby inflicting avoidable loss on a ship owner or other persons affected by such detention. Equally, it safeguards the interests of the coastal State by providing for release only upon the posting of a reasonable bond or other financial security determined by a court or tribunal referred to in Article 292, without prejudice to the merits of the case in the domestic forum against the vessel, its owner, or its crew. Since Article 292 provides for an independent remedy and not an appeal against a decision of a national court, no limitation should be read into Article 292 that would have the effect of defeating its very object and purpose. Indeed, Article 292 permits the making of an application within a short period from the date of detention and it is not normally the case that local remedies could be exhausted in such a short period.[32]

---

[29] *'Hoshinmaru'* (Prompt Release) (n 3) 42 [64]–[66], reaffirming *M/V 'Saiga'* (Prompt Release) (n 6) 35 [77].

[30] *'Camouco'* (Prompt Release) (n 24) 28 [54].

[31] *'Hoshinmaru'* (Prompt Release) (n 3) 44 [80].

[32] *'Camouco'* (Prompt Release) (n 24) 29 [57]–[58].

5. Detention and confiscation

Whether a vessel and/or its crew is/are detained is a question of fact in the light of the prevailing circumstances. In 'Monte Confurco' (Prompt Release), the Master of the vessel was then under court supervision, his passport had also been taken away from him by the respondent's authorities, and, consequently, he was not in a position to leave the detaining State's territory. ITLOS considered it appropriate, in the circumstances of the case, to order the release of the Master in accordance with Article 292(1) of UNCLOS.[33]

To date, ITLOS has ruled an application for prompt release to be without object in only one case, in 'Tomimaru' (Japan v Russian Federation) (Prompt Release). A Russian City Court, on 28 December 2006, after deciding the shipowner had violated the terms and conditions of the fishing licence, imposed a fine on the shipowner and ordered the confiscation of the vessel. This decision was upheld on appeal. At the time of filing of the application for prompt release with ITLOS, a supervisory review procedure was pending before the Russian Supreme Court. After the closure of the hearing before ITLOS, on 26 July 2007, Russia informed ITLOS that the Russian Supreme Court had dismissed the complaint concerning the confiscation of the vessel. In such circumstances, ITLOS proceeds as follows. It emphasizes the distinction between two questions: first, whether confiscation may have an impact on the nationality of a vessel and, second, whether confiscation renders an application for the prompt release of a vessel without object. As regards the first question, the confiscation of a vessel does not result per se in an automatic change of the flag or in its loss. Confiscation changes the ownership of a vessel but ownership of a vessel and the nationality of a vessel are different issues. According to Article 91 of UNCLOS, it is for each State to establish the conditions for the granting of its nationality to ships and for the registration of ships. The State of nationality of the ship is the flag State or the State whose flag the ship is entitled to fly. The juridical link between a State and a ship entitled to fly its flag produces a network of mutual rights and obligations, as indicated in Article 94 of UNCLOS. In view of the important functions of the flag State and the pivotal role played by the flag State in the initiation of the procedure for the prompt release of a ship under Article 292, a change in ownership cannot be presumed to lead automatically to the change or loss of its flag.

---

[33] 'Monte Confurco' (Prompt Release) (n 18) 112 [90]. The same situation occurred in 'Camouco' (Prompt Release) (n 24) 32–33 [71].

With regard to the second question, Article 73 of UNCLOS makes no reference to confiscation of vessels although ITLOS is aware many States have provided for measures of confiscation of fishing vessels in their legislation with respect to the management and conservation of marine living resources. In considering whether confiscation renders an application for the prompt release of a vessel without object ITLOS has to take into account the object and purpose of the prompt release procedure as well as Article 292(3). In particular, a judgment under Article 292 must be 'without prejudice to the merits of any case' before the appropriate domestic forum against the vessel or its crew, and this is a factor in maintaining the balance between the interests of the coastal State and of the flag State. Confiscation of a fishing vessel must not be used in such a manner as to upset the balance of the interests of the flag State and of the coastal State established in UNCLOS. Because a decision to confiscate eliminates the provisional character of the detention of the vessel rendering the procedure for its prompt release without object, such a decision should not be taken in such a way as to prevent the shipowner from having recourse to available domestic judicial remedies, nor as to prevent the flag State from resorting to the prompt release procedure under UNCLOS; nor should it be taken through proceedings inconsistent with international standards of due process of law. In particular, a confiscation decided in unjustified haste would jeopardize the operation of Article 292. In this context, in the light of the objective of Article 292, it is incumbent upon the flag State to act in a timely manner, and this objective can only be achieved if the shipowner and the flag State take action within reasonable time either to have recourse to the national judicial system of the detaining State or to initiate the prompt release procedure under Article 292. Considering the object and purpose of the prompt release procedure, a decision to confiscate a vessel does not prevent ITLOS from considering an application for prompt release of such vessel while proceedings are still before the domestic courts of the detaining State.

In 'Tomimaru' (Japan v Russian Federation) (Prompt Release), the respondent did not claim to have initiated procedures leading to a change or loss of the flag of the 'Tomimaru'. Furthermore, the decision of the Russian Supreme Court brought to an end the procedures before the Russian domestic courts. ITLOS also noted that no inconsistency with international standards of due process of law was argued and no allegation was raised that the proceedings resulting in the confiscation were such as to frustrate the possibility of recourse to national or international remedies. ITLOS considered its decision under Article 292 to release the vessel in that case would contradict the decision which concluded the proceedings before the appropriate domestic forums and encroach upon national competences, thus contravening Article 292(3). Therefore, the application for prompt release was held to be without object in that particular case.[34]

6. Bond or other security and its reasonableness

In interpreting the expression 'bond or other security' in Article 73(2) of UNCLOS, ITLOS considers this expression must be seen in its context and in the light of its object and purpose. The relevant context includes the provisions of UNCLOS concerning the prompt release of vessels and crews upon the posting of a bond or security; namely, Article 292, Article 220(7), and Article 226(1)(b) and they use the expressions 'bond or other financial security' and 'bonding or other appropriate financial security'. Seen in this context, the expression 'bond or other security' in Article 73(2) should be interpreted as referring to a bond or security of a financial nature. Where UNCLOS envisages the imposition of conditions additional to a bond or other financial security, it expressly stipulates so, as in Article 226(1)(c) according to which 'the release of a vessel may, whenever it would present an unreasonable threat of damage to the marine environment, be refused or made conditional upon proceeding to the nearest appropriate repair yard'. Therefore, the non-financial conditions cannot be considered components of a bond or other financial security for the purpose of applying Article 292 in respect of an alleged violation of Article 73(2), whose object and purpose as read in conjunction with Article 292 is to provide the flag State with a mechanism for obtaining the prompt release of a vessel and crew arrested for alleged fisheries violations by posting a security of a financial nature whose reasonableness can be assessed in financial terms. The inclusion of additional non-financial conditions in such a security would defeat such object and purpose.[35]

In 'Volga' (Russian Federation v Australia) (Prompt Release), besides requiring a bond, the respondent made the release of the vessel conditional upon the fulfilment of two conditions: that the vessel carried a VMS, and that information concerning particulars about the owner and ultimate

---

[34] 'Tomimaru' (Prompt Release) (n 20) 95–7 [69]–[81].
[35] 'Volga' (Prompt Release) (n 6) 34–35 [77].

beneficial owners of the ship was to be submitted to its authorities. The respondent required, as part of the security for obtaining the release of the Volga and its crew, payment by the owner of one million Australian dollars to guarantee the carriage of a fully operational monitoring system and observance of the Commission for the Conservation of Antarctic Marine Living Resources' conservation measures until the conclusion of legal proceedings. The respondent explained this component of the bond was to ensure that the Volga comply with Australian law and relevant treaties to which Australia was a party until the completion of the domestic legal proceedings; that the ship not enter Australian territorial waters other than with permission or for the purpose of innocent passage prior to the conclusion of the forfeiture proceedings; and that the vessel not be used to commit further criminal offences. ITLOS held that a 'good behaviour bond' to prevent future violations of the laws of a coastal State could not be considered as a bond or security within the meaning of Article 73(2) read in conjunction with Article 292. Therefore, concluded ITLOS, the bond sought by the respondent was not reasonable.[36] Instead, ITLOS ordered a bond for the release of the 'Volga', the fuel, lubricants, and fishing equipment in the amount of A$1,920,000—in the form of a bank guarantee from a bank present in Australia or having corresponding arrangements with an Australian bank or, if agreed to by the parties, in any other form—be posted with the respondent for the prompt release of the vessel.[37]

Likewise, ITLOS has rejected the contention by applicants that no bond or financial security (or only a 'symbolic bond') should be posted. ITLOS considers the actual posting of a bond or security to be necessary in view of the nature of the prompt release proceedings.[38]

On the whole, the amounts of sanction evaluation and methods of calculation, and the amount of security demanded, by detaining coastal States for the release of detained foreign vessels and their crews vary so considerably from one State to another and even from one court to another court in the same State that there is no consistent, generalized, or widespread common pattern in this respect so as to form a rule of customary international law of general or even regional application. ITLOS thus has to approach applications for prompt release on a case-by-case basis, using the criteria ITLOS

---

[36]   ibid 34–36 [75]–[80], 37 [88].
[37]   ibid 37 [90], 39 [95(5) and (6)].
[38]   *M/V 'Saiga'* (Prompt Release) (n 6) 35 [81], reaffirmed in *'Juno Trader'* (Prompt Release) (n 3) 43 [97].

itself has honed. A number of factors are relevant in an assessment of the reasonableness of bonds or other financial security, including the gravity of the alleged offences, the penalties imposed or imposable under the laws of the detaining State, the value of the detained vessel and of the cargo seized, and the amount of the bond imposed by the detaining State and its form.[39] This is by no means a complete list of factors, nor does ITLOS intend to lay down rigid rules as to the exact weight to be attached to each of them—they complement the criterion of reasonableness that encompasses the amount, the nature, and the form of the bond or financial security whose overall balance must be reasonable.[40] The assessment of the relevant factors must be an objective one, taking into account all information provided to ITLOS by the parties.[41] Above all, the obligation of prompt release of vessels and crews in ITLOS case law includes 'elementary considerations of humanity and due process of law', and the requirement for the bond or other financial security to be reasonable indicates that 'a concern for fairness is one of the purposes of [Article 73(2)]'.[42]

Indeed, the value of the vessel alone may not be the controlling factor in the determination of the amount of the bond or other financial security.[43] As regards the value of the fish and of the fishing gear seized, it is also to be taken into account as a factor relevant in the assessment of the reasonableness of the bond.[44] In *Volga* (Prompt Release), although the proceeds of the sale of the catch represented a guarantee to the respondent, they had no relevance to the bond to be set for the release of the vessel and the members of the crew, and the question of their inclusion or exclusion from the bond did not arise in that case.[45] In another case, ITLOS ruled that the amount of €8,770 previously paid to the respondent for the fine imposed on the Master was to be considered as bond or financial security since the payment of the

---

[39] *'Camouco'* (Prompt Release) (n 24) 31 [67].

[40] *M/V 'Saiga'* (Prompt Release) (n 6) 35 [82]; *'Monte Confurco'* (Prompt Release) (n 18) 109 [76]; *'Volga'* (Prompt Release) (n 6) 32 [64]–[65]; *'Hoshinmaru'* (Prompt Release) (n 3) 45 [82].

[41] *'Juno Trader'* (Prompt Release) (n 3) 41 [85]; *'Hoshinmaru'* (Prompt Release) (n 3) 45 [82]. One commentator suggests that ITLOS should pay more attention to the interests of the detaining coastal States in a prompt release analysis as well as exercise restraint in questioning domestic courts or authorities' decisions in imposing bonds or other financial security: Anastasia Telesetsky, 'The International Tribunal for the Law of the Sea: Seeking the Legitimacy of State Consent' in Nienke Grossman and others (eds), *Legitimacy and International Courts* (Cambridge University Press 2018) 206–09.

[42] *'Juno Trader'* (Prompt Release) (n 3) 38–39 [77].

[43] *'Camouco'* (Prompt Release) (n 24) 32 [69].

[44] *'Monte Confurco'* (Prompt Release) (n 18) 111 [86].

[45] *'Volga'* (Prompt Release) (n 6) 37 [86].

said fine had been suspended by the decision of a competent court of the respondent, and that the letter of guarantee in the amount of €50,000 and in a form not acceptable to the respondent were to be returned to the applicant upon the posting of the bond ordered by ITLOS.[46] In yet another case, after taking into consideration the commercial value of the gasoil discharged and the difficulties that might be incurred in restoring the gasoil to the holds of the detained vessel, ITLOS found it reasonable for the discharged gasoil to be considered as a security to be held and, as the case might be, returned by the respondent, in kind or in its equivalent in US dollars at the time of judgment.[47] ITLOS also considered it reasonable to add to this security a financial security in the amount of US$400,000, to be posted in the form of a letter of credit or bank guarantee, or, if agreed by the parties, in any other form.[48]

Prompt release proceedings have been resorted to in connection with the arrest and detention of foreign fishing vessels and their crews accused of illegal fishing in the maritime zone of the arresting State.[49] In 'Monte Confurco' (Prompt Release), ITLOS took note of the respondent's contention that the fundamental factual background in the general context of unlawful fishing in the maritime region concerned should also constitute one of the factors to be taken into account in assessing the reasonableness of the bond as this illegal fishing was a threat to the future resources and the measures taken under for the conservation of toothfish.[50] In 'Juno Trader' (Prompt Release), ITLOS similarly took note of the respondent's concern that illegal, unregulated, and unreported fishing in its exclusive economic zone had resulted in a serious depletion of its fisheries resources.[51] However, matters relating to the circumstances of the seizure of the vessel are not relevant to proceedings for prompt release under Article 292, and

---

[46] 'Juno Trader' (Prompt Release) (n 3) 43–44 [99]. In the end, the bond or other security as determined by ITLOS comprised €8,770 already paid to Guinea-Bissau and €300,000 to be posted with Guinea-Bissau (ibid 45 [104(5)]).

[47] M/V 'Saiga' (Prompt Release) (n 6) 36 [84].

[48] ibid 36 [85].

[49] 'Camouco' (Prompt Release) (n 24); 'Monte Confurco' (Prompt Release) (n 18); 'Grand Prince' (Prompt Release) (n 2); 'Volga' (Prompt Release) (n 6); 'Juno Trader' (Prompt Release) (n 3); 'Hoshinmaru' (Prompt Release) (n 3); 'Tomimaru' (Prompt Release) (n 20). Unlike the other cases, the vessels in the last two cases held valid fishing licences and were authorized to be present and to fish in the Russian exclusive economic zone but were arrested for the inaccurate reporting of the species caught and illegal catch in violation of the terms and conditions of their respective licences.

[50] 'Monte Confurco' (Prompt Release) (n 18) 110 [79].

[51] 'Juno Trader' (Prompt Release) (n 3) 41 [87].

ITLOS, therefore, cannot take into account the circumstances of the seizure of the vessel in assessing the reasonableness of the bond.[52]

While ITLOS understands the international concerns about illegal, unregulated, and unreported fishing and appreciates the objectives behind the measures taken by States to deal with the problem, in the Article 292 proceedings ITLOS is called upon to assess whether the bond set by the respondent is reasonable in terms of Article 292, whose purpose is to secure the prompt release of the vessel and crew upon the posting of a reasonable bond, pending completion of the judicial procedures before the courts of the detaining State.[53] Among the factors to be considered in making the assessment are the penalties which may be imposed for the alleged offences under the laws of the respondent. It is by reference to these penalties that ITLOS may evaluate the gravity of the alleged offences,[54] and the amount of a bond should not be excessive and unrelated to the gravity of the alleged offences.[55] ITLOS in 'Monte Confurco' (Prompt Release) considered the bond of 56,400,000 FF imposed by the French court not 'reasonable' within the meaning of Article 292.[56] Instead, the security was to be in the total amount of 18,000,000 FF. In considering the overall balance of amount, form, and nature of the bond or financial security, ITLOS ruled that the monetary equivalent of the 158 tonnes of fish on board the 'Monte Confurco' held by the French authorities (ie, 9,000,000 FF) was to be considered as security to be held or, as the case might be, returned by France to the applicant. The remaining security, in the amount of 9,000,000 FF was, unless the parties otherwise agreed, to be in the form of a bank guarantee, to be posted with France.[57] In 'Hoshinmaru' (Prompt Release), ITLOS did not consider the bond of 22,000,000 roubles (approximately US$862,000) to be reasonable. Although ITLOS accepted that inaccurate reporting of the species caught in violation of the terms and conditions of the vessel's fishing licence could be sanctioned by Russia, the detaining State, ITLOS did not consider it reasonable that a bond should be set on the basis of the maximum penalties that could be applicable to the owner and the Master, nor did it consider

---

[52] 'Volga' (Prompt Release) (n 6) 36 [83]; 'Juno Trader' (Prompt Release) (n 3) 43 [95].

[53] 'Volga' (Prompt Release) (n 6) 33 [68]–[69].

[54] ibid 33 [69], echoing 'Monte Confurco' (Prompt Release) (n 18) 108 [73] and 'Juno Trader' (Prompt Release) (n 3) 41 [89]. See also Gabriela A Oonta, 'The International Tribunal for the Law of the Sea and the Polar Region' (2014) 13 Law & Practice of Int'l Courts and Tribunals 286, 299.

[55] 'Monte Confurco' (Prompt Release) (n 18) 108 [73].

[56] ibid 112 [89].

[57] ibid 113 [93].

it reasonable that the bond should be calculated on the basis of the confiscation of the vessel, given the circumstances of that case. ITLOS noted in this respect that the applicable Russian regulations did not foresee automatic inclusion of the value of the arrested vessel in the assessment of the bond.[58] ITLOS determined that the bond in that case was to be 10,000,000 roubles.[59] 'Hoshinmaru' (Prompt Release), decided in August 2007, is the last case, as of this writing, of prompt release proceedings in which ITLOS determined the amount of a bond or other financial security.

When, eventually, there is no legitimate ground to detain the vessel and its crew subject to a prompt release proceeding, as when ITLOS rules the respondent's acts against them to be in breach of UNCLOS, the bond or other financial security posted with the respondent is to be treated as no longer effective, and, accordingly, the relevant document should be returned by the respondent forthwith to the applicant.[60]

7. Promptness of the release

The promptness of the release upon the posting of a reasonable bond or security must be considered in the circumstances of each case. For instance, in 'Saiga' (No 2) (Merits), in rejecting the applicant's contention that a release of the ship 80 days after the posting of the bond could not be considered as prompt release, ITLOS found a number of factors contributing to the delay in releasing the ship and not all of them could be said to have been due to the fault of the respondent.[61]

---

[58]   'Hoshinmaru' (Prompt Release) (n 3) 48 [93].

[59]   ibid 51 [102(5)].

[60]   M/V 'Saiga' (No 2) (Saint Vincent and the Grenadines v Guinea) (Merits) ITLOS Reports 1999, 10, 68 [180].

[61]   ibid 64 [165]. ITLOS did not elaborate the factors contributing to the delay in releasing the ship. According to Judge Laing's Separate Opinion (ibid 192–93), these factors included the parties' disagreement about the implementation of the requirements of the prompt release Judgment, the actual wording on the bank guarantee (originally written in English), communications difficulties, travel by the representatives of the parties, and the novelty in the international community of the prompt release requirement under UNCLOS. In that case, ITLOS fixed the amount and broadly determined the 'nature and form' of the security, leaving the latter details to the parties, causing 'considerable scope for delay'. In subsequent cases of prompt release, ITLOS laid down specific indications about the terms and content of the bond or financial security to be posted and the conditions of its payment: P Chandrasekhara Rao and Philippe Gautier (eds), The Rules of the International Tribunal for the Law of the Sea: A Commentary (Martinus Nijhoff 2006) 328. For its part, Guinea also cited 'communication difficulties of a technical nature' between the parties as another major reason for the considerable delay in the release of the ship: paras 114–25 of Guinea's Rejoinder of 28 December 1998 in M/V 'Saiga' (No 2) (Merits) (n 60).

6

Applications for Provisional Measures

Provisional measures of protection are the international equivalent of an interim injunction designed to protect the rights of the parties pending the final decision in a dispute. They have been widely resorted to in international adjudication.[1] In the context of the law of the sea disputes, two high-profile cases in which provisional measures were requested may be cited as examples. The first concerns the arrest in September 2013 by the Russian authorities of the Dutch-flagged ship 'Arctic Sunrise' used by Greenpeace International to stage a protest against Russia's oil production in the Barents Sea, with 30 crew members of various nationalities on board. The second case concerns the arrest and detention in November 2018 by the Russian authorities of three Ukrainian naval vessels and the 24 Ukrainian servicemen on board while travelling in the Black Sea towards their home port of Odesa.

At the Third UN Conference on the Law of the Sea, the need for courts or tribunals having jurisdiction under UNCLOS to have the power to prescribe provisional measures was beyond dispute although there was considerable debate concerning the details of the regime associated with such measures. The finally adopted Article 290 of UNCLOS, under the heading 'Provisional measures', represents the best possible compromise.[2] It reads:

---

[1] Lawrence Collins, 'Provisional and Protective Measures in International Litigation' (1992) 234 Recueil des Cours de l'Académie de Droit International 9; Antonio Augusto Cançado Trindade, 'The Evolution of Provisional Measures of Protection under the Case-Law of the Inter-American Court of Human Rights (1987–2002)' (2003) 24 Human Rights LJ 162; Shabtai Rosenne, *Provisional Measures in International Law: The International Court of Justice and the International Tribunal for the Law of the Sea* (OUP 2005) ch 1; Cameron A Miles, *Provisional Measures before International Courts and Tribunals* (CUP 2017).

[2] Myron H Nordquist, Shabtai Rosenne, and Louis B Sohn (eds), *United Nations Convention on the Law of the Sea 1982: A Commentary*, vol 5 (Brill 1989) ('Virginia Commentary') 53–59.

1. If a dispute has been duly submitted to a court or tribunal which considers that *prima facie* it has jurisdiction under this Part [XV] or Part XI, section 5 [Settlement of disputes and advisory opinions by the Seabed Disputes Chamber], the court or tribunal may prescribe any provisional measures which it considers appropriate under the circumstances to preserve the respective rights of the parties to the dispute or to prevent serious harm to the marine environment, pending the final decision.

2. Provisional measures may be modified or revoked as soon as the circumstances justifying them have changed or ceased to exist.

3. Provisional measures may be prescribed, modified, or revoked under this article only at the request of a party to the dispute and after the parties have been given an opportunity to be heard.

4. The court or tribunal shall forthwith give notice to the parties to the dispute, and to such other States Parties as it considers appropriate, of the prescription, modification, or revocation of provisional measures.

5. Pending the constitution of an arbitral tribunal to which a dispute is being submitted under this section [2 of Part XV on compulsory procedures entailing binding decisions], any court or tribunal agreed upon by the parties or, failing such agreement within two weeks from the date of the request for provisional measures, the International Tribunal for the Law of the Sea or, with respect to activities in the Area, the Seabed Disputes Chamber, may prescribe, modify, or revoke provisional measures in accordance with this article if it considers that *prima facie* the tribunal which is to be constituted would have jurisdiction and that the urgency of the situation so requires. Once constituted, the tribunal to which the dispute has been submitted may modify, revoke, or affirm those provisional measures, acting in conformity with paragraphs 1 to 4.

6. The parties to the dispute shall comply promptly with any provisional measures prescribed under this article.

It should be noted that, according to Article 290(3), provisional measures may be prescribed only at a request of a party to the dispute, and not *proprio motu*.[3]

---

[3] Unlike the International Court of Justice, which is authorized by Art 75(1) of its Rules to decide at any time to examine *proprio motu* whether the circumstances of the case require the indication of provisional measures which ought to be taken or complied with by any or all of the parties.

1. Initiation of the application for provisional measures

By virtue of Article 89 of ITLOS's Rules, a party may submit a request to ITLOS for the prescription of provisional measures under Article 290(1) of UNCLOS 'at any time during the course of the proceedings in a dispute submitted to [ITLOS]'. In the case of a dispute submitted to an arbitral tribunal under UNCLOS, pending the constitution of that tribunal a party may submit a request for the prescription of provisional measures under Article 290(5) to ITLOS (a) at any time if the parties have so agreed; or (b) at any time after two weeks from the notification to the other party of a request for provisional measures if the parties have not agreed that such measures may be prescribed by another court or tribunal. The request shall be in writing and specify the measures requested, the reasons therefor, and the possible consequences, if the request is not granted, for the preservation of the respective rights of the parties or for the prevention of serious harm to the marine environment. A request for the prescription of provisional measures under Article 290(5) of UNCLOS shall indicate the urgency of the situation and the legal grounds upon which the arbitral tribunal which is to be constituted would have jurisdiction, and a certified copy of the notification or of any other document instituting the proceedings before the arbitral tribunal shall be annexed to the request.

If ITLOS is not in session or a sufficient number of judges are not available to constitute a quorum, the provisional measures under Article 290 of UNCLOS shall be prescribed by the Chamber of Summary Procedure. Such provisional measures may be adopted at the request of any party to the dispute. They shall be subject to review and revision by ITLOS at the written request of a party within 15 days of the prescription of the measures, and ITLOS itself may also at any time decide *proprio motu* to review or revise the measures.[4] Despite the logic of having the Chamber of Summary Procedure to expedite dispatch of business, it has never been utilized as of this writing. In *M/V 'Louisa' (Saint Vincent and the Grenadines v Kingdom of Spain)*, the applicant proposed that its application and request for provisional measures be referred to ITLOS's Chamber of Summary Procedure but this was opposed by the respondent who, instead, requested the full-bench ITLOS to hear and determine the case.[5]

---

[4] Statute Art 25(2) and Rules Art 91.

[5] *M/V 'Louisa' (Saint Vincent and the Grenadines v Kingdom of Spain)* (Provisional Measures, Order of 23 December 2010) ITLOS Reports 2008–10, 58, 60 [7]–[9].

Article 290 of UNCLOS applies independently of any other procedure which may have been instituted at the domestic level. In other words, if proceedings are instituted at the domestic level, this does not deprive the applicant of recourse to international proceedings under Article 290.[6]

When fixing the dates for the hearing, the ITLOS President, in accordance with Article 27 of the Statute and Articles 45 and 90(2) of the Rules, must duly bear in mind that applications for provisional measures are urgent proceedings with priority over all other proceedings subject to Article 112(1) of the ITLOS Rules.[7] ITLOS, or its President if ITLOS is not sitting, shall fix the earliest possible date for a hearing.[8]

The entire duration from the initiation of the provisional measures proceedings before ITLOS to the rendering of the Order by ITLOS lasted 39 days and 46 days, respectively, in the two requests for provisional measures in 2019.[9]

2. Pre-conditions: prima facie jurisdiction and urgency of the situation

First of all, ITLOS shall ascertain whether the parties are party to UNCLOS; whether either of them has made declarations pursuant to Article 287(1) upon their ratification/accession that will prima facie give ITLOS, in an application under Article 290(1), or the Annex VII arbitral tribunal, in an application under Article 290(5), jurisdiction over the dispute between them relating to the interpretation or application of UNCLOS.[10] Where several provisions of UNCLOS related to the dispute are invoked, at least some of these provisions must appear to afford a basis for such prima facie

---

[6] *'Enrica Lexie' (Italy v India)* (Provisional Measures, Order of 24 August 2015) ITLOS Reports 2015, 182, 195 [73].

[7] Rules Art 112(1):

> The Tribunal shall give priority to applications for release of vessels or crews over all other proceedings before the Tribunal. However, if the Tribunal is seized of an application for release of a vessel or its crew and of a request for the prescription of provisional measures, it shall take the necessary measures to ensure that both the application and the request are dealt with without delay.

[8] Rules Art 90(1) and (2).

[9] *Detention of three Ukrainian naval vessels (Ukraine v Russian Federation)* ITLOS Case No 26 (Provisional Measures, Order of 25 May 2019); *M/T 'San Padre Pio' (Switzerland v Nigeria)* ITLOS Case No 27 (Provisional Measures, Order of 6 July 2019).

[10] *'Enrica Lexie'* (n 6) 189–90 [34]–[35]; *M/T 'San Padre Pio'* (n 9) para 46.

jurisdiction.[11] In addition, ITLOS will proceed to determine whether, prima facie, the requirements under Article 283 relating to an exchange of views are met before the request for the prescription of provisional measures by ITLOS.[12]

At this stage of the proceedings, ITLOS does not need to establish definitively the existence of the rights claimed by the applicant and, before prescribing provisional measures, ITLOS need not finally satisfy itself that ITLOS or the Annex VII arbitral tribunal, as the case may be, has jurisdiction on the merits of the case.[13] The question of jurisdiction to deal with the merits can be decided only after consideration of the written and oral proceedings, and not on the basis of the decision on prima facie jurisdiction in connection with a request for the prescription of provisional measures.[14] Therefore, an Order for provisional measures in no way prejudges any questions relating to the court or tribunal's jurisdiction or to the merits of the case, and leaves unaffected the right of both parties to submit arguments in respect of such questions.[15] For example, in in *Detention of three Ukrainian naval vessels (Ukraine v Russian Federation)*, a case concerning the apprehension and detention by Russia of three Ukrainian naval vessels and the 24 Ukrainian servicemen on board, ITLOS did not have to rule definitively on the existence (or not) of an armed conflict between the parties that would implicate the applicability of the law of naval warfare as *lex specialis* replacing the law of the sea under UNCLOS and allow targeting military objectives such as enemy warships which are not immune from capture, attack, or destruction to achieve a military advantage for Russia.[16] ITLOS had only had to find prima facie that this was not a situation of armed conflict which would exclude dispute settlement.

---

[11] *M/T 'San Padre Pio'* (n 9) paras 46–61, See also *'ARA Libertad' (Argentina v Ghana)* (Provisional Measures, Order of 15 December 2012) ITLOS Reports 2012, 332, 343–44 [61]–[67].

[12] *M/T 'San Padre Pio'* (n 9) paras 62–76.

[13] *M/V 'Louisa'* (Provisional Measures) (n 5) 69 [69], quoting *M/V 'Saiga' (No 2)* (Provisional Measures, Order of 11 March 1998) ITLOS Reports 1998, 24, 37 [29]. See also *'Arctic Sunrise' (Kingdom of the Netherlands v Russian Federation)* (Provisional Measures, Order of 22 November 2013) ITLOS Reports 2013, 230, 246 [69].

[14] *M/V 'Louisa' (Saint Vincent and the Grenadines v Kingdom of Spain)* (Merits) [2013] ITLOS Rep 4, 33 [92]; *Delimitation of the Maritime Boundary in the Atlantic Ocean (Ghana/ Côte d'Ivoire)* (Provisional Measures, Order of 25 April 2015) ITLOS Reports 2015, 146, 164– 65 [98], [104].

[15] *M/V 'Saiga' (No 2)* (n 13) 24, 39 [46].

[16] See *Detention of three Ukrainian naval vessels* (n 9) Declaration of Judge Kittichaisaree paras 26–29, Declaration of Judge Lijnzaad paras 5–8.

The threshold of prima facie means a court or tribunal called upon to rule on a request for provisional measures does not need, at this stage of the proceedings, to settle the parties' claims in respect of the rights and obligations in dispute and is not called upon to determine definitively whether the rights which they each wish to see protected exist. In other words, ITLOS need not concern itself with the competing claims of the parties but need only to satisfy itself that the rights the requesting party claims on the merits and seeks to protect are 'at least plausible',[17] taking into account the legal arguments made by the parties and evidence available before it,[18] and that there is a link between the rights claimed by the requesting party and the provisional measures it seeks.[19] Where the plausibility of one or more of the rights asserted by the applicant would have required the examination of legal and factual issues which were not fully addressed by the parties in the proceedings before ITLOS, ITLOS need not determine the plausible character of such right(s) at this stage of the proceedings provided that it has established that the other right(s) asserted by the applicant is/are plausible.[20]

The issue of exhaustion of local remedies should be examined at a future stage of the proceedings.[21]

ITLOS may not prescribe provisional measures unless it finds there is 'a real and imminent risk that irreparable prejudice may be caused to the rights of the parties in dispute'. In this regard, urgency is required in order to exercise the power to prescribe provisional measures—that is to say 'the need to avert a real and imminent risk that irreparable prejudice may be caused to rights at issue before the final decision is delivered', and the decision whether there exists imminent risk of irreparable prejudice can only be taken on a case-by-case basis in light of all relevant factors.[22] For instance, in *Detention of three Ukrainian naval vessels (Ukraine v Russian Federation)*, ITLOS found a real and imminent risk of irreparable prejudice to Ukraine's

---

[17] *Delimitation of the Maritime Boundary in the Atlantic Ocean* (n 14) 158 [58]; *'Enrica Lexie'* (n 6) 197 [83]–[84].

[18] *M/T 'San Padre Pio'* (n 9) para 108.

[19] *Delimitation of the Maritime Boundary in the Atlantic Ocean* (n 14) 159 [63].

[20] *M/T 'San Padre Pio'* (n 9) para 110.

[21] *M/V 'Louisa'* (Provisional Measures) (n 5) 69 [68]. See also *'Enrica Lexie'* (n 6) 194 [67].

[22] *Delimitation of the Maritime Boundary in the Atlantic Ocean* (n 14) 155–56 [39]–[43], citing, inter alia, *M/V 'Louisa'* (Provisional Measures) (n 5) 69 [72]. For a criticism of ITLOS's 'non-uniform' practice in taking account of the urgency in prescribing or not prescribing provisional measures, see Yoshifumi Tanaka, 'The Requirement of Urgency in the Jurisprudence of ITLOS Concerning Provisional Measures' in Angela Del Vecchio and Roberto Virzo (eds), *Interpretation of the United Nations Convention on the Law of the Sea by International Courts and Tribunals* (Springer 2019) 107–24.

rights pending the constitution and functioning of the Annex VII arbitral tribunal; hence, the urgency of the situation requiring the prescription of provisional measures under Article 290(5) due to the seriousness of the circumstances. In reaching this conclusion, ITLOS considered a warship an expression of the sovereignty of the State whose flag it flew and enjoyed immunity under UNCLOS and general international law. Since any action affecting the immunity of warships was capable of causing serious harm to the dignity and sovereignty of a State and had the potential to undermine its national security, the actions taken by Russia could irreparably prejudice the rights claimed by Ukraine to the immunity of its naval vessels and their servicemen if the Annex VII arbitral tribunal adjudged those rights to belong to Ukraine. In addition, the risk of irreparable prejudice was real and ongoing under the circumstances of the case. The continued deprivation of liberty and freedom of Ukraine's 24 servicemen arrested while on board the vessels also raised humanitarian concerns.[23]

In prescribing provisional measures to prevent 'serious harm to the marine environment', ITLOS need not require such harm to be irreparable.[24] In one case, ITLOS prescribed provisional measures ordering the parties to act with 'prudence and caution' to ensure effective conservation measures were taken to prevent serious harm to the stock of southern bluefin tuna.[25] In another case, ITLOS reasoned that 'prudence and caution' required Ireland and the UK to cooperate in exchanging information concerning risks or effects of the operation of the Mixed Oxide Fuel (MOX) plant in Sellafield, UK, on the coast of the Irish Sea and in devising ways to deal with them, as appropriate.[26] In yet another case, ITLOS found the impugned land reclamation works by Singapore might have adverse effects on the marine environment, and, therefore, 'prudence and caution' required Malaysia and Singapore to establish mechanisms for exchanging information and assessing the risks or effects of land reclamation works and devising ways to deal with them in the areas concerned. ITLOS, consequently, directed Singapore not to conduct its land reclamation in ways that might cause irreparable prejudice to Malaysia's rights or serious harm

---

[23] *Detention of three Ukrainian naval vessels* (n 9) paras 110–13.

[24] P Chandrasekhara Rao and Philippe Gautier, *The International Tribunal for the Law of the Sea: Law, Practice and Procedure* (Edward Elgar 2018) 132.

[25] *Southern Bluefin Tuna (Australia v Japan; New Zealand v Japan)* (Provisional Measures, Order of 27 August 1999) ITLOS Reports 1999, 280, 295 [77].

[26] *MOX Plant (Ireland v UK)* (Provisional Measures, Order of 3 December 2001) ITLOS Reports 2001, 95, 110 [84].

to the marine environment, taking especially into account the reports of the group of independent experts.[27] In the only provisional measure application to date in which ITLOS did not prescribe provisional measures, ITLOS, while noting that Article 192 of UNCLOS imposes an obligation on States to protect and preserve the marine environment, was satisfied with the respondent's assurances that there was no imminent threat or harm to the marine environment due to the presence of the applicant's vessel in question in the commercial dock where it was present, that the respondent's port authorities were continuously monitoring the situation, paying special attention to the fuel still loaded in the vessel and the oil spread in the different conducts and pipes on board, and that the respondent's authority concerned had an updated protocol for reacting against threats of any kind of environmental accident within the port and the maritime area in question.[28]

Finally, ITLOS may exercise jurisdiction to prescribe provisional measures where an international agreement other than UNCLOS so authorizes. This is the case of, for example, Article 31(2) of the 1995 UN Agreement for the Implementation of the Provisions of the UN Convention on the Law of the Sea of 10 December 1982 relating to the Conservation and Management of Straddling Fish Stocks and Highly Migratory Species Fish Stocks ('FSA').[29] Article 31(3) of the FSA stipulates, however, that a State Party to the FSA which is not party to UNCLOS may declare that, notwithstanding Article 290(5) of UNCLOS, ITLOS shall not be entitled to prescribe, modify, or revoke provisional measures without the agreement of such State.

3. Difference between Article 290(1) and Article 290(5) proceedings

As of this writing, 11 of the 29 cases before ITLOS involve requests for provisional measures. These requests are further divided into provisional measures prescribed by ITLOS under Article 290(1) pending ITLOS's judgment on the merits of the dispute, on the one hand, and provisional

---

[27] *Land Reclamation in and around the Straits of Johor (Malaysia v Singapore)* (Provisional Measures, Order of 8 October 2003) ITLOS Reports 2002, 10, 26 [96]–[99], 28 [106(2)].

[28] *M/V 'Louisa'* (Provisional Measures) (n 5) 69–70 [74]–[78].

[29] 2167 UNTS 88.

measures prescribed by ITLOS under Article 290(5) pending the constitution of an arbitral tribunal to which a dispute is being submitted, on the other hand. They differ in the following aspects.

First, provisional measures under Article 290(1) are incidental proceedings, whereas those under Article 290(5) are self-contained proceedings.[30] With regard to the latter, the applicant must first institute proceedings under Annex VII of UNCLOS against the respondent in a dispute concerning the interpretation or application of UNCLOS which appears to have existed between the parties on the date of the institution of arbitral proceedings. After the expiry of the two-week time limit provided for in Article 290(5) and pending the constitution of the Annex VII arbitral tribunal, the applicant may submit a request to ITLOS for prescription of provisional measures.[31] Article 89(4) of ITLOS's Rules requires a request for the prescription of provisional measures under Article 290(5) to also indicate the legal grounds upon which the arbitral tribunal which is to be constituted would have jurisdiction and the urgency of the situation, and a certified copy of the notification or of any other document instituting the proceedings before the arbitral tribunal to be annexed to the request.

Second, in Article 290(5) proceedings ITLOS has to ascertain whether the Annex VII arbitral tribunal to be constituted would have prima facie jurisdiction over the dispute. By contrast, in Article 290(1) proceedings ITLOS must determine whether, prima facie, ITLOS itself has jurisdiction over the dispute between the parties.[32] With regard to Article 290(5) proceedings, ITLOS's power to prescribe provisional measures has as its object the preservation of the rights of the parties pending the constitution and functioning of the Annex VII arbitral tribunal and, therefore, before prescribing provisional measures, ITLOS needs to satisfy itself that the rights which the applicant seeks to protect are at least plausible before the Annex VII arbitral tribunal.[33] ITLOS's Order prescribing provisional measures under Article 290(5) in no way prejudges the question of the jurisdiction of the Annex VII arbitral tribunal to deal with the merits of the case, or any

---

[30] Rao and Gautier (n 24) 129.

[31] *M/T 'San Padre Pio'* (n 9) para 44.

[32] *M/V 'Saiga' (No 2)* (n 13) 24 [25]–[30]; *Southern Bluefin Tuna* (n 25) 293 [40]; *MOX Plant* (n 26) 104 [35]; *Land Reclamation in and around the Straits of Johor* (n 27) 18 [30]; *'ARA Libertad'* (n 11) 340 [37]; *'Arctic Sunrise'* (n 13) 243 [58]; *'Enrica Lexie'* (n 6) 189 [33]; *Detention of three Ukrainian naval vessels* (n 9) para 36; *M/T 'San Padre Pio'* (n 9) para 45.

[33] *M/T 'San Padre Pio'* (n 9) para 77, citing *Delimitation of the Maritime Boundary in the Atlantic Ocean* (n 14) 158 [58]; *'Enrica Lexie'* (n 6) 197 [84]; *Detention of three Ukrainian naval vessels* (n 9) para 91.

questions relating to the admissibility of the applicant's claims or relating to the merits themselves, and leaves unaffected the rights of the applicant and the respondent to submit arguments in respect of those questions.[34] For instance, the Annex VII arbitral tribunal in *Southern Bluefin Tuna (New Zealand–Japan, Australia–Japan)*, finding it has no jurisdiction to entertain the merits of the dispute brought by Australia and New Zealand against Japan, revoked the provisional measures prescribed by ITLOS pursuant to Article 290(5).[35]

Third, any provisional measures to be prescribed by ITLOS under Article 290(5) will cover the duration between the date of the Order and the constitution and functioning of the Annex VII arbitral tribunal. However, ITLOS has held that there is nothing in Article 290 to suggest the measures prescribed by ITLOS must be confined to the period pending the constitution of the Annex VII arbitral tribunal—the provisional measures prescribed by ITLOS pursuant to Article 290(5) may remain applicable beyond that period.[36]

Fourth, the Annex VII arbitral tribunal may modify, revoke, or affirm those provisional measures prescribed by ITLOS in that case pursuant to Article 290(5).

Otherwise, the procedural rules and reasoning utilized by ITLOS apply to both types of provisional orders. This includes the precondition of urgency, which is specifically mentioned in paragraph 5 of Article 290, but not in the other paragraphs of that Article. As a special chamber of ITLOS has held in response to a request for the prescription of provisional measures under Article 290(1), 'urgency is required in order to exercise the power to prescribe provisional measures, that is to say the need to avert a real and imminent risk that irreparable prejudice may be caused to rights at issue before the final decision is delivered'.[37]

---

[34] *M/T 'San Padre Pio'* (n 9) para 145.

[35] *Southern Bluefin Tuna (New Zealand–Japan, Australia–Japan)* Award of 4 August 2000, RIAA vol VII, 1, 46–47 [65]–[66].

[36] *Land Reclamation in and around the Straits of Johor* (n 27) 22 [67]–[69]; *'Arctic Sunrise'* (n 13) 248 [84]–[85].

[37] *Delimitation of the Maritime Boundary in the Atlantic Ocean* (n 14) 156 [42], citing *Certain Activities Carried Out by Nicaragua in the Border Area (Costa Rica v Nicaragua)* (Request for the Indication of Provisional Measures: Order) [2013] ICJ Rep 398, 405 [25]. See also *M/T 'San Padre Pio'* (n 9) paras 77–131. According to Judge Treves's Separate Opinion in *Southern Bluefin Tuna* (n 25) 316 [2], '[t]he requirement of urgency is part of the very nature of provisional measures, as these measures are meant to preserve the rights of the parties pending the final decision (Article 290, paragraph 1, of the Convention)'.

The urgency factor in the context of Article 290(5) proceedings must be seen in the light of the fact that any provisional measures to be prescribed by ITLOS must be necessary pending the constitution of the Annex VII arbitral tribunal which, once constituted, may modify, revoke, or affirm those provisional measures. Yet, the duration between the date of ITLOS's Order prescribing provisional measures and the constitution and functioning of the Annex VII arbitral tribunal is not necessarily determinative for the assessment of the urgency of the situation or the period during which the prescribed measures are applicable. ITLOS carefully takes into account the fact that in practice the process of constituting an Annex VII arbitral tribunal pursuant to Article 3 of Annex VII may take several months and, once constituted, the arbitral tribunal will have to formulate its own rules of procedure and take other preparatory steps before it can become fully operational. For example, in *The 'Enrica Lexie' Incident (Italy v India)*, Italy instituted the Annex VII arbitral proceedings against India on 26 June 2015 and requested ITLOS to prescribe provisional measures under Article 290(5) of UNCLOS on 21 July 2015. ITLOS prescribed provisional measures on 24 August 2015. The Annex VII arbitral tribunal was constituted on 30 September 2015 and held its first procedural meeting with both parties on 18 January 2016. The arbitral tribunal had received Italy's request for prescription of provisional measures on 11 December 2015, but not until 29 April 2016 could the arbitral tribunal adopt an Order in respect of Italy's request—almost 10 months after Italy's instituting the Annex VII arbitral proceedings against India and eight months and five days after ITLOS's prescription of provisional measures pursuant to Article 290(5).

4. Default of appearance by one party

Of the 29 cases before ITLOS as of this writing, in only two cases did the respondent refuse to participate in the proceedings. The Russian Federation was the non-participating respondent in both cases, which concerned requests for provisional measures under Article 290(5) of UNCLOS.

ITLOS has explained in these two cases of default of appearance by the respondent that the absence of a party or failure of a party to defend its case does not constitute a bar to the proceedings and does not preclude ITLOS from prescribing provisional measures, provided the parties have been given an opportunity of presenting their observations on the subject. Where a party refuses to participate in the proceedings, the prescription of provisional measures must also take into account the procedural rights of both parties and ensure full implementation of the principle of equality of the parties in a situation where the absence of a party may hinder the regular conduct of the proceedings and affect the good administration of justice. The non-participating party could have facilitated ITLOS's task by furnishing ITLOS with fuller information on questions of fact and of law. However, the difficulty for ITLOS, in such circumstances, to evaluate the nature and scope of the respective rights of the parties to be preserved by provisional measures should not put the applicant at a disadvantage because of the non-appearance of the respondent in the proceedings. Therefore, ITLOS must identify and assess the respective rights of the parties involved on the best available evidence.[38]

In *Artic Sunrise (Kingdom of the Netherlands v Russian Federation)*, all communications pertaining to the case were transmitted by ITLOS to Russia and Russia was informed that, pursuant to Article 90(3) of the Rules of ITLOS, ITLOS was ready to take into account any observations that might be presented to it by a party before the closure of the hearing. Russia was thus given ample opportunity to present its observations, but declined to do so.[39] In *Detention of three Ukrainian naval vessels (Ukraine v Russian Federation)*, Russia declined to participate in the hearings in the case initiated by Ukraine. All communications relevant to the case were transmitted by ITLOS to Russia. Before the closure of the oral proceedings, Russia submitted a Memorandum to ITLOS, which ITLOS took into account pursuant to Article 90(3) of its Rules. ITLOS, therefore, considered that Russia was given ample opportunity to present its observations.[40]

5. Provisional measures to be prescribed

In considering whether to prescribe provisional measures, ITLOS must safeguard and balance the respective rights which may be adjudged in its judgment on the merits to belong to either party. In accordance with Article 89(5) of its Rules, ITLOS may prescribe measures different in whole

---

[38] 'Arctic Sunrise' (n 13) 242 [48], 243 [53]–[57]; *Detention of three Ukrainian naval vessels* (n 9) paras 26–29.

[39] 'Arctic Sunrise' (n 13) 242 [49]. See also Alex G Oude Elferink, 'The Russian Federation and the *Arctic Sunrise* Case: Hot Pursuit and Other Issues under the LOSC' (2016) 92 International Law Studies 381, 386–90, 405–06.

[40] *Detention of three Ukrainian naval vessels* (n 9) para 28.

or in part from those requested.[41] ITLOS has also ruled it may prescribe a bond or other financial security as a provisional measure for the release of the vessel and the persons detained although this is not requested by the applicant.[42]

Southern Bluefin Tuna concerns the dispute between Australia and New Zealand on one side and Japan on the other regarding the conservation of the population of southern bluefin tuna which was, according to the applicants, significantly overfished and was below commonly accepted thresholds for biologically safe parental biomass. Australia and New Zealand claimed that Japan's actions amounted to a failure to conserve and to cooperate in the conservation of the southern bluefin tuna stock. ITLOS ordered the parties to, inter alia, keep southern bluefin tuna catches to levels last agreed among them; ensure, unless they agreed otherwise, that their annual catches not exceed the annual national allocations at the levels last agreed by the parties of 5,265 tonnes, 6,065 tonnes, and 420 tonnes, respectively. Such precise measures might not have been ordered absent a prior agreement between the parties. The parties were also ordered to refrain from conducting an experimental fishing programme involving the taking of a catch of southern bluefin tuna, except with the agreement of the other parties or unless the experimental catch was counted against its annual national allocation. In addition, the parties were to resume negotiations without delay with a view to reaching agreement on measures for the conservation and management of southern bluefin tuna, as well as make further efforts to reach agreement with other States and fishing entities engaged in fishing for southern bluefin tuna, with a view to ensuring conservation and promoting the objective of optimum utilization of the stock.[43]

Land Reclamation in and around the Straits of Johor concerns land reclamation activities carried out by Singapore which allegedly impinged upon Malaysia's rights in and around the Straits of Johor that separate the island of Singapore from Malaysia. ITLOS ordered the parties to, inter alia, cooperate and, for this purpose, enter into consultations forthwith in order to establish promptly a group of independent experts entrusted with conducting a study to determine, within a period not exceeding one year from the date of this Order, the effects of the respondent's land reclamation, and with proposing, as appropriate, measures to deal with any adverse effects of

---

[41]   As in, eg, *M/V 'Saiga' (No 2)* (n 13) 39 [47]; *MOX Plant* (n 26) 110 [83].

[42]   *'Arctic Sunrise'* (n 13) 250 [93]; *M/T 'San Padre Pio'* (n 9) paras 137–38.

[43]   *Southern Bluefin Tuna* (n 25) 297–300 [90].

such land reclamation. The parties were ordered to exchange, on a regular basis, information on, and assess risks or effects of, the respondent's land reclamation works as well as implement their commitments noted in this Order and avoid any action incompatible with their effective implementation. The respondent was specifically directed by the Order not to conduct its land reclamation in ways that might cause irreparable prejudice to the applicant's rights or serious harm to the marine environment, taking especially into account the reports of the group of independent experts.[44]

In its request for provisional measures in 'ARA Libertad', Argentina claimed that the frigate 'ARA Libertad' was being illegally detained by the authorities of Ghana although the 'ARA Libertad' was a warship and the flagship of the Argentine Navy. It alleged that, at the time of its detention, the frigate was on an official visit to Ghana and that the Government of Argentina and the Government of Ghana had agreed upon the vessel's arrival at a designated port in Ghana. The captain of the ship and 44 crew members were still on board the ARA Libertad at the time of Argentina's application to ITLOS for provisional measures. Argentina submitted that the frigate was detained pursuant to an order rendered by a Ghanaian court in violation of international law and, in particular, of the immunities enjoyed by warships. ITLOS ordered the respondent to forthwith and unconditionally release the frigate as well as ensure the frigate, its Commander, and crew were able to leave the port where they were being detained and the maritime areas under the respondent's jurisdiction, and, for this purpose, ensure the frigate was resupplied.[45]

In 'Arctic Sunrise' the respondent was ordered to immediately release the vessel 'Arctic Sunrise' and all persons who had been detained, upon the posting of a bond or other financial security by the applicant in the amount of €3.6 million. Upon the posting of the bond or other financial security, the respondent was ordered to ensure the vessel and all persons who had been detained were allowed to leave the respondent's territory and maritime areas under its jurisdiction.[46]

In *Detention of three Ukrainian naval vessels* ITLOS ordered Russia to immediately release the three detained Ukrainian naval vessels and return them to Ukraine's custody as well as immediately release the 24 detained Ukrainian servicemen and allow them to return to Ukraine.[47]

---

[44] *Land Reclamation in and around the Straits of Johor* (n 27) 27–28 [106].
[45] *'ARA Libertad'* (n 11) 350 [108].
[46] *'Arctic Sunrise'* (n 13) 252 [105].
[47] *Detention of three Ukrainian naval vessels* (n 9) para 124.

M/T 'San Padre Pio' concerns Nigeria's arrest and detention of the M/T 'San Padre Pio', a motor tanker flying the flag of Switzerland, its crew, and cargo, for having allegedly engaged in ship-to-ship transfers of gasoil in Nigeria's exclusive economic zone. ITLOS accepted Switzerland's request for Nigeria to immediately release the vessel, its cargo, the Master, and the three officers and to ensure the M/T 'San Padre Pio', its cargo, the Master, and the three officers were allowed to leave the territory and maritime areas under Nigeria's jurisdiction. This was because the vessel and the crew and other persons on board appeared to remain vulnerable to the constant danger to their safety and security, including having been subject to armed attack on 15 April 2019, endangering the lives of those on board the vessel, while piracy and armed robbery against ships were reportedly frequent in the maritime region where the vessel was kept in detention.[48] In order to preserve Nigeria's rights, ITLOS ordered Switzerland to post a bond or other financial security in the amount of US$14 million with Nigeria in the form of a bank guarantee and to undertake to ensure the Master and the three officers were available and present at the criminal proceedings in Nigeria, if the Annex VII arbitral tribunal was to find the arrest and detention of the vessel, its cargo, and its crew and the exercise of jurisdiction by Nigeria in relation to the event in question did not violate UNCLOS. This Order duly took into consideration the value of the vessel and its cargo as well as the fact that the vessel's Master and three officers were of Ukrainian nationality and Ukraine, which was a third party to the dispute, did not extradite its own nationals.[49]

In *Delimitation of the Maritime Boundary in the Atlantic Ocean (Ghana/ Côte d'Ivoire)* the special chamber of ITLOS declined to prescribe an order suspending all exploration or exploitation activities conducted by or on behalf of Ghana in the disputed maritime area, including activities in respect of which drilling has already taken place, as requested by Côte d'Ivoire, because this would entail the risk of financial loss to Ghana, cause prejudice to the rights claimed by Ghana, and create an undue burden upon Ghana.[50] Nonetheless, in assessing the real and imminent risk of irreparable prejudice, ITLOS reasoned that while the alleged loss of the revenues derived from oil exploration or exploitation permits in the disputed area issued by Ghana could be the subject of adequate financial compensation in the

---

[48] *M/T 'San Padre Pio'* (n 9) paras 128–31.
[49] ibid para 146.
[50] *Delimitation of the Maritime Boundary in the Atlantic Ocean* (n 14) 164 [100].

future, the ongoing exploration and exploitation activities conducted by Ghana in the disputed area would result in a modification of the physical characteristics of the continental shelf; hence, a risk of irreparable prejudice which could not be fully compensated by financial reparations since it would never be able to restore the status quo in respect of the seabed and subsoil.[51]

Ghana was, therefore, ordered to (a) take all necessary steps to ensure no new drilling either by Ghana or under its control take place in the disputed area; (b) take all necessary steps to prevent information resulting from past, ongoing, or future exploration activities conducted by Ghana, or with its authorization, in the disputed area which was not already in the public domain from being used in any way whatsoever to the detriment of Côte d'Ivoire; and (c) carry out strict and continuous monitoring of all activities undertaken by Ghana or with its authorization in the disputed area with a view to ensuring the prevention of serious harm to the marine environment. Both parties were ordered to take all necessary steps to prevent serious harm to the marine environment, including the continental shelf and its superjacent waters, in the disputed area and to cooperate to that end as well as to pursue cooperation and refrain from any unilateral action that might lead to aggravating the dispute.[52]

In 'MOX' Plant Ireland claimed that the UK's authorization to open a new facility in Sellafield bordering the Irish Sea in order to reprocess spent nuclear fuel into a new fuel, known as mixed oxide fuel, or MOX, would contribute to the pollution of the Irish Sea, and Ireland underlined the potential risks involved in the transportation of radioactive material to and from the plant. ITLOS did not accede to Ireland's request for ITLOS to order the UK to immediately suspend the UK's authorization of the MOX plant or, alternatively, take such other measures as are necessary to prevent with immediate effect the operation of the MOX plant, as well as to take other related measures. The dispute was characterized by an almost total lack of agreement on the scientific evidence with respect to the possible consequences of the operation of the MOX plant on the marine environment of the Irish Sea. Under these circumstances of scientific uncertainty and the short period before the constitution of the Annex VII arbitral tribunal, ITLOS decided the urgency of the situation did not require it to lay down, as binding legal obligations, the measures requested by Ireland.

---

[51] ibid 163 [88]–[90].
[52] ibid 166 [108(1)].

Instead, ITLOS ordered the parties to cooperate, convinced that the results of the consultations prescribed would include a common understanding of the scientific evidence and a common appreciation of the measures which had to be taken with respect to the MOX plant to prevent harm to the marine environment.[53] That duty to cooperate is a fundamental principle in the prevention of pollution of the marine environment under Part XII of UNCLOS and general international law.[54] Ireland and the UK were ordered to cooperate and, for this purpose, to enter into consultations forthwith in order to (a) exchange further information with regard to possible consequences for the Irish Sea arising out of the commissioning of the MOX plant; (b) monitor risks or the effects of the operation of the MOX plant for the Irish Sea; and (c) devise, as appropriate, measures to prevent pollution of the marine environment which might result from the operation of the MOX plant.[55] In the same vein, in *Delimitation of the Maritime Boundary in the Atlantic Ocean*, a case concerning Article 290(1), the special chamber of ITLOS ruled that even where there was insufficient evidence to support the applicant's allegations that the impugned activities by the respondent were such as to create an imminent risk of serious harm to the environment, the parties had the duty to cooperate since they should 'act with prudence and caution to prevent serious harm to the marine environment' thanks to, inter alia, Article 192 of UNCLOS imposing an obligation on States to protect the marine environment and the general obligation of States to ensure activities within their jurisdiction and control respect the environment of other States.[56] Therefore, ITLOS ordered the respondent to carry out strict and continuous monitoring of all activities undertaken by the respondent or with its authorization in the disputed maritime area so as to ensure the prevention of the serious harm to the marine environment.[57]

In its Orders prescribing provisional measures, ITLOS frequently orders or recommends the parties to ensure no action shall be taken by their

---

[53] Joint declaration of Judges Caminos, Yamamoto, Park, Akl, Marsit, Eiriksson, and Jesus in *MOX Plant* (n 26) 113.

[54] *MOX Plant* (n 26) 110 [81]–[82].

[55] ibid 111 [89].

[56] *Delimitation of the Maritime Boundary in the Atlantic Ocean* (n 14) 159–61 [67]–[73], citing *Legality of the Threat or Use of Nuclear Weapons* (Advisory Opinion) [1996] ICJ Rep 226, 241–42 [29]; *M/V 'Louisa'* (Provisional Measures) (n 5) 70 [76]–[77]; *Southern Bluefin Tuna* (n 25) 296 [77]; *Responsibilities and obligations of States with respect to activities in the Area* (Advisory Opinion) ITLOS Reports 2011, 10, 46 [132].

[57] *Delimitation of the Maritime Boundary in the Atlantic Ocean* (n 14) 166 [108(1)(c)].

respective authorities or, as the case may be, vessels flying their flag which might aggravate or extend the dispute.[58]

A sensitive issue is whether ITLOS should order the respondent to refrain from or suspend its domestic court proceedings pending the eventual settlement of the dispute between the parties, as this might be seen as interfering in the judicial process of a State and its domestic court that enforces its law protect its rights.[59] In 'Saiga' (No 2) ITLOS ordered Guinea to refrain from taking or enforcing any judicial or administrative measure against the 'Saiga', its Master and the other members of the crew, its owners, or operators, in connection with the incidents leading to the arrest and detention of the vessel on 28 October 1997 and to the subsequent prosecution and conviction of the Master.[60]

'Enrica Lexie' concerns the dispute arising from an incident on 15 February 2012 approximately 20.5 nm off the Western coast of India involving the 'Enrica Lexie', an oil tanker flying the Italian flag, and India's subsequent exercise of criminal jurisdiction over the incident and over two Italian marines from the Italian Navy who were deployed on board the oil tanker to protect it against piracy. The oil tanker was intercepted by the Indian Navy shortly after the incident. According to India, the two Italian marines shot and killed two Indian fishermen on board an Indian fishing vessel on suspicion that the latter were pirates. The two Italian marines were formally subject to the custody of the Indian courts and were still being deprived of liberty at the time of Italy's application to ITLOS for prescription

---

[58] eg, *M/V 'Saiga' (No 2)* (n 13) 40 [52]; *Southern Bluefin Tuna* (n 25) 297 [90]. This is in line with

> the principle universally accepted by international tribunals ... to the effect that the parties to a case must abstain from any measure capable of exercising a prejudicial effect in regard to the execution of the decision to be given, and, in general, not allow any step of any kind to be taken which might aggravate or extend the dispute. *Electricity Company of Sofia and Bulgaria*, Order of 5 December 1939, PCIJ Series A/B, No 79 p 199,

quoted in *LaGrand (Germany v United States of America)* (Merits) [2001] ICJ Rep 466, 503 [103] and see also the ICJ judgments cited in that paragraph.

[59] cf, eg, paras 16–18 of Judge Lucky's separate opinion in *Detention of three Ukrainian naval vessels* (n 9); para 44 of Judge Lucky's dissenting opinion and para 82 of Judge Gao's dissenting opinion in *M/T 'San Padre Pio'* (n 9). See also Douglas Guilfoyle and Cameron A Miles, 'Provisional Measures and the MV *Arctic Sunrise*' (2014) 108 American JIL 271, 276, 281–82, 286 criticizing ITLOS's prioritization of human rights and the applicant's interest in freedom of navigation over the respondent's potentially legitimate concerns to enforce its own laws in *Arctic Sunrise* (n 13).

[60] *M/V 'Saiga' (No 2)* (n 13) 39–40 [52(1)]. ITLOS reasoned that otherwise the rights of the applicant would not be fully preserved pending the final decision of ITLOS on the merits in that case (ibid 38 [41]).

of provisional measures on 21 July 2015. On 24 August 2015 ITLOS ordered both Italy and India to suspend all court proceedings and to refrain from initiating new ones which might aggravate or extend the dispute submitted to the Annex VII arbitral tribunal, jeopardize, or prejudice the carrying out of any decision which the arbitral tribunal might render.[61]

In the two most recent provisional measures cases in 2019, after duly taking all relevant factors into consideration ITLOS did not consider it necessary to require the respective respondents to suspend all court and administrative proceedings against the vessels and crews that were the subjects of the respective applicants' requests and to refrain from initiating new proceedings against them. —Nonetheless, ITLOS considered it appropriate to order the parties to refrain from taking any action which might aggravate or extend the disputes submitted to the Annex VII arbitral tribunal.[62]

6. Implementation of orders for provisional measures

Article 290(6) of UNCLOS obliges the parties to the dispute to comply promptly with any provisional measures prescribed under Article 290. For this purpose, Article 95 of the Rules of ITLOS requires each party to submit to ITLOS reports and information on compliance with any provisional measures prescribed, and it may be necessary for ITLOS to request further information from the parties on the implementation of provisional measures.[63] In practice, ITLOS authorizes its President to request such information from the parties within a specified period.[64] ITLOS also deems it consistent with the purpose of proceedings under Article 290(5) for the parties to also submit reports and information to the Annex VII arbitral tribunal, unless the arbitral tribunal decides otherwise.[65]

---

[61] 'Enrica Lexie' (n 6) 205 [141].

[62] M/T 'San Padre Pio' (n 9) paras 142, 146(2); Detention of three Ukrainian naval vessels (n 9) paras 119–20, 124(1)(c).

[63] eg, M/V 'Saiga' (No 2) (n 13) 39 [50].

[64] In Detention of three Ukrainian naval vessels (n 9) the parties were to submit an initial report no later than one calendar month after the rendering of the Order, whereas in M/T 'San Padre Pio' (n 9) the parties were to submit an initial report no later than 16 days after the rendering of the Order. In fact, ITLOS intended to order the parties in the latter case to submit the initial report within two weeks but since the Order was rendered on a Saturday, the deadline for the submission of the initial report was extended until the following Monday, making it 16 days in total.

[65] M/T 'San Padre Pio' (n 9) para 144.

In *Detention of three Ukrainian naval vessels*, in which Russia declined to participate in the oral hearings, ITLOS ordered Russia to immediately release the three detained Ukrainian naval vessels and return them to Ukraine's custody as well as immediately release the 24 detained Ukrainian servicemen and allow them to return to Ukraine. Russia reported to ITLOS on 25 June 2019 that ITLOS's Order had been translated into Russian and communicated to its competent authorities in charge of the criminal proceedings in respect of the 24 Ukrainian servicemen and naval vessels, adding that the Russian authorities had proposed to their Ukrainian counterparts specific procedural measures which, within the framework of the Russian legislation, would allow the release of the servicemen from Russian custody and the handover of the naval vessels to Ukraine. For its part, Ukraine immediately reported to ITLOS on 26 June 2019 that Russia had just requested Ukraine to offer 'written guarantees' to the Russian authorities, inconsistent with ITLOS's Order for Russia to 'immediately release' the vessels and servicemen without any condition unilaterally imposed by Russia to further aggravate the dispute. Russia subsequently released the 24 servicemen three months and a half after ITLOS's Order, without the parties submitting reports to ITLOS on the release of these servicemen. ITLOS received another report from Russia on 22 November 2019, stating the three Ukrainian naval vessels had been 'handed over to Ukraine' on 18 November 2019.[66]

In *M/T 'San Padre Pio'* both parties submitted several reports to ITLOS because many months after the Order Switzerland still could not fulfil the conditions for the release of the vessel and its crew since the steps to be taken by Switzerland 'involve[d] various actors'.[67] Not until 7 November 2019 did Switzerland send by way of a diplomatic note a copy of the contract for a bank guarantee for the sum of US$14 million to Nigeria for approval. At the same time, the contract was sent by the Swiss bank responsible for organizing the bank guarantee to the Nigerian bank where the guarantee would be deposited. Switzerland also submitted to ITLOS a copy of the assurances received from the four officers concerned regarding their undertaking to be available and present at the criminal proceedings in Nigeria should the Annex VII arbitral tribunal find Nigeria did not violate UNCLOS. In

---

[66] By note verbale No 4562/H dated 22 November 2019 from the Russian Embassy in Berlin addressed to ITLOS.

[67] Notes from the Agent of Switzerland dated 22 July 2019 and 16 August 2019 addressed to the ITLOS Registrar.

addition, Switzerland enclosed a copy of the diplomatic note dated 19 July 2019 from the Ministry of Foreign Affairs of Ukraine addressed to the Federal Department of Foreign Affairs of Switzerland declaring it would 'cooperate with Nigeria for international legal assistance in accordance with international treaties' to which both Ukraine and Nigeria were parties 'and with norms and rules of national legislation of Ukraine' should the Annex VII arbitral tribunal find Nigeria's impugned acts not in breach of UNCLOS. However, the parties let the time limit for the constitution of the Annex VII arbitral tribunal[68] elapse. Nigeria subsequently declared on 2 December 2019 its acceptance of ITLOS's jurisdiction over the dispute. On 17 December 2019, Switzerland and Nigeria transmitted a special agreement and notification to ITLOS, thereby transferring their dispute from the Annex VII arbitral tribunal to ITLOS.

7. Provisional measures by the Seabed Disputes Chamber

By virtue of Article 290(5), the Seabed Disputes Chamber may, with respect to the activities in the Area, prescribe, modify, or revoke provisional measures in accordance with Article 290 if it considers that prima facie the tribunal which is to be constituted would have jurisdiction and that the urgency of the situation so requires. Therefore, the other paragraphs of Article 290, including paragraph 1, applies *mutatis mutandis* to the Chamber and the Chamber may exercise jurisdiction regarding provisional measures in disputes duly submitted to it under Part XI (The Area) of UNCLOS.[69]

---

[68] Art 3 of Annex VII requires the party instituting the proceedings before the Annex VII arbitral tribunal to appoint one member of the arbitral tribunal at the time of the notification of the initiation of the arbitration, after which the other party shall, within 30 days of receipt of the said notification, appoint one member of the arbitral tribunal. The other member(s) shall be appointed by agreement between the parties. If, within 60 days of receipt of the said notification, the parties are unable to reach agreement on the appointment of one or more of the members of the tribunal to be appointed by agreement, or on the appointment of the President, the remaining appointment or appointments shall be made at the request of a party to the dispute within two weeks of the expiration of the aforementioned 60-day period, as follows. Unless the parties agree that any appointment shall be made by a person or a third State chosen by the parties, the President of ITLOS shall make the necessary appointments within a period of 30 days of the receipt of the request and in consultation with the parties. If the President is unable to act or is a national of one of the parties to the dispute, the appointment shall be made by the next senior ITLOS judge who is available and is not a national of one of the parties.

[69] Tullio Treves, 'Article 290 Provisional Measures' in Alexander Proelss (ed), *United Nations Convention on the Law of the Sea: A Commentary* (Hart 2017) 1868.

There is no discrete procedure governing requests for provisional measures to be prescribed by the Seabed Disputes Chamber. Article 115 of the Rules of ITLOS stipulates that proceedings in contentious cases before the Seabed Disputes Chamber and its ad hoc chambers shall, subject to the provisions of UNCLOS, the Statute, and these Rules relating specifically to the Seabed Disputes Chamber and its ad hoc chambers, be governed by the Rules applicable in contentious cases before ITLOS. A question has been raised as to whether Article 25(2) of the ITLOS Statute and Article 91 of the Rules of ITLOS governing the use of the Chamber of Summary Procedure when ITLOS is not in session or there is an insufficient number of ITLOS judges to constitute a quorum would also apply to cases before the Seabed Disputes Chamber. According to some commentators, these provisions would not apply to the Seabed Disputes Chamber due to its special jurisdictional status.[70]

---

[70] Sotiorios-Ioannis Lekkas and Christopher Staker, 'Art 25 Annex VI' in Proelss (n 69) 2399.

7

ITLOS's Jurisprudential Contributions

Present and Future

1. Present

a) Resolution of ongoing disputes

The existence of ITLOS and the willingness of States to utilize ITLOS[1] may play an important role in the resolution of ongoing disputes even prior to the start of the actual, initial written, proceedings at ITLOS.[2] This happened in the *'Chaisiri Reefer 2' (Panama v Yemen)* (Prompt Release) case.[3] On 3 July 2001, an application was submitted to ITLOS for the prompt release of the 'Chaisiri Reefer 2', a vessel flying the flag of Panama, and its crew arrested by Yemeni coastguard officials on 3 May 2001 for alleged violation of Yemen's fishery laws. According to Panama's application, the vessel's cargo of 765.74 metric tons of frozen fish, valued at US$950,332, was offloaded after arriving at the designated Yemeni port. On 16 June 2001 Yemen's Court of Public Assets delivered a judgment ordering the release of the vessel and the payment of a commercial guarantee which the vessel's shipowners furnished on the same day. However, the vessel was not released and its captain and 15 crew members were held on board. Panama requested ITLOS to order the immediate release of the vessel, its cargo, and crew. On 13 July

---

[1] See also International Tribunal for the Law of the Sea, *The Contribution of the International Tribunal for the Law of the Sea to the Rule of Law: 1996–2016* (Brill/Nijhoff 2017), which contains the proceedings of the Symposium on 'The Contribution of the Tribunal to the Rule of Law' to celebrate the twentieth anniversary of ITLOS, held at ITLOS on 5 October 2016; P Chandrasekhara Rao and Philippe Gautier, *The International Tribunal for the Law of the Sea: Law, Practice and Procedure* (Edward Elgar2018) ch 5.

[2] Ted L McDorman, 'An Overview of International Fisheries Disputes and the International Tribunal for the Law of the Sea' (2002) 40 Canadian YBIL 119, 148.

[3] *'Chaisiri Reefer 2' (Panama v Yemen)*, Order of 13 July 2001, ITLOS Reports 2001, 82.

2001, following an agreement between Panama and Yemen according to which the vessel, its cargo, and crew were released with the guarantee from the Government of Yemen that the same load which had been unloaded from the vessel would be loaded back, the case was discontinued and removed from ITLOS's List of cases. The same may be said of the *Swordfish Stocks* case,[4] discussed in Chapter 3, which was brought before ITLOS and then withdrawn.

Provisional measures ordered by ITLOS have been instrumental in bringing the disputing parties together and paved the way for the eventual resolution of their disputes, including by diplomatic means even when such provisional measures prescribed by ITLOS pursuant to Article 290(5) of UNCLOS may be subsequently revoked by Annex VII arbitral tribunals, as in *Southern Bluefin Tuna (New Zealand–Japan, Australia–Japan)* where the Annex VII arbitral tribunal, finding it had no jurisdiction to entertain the merits of the dispute brought by Australia and New Zealand against Japan, revoked the provisional measures prescribed by ITLOS. However, the tribunal considered the provisional measure proceedings brought before ITLOS to be constructive. It added that its revocation of ITLOS's Order prescribing provisional measures did not mean the parties could disregard the effects of that Order or their own decisions made in conformity with it. ITLOS's Order and those decisions— and the recourse to ITLOS that had given rise to them—as well as the consequential proceedings before the Annex VII tribunal, had had an impact; not merely in the suspension of Japan's unilateral experimental fishing programme during the period ITLOS's Order was in force, but also on the perspectives and actions of the parties which increasingly manifested flexibility of approach to the problems dividing them, thus making them close to the conclusion of an agreement on the principle of having an experimental fishing programme and on the tonnage of that programme. Furthermore, the possibility of renewed negotiations on other elements of their differences was real, with ITLOS's aforesaid Order having played a significant role in encouraging the parties to make progress on the issue of third-party fishing and ensuring progress in settling the dispute between the parties.[5]

---

[4] *Conservation and Sustainable Exploitation of Swordfish Stocks (Chile/European Union)*, Order of 16 December 2009, ITLOS Reports 2008–10, 13.

[5] *Southern Bluefin Tuna (New Zealand–Japan, Australia–Japan)* Award of 4 August 2000, RIAA vol VII, 1, 46–47 [65]–[69].

In *Land Reclamation in and around the Straits of Johor (Malaysia v Singapore)*,[6] the work by the group of experts established by both parties pursuant to ITLOS's Order formed the basis of the Settlement Agreement between the parties for the Annex VII arbitral tribunal in that case to endorse as a final award according to the joint request of the parties.[7]

Detention of three Ukrainian naval vessels (Ukraine v Russian Federation),[8] is the ITLOS case with the highest profile to date. It has played a role in a breakthrough in the process of normalization of Ukrainian–Russian relations after the armed conflict in Crimea starting in early 2014. Before the functioning of the Annex VII arbitral tribunal, Russia released the 24 servicemen as part of a prisoner exchange agreement on 7 September 2019, three months and a half after ITLOS's prescription of provisional measures ordering Russia to immediately release the three detained Ukrainian naval vessels and return them to Ukraine's custody as well as immediately release the 24 detained Ukrainian servicemen and allow them to return to Ukraine. ITLOS's Order gave weight to Ukraine and its allies in pressuring Russia to release these servicemen. Although their release was part of a prisoner exchange deal between Russia and Ukraine, that could be seen as a face-saving measure by the former. On 18 November 2019, three days before the parties were to appear before the Annex VII arbitral tribunal in that case, the three Ukrainian naval vessels were unconditionally released by Russia and returned to Ukraine. Subsequently, Russia officially notified ITLOS that the vessels had been 'handed over to Ukraine'.[9] Admittedly, the release of the vessels and servicemen did not lay to rest the dispute between the parties, as Ukraine wanted the arbitral tribunal to rule that Russia had violated Articles 32 (immunities of warships and other government ships operated for non-commercial purposes), 58 (rights and duties of other States in the exclusive economic zone), 95 (immunity of warships on the high seas), and 96 (immunity of ships used only on government non-commercial service) of UNCLOS, and that Russia was obligated to pay appropriate compensation to Ukraine. In Ukraine's submission to the arbitral tribunal, although Russia had released the servicemen, criminal proceedings against them

---

[6] *Land Reclamation in and around the Straits of Johor (Malaysia v Singapore)* (Provisional Measures, Order of 8 October 2003) ITLOS Reports 2003, 10.

[7] *Case concerning Land Reclamation by Singapore in and around the Straits of Johor (Malaysia v Singapore)*, decision of 1 September 2005, RIAAA vol XXVII, 133, 139–41 [18]–[25].

[8] *Detention of three Ukrainian naval vessels* (Ukraine v Russian Federation) (Provisional Measures, Order of 25 May 2019).

[9] By note verbale No 4562/H dated 22 Nov 2019 from the Russian Embassy in Berlin addressed to ITLOS.

continued, thereby denying the immunity of the Ukrainian servicemen, and Russia had seized weapons, communication equipment, and documents from the vessels before returning them to Ukraine, in violation of ITLOS's Order of 25 May 2019.[10] Nevertheless, the developments after ITLOS had issued its Order in May 2019 were positive enough to enable the Ukrainian President and his Russian counterpart to meet face-to-face in Paris on 9 and 10 December 2019 in the presence of the French President and the German Chancellor in a renewed effort to end the conflict between Ukraine and Russia.

One of the major perennial challenges for international law is compliance with international legal obligations, including judgments and orders of international courts and tribunals.[11] Compliance with ITLOS's judgments and Orders is to be expected as a matter of course even in cases of non-appearance by the respondent. In *'Arctic Sunrise' (Kingdom of the Netherlands v Russian Federation)*,[12] Russia informed the Netherlands that since Russia did not accept the arbitration procedure under Annex VII to UNCLOS initiated by the Netherlands concerning Russia's arrest and detention of the 'Arctic Sunrise', an icebreaker flying the flag of the Netherlands operated by Greenpeace International, and its crew, Russia would not participate in the proceedings before ITLOS in respect of the Netherlands' request for the prescription of provisional measures under Article 290(5) of UNCLOS. Despite Russia's non-participation in the proceedings before ITLOS and the subsequently constituted Annex VII arbitral tribunal, a full and final settlement in that case was reportedly reached between the Netherlands and Russia on 17 May 2019, whereby Greenpeace International would be paid €2.7 million by Russia. This final

---

[10] *Dispute Concerning the Detention of Ukrainian Naval Vessels and Servicemen (Ukraine v the Russian Federation)* Permanent Court of Arbitration Case No 2019–28.

[11] Oscar Schachter, *International Law in Theory and Practice* (Martinus Nijhoff 1991) 184–249, 389–417; Joseph Sinde Warioba, 'Monitoring Compliance with and Enforcement of Binding Decisions of International Courts' (2001) 5 Max Planck YB United Nations Law 41; Karen J Alter, 'Do International Courts Enhance Compliance with International Law?' (2002) 25 Review of Asian & Pacific Studies 51; Andrew T Guzman, 'A Compliance-Based Theory of International Law' (2002) 90 California L Rev 1823; Carmela Lutmar, Cristiane L Carneiro, and Sarah McLaughlin Mitchell, 'Formal Commitments and States' Interests: Compliance in International Relations' (2016) 42 Int'l Interactions 559.

[12] *'Arctic Sunrise' (Kingdom of the Netherlands v Russian Federation)* (Provisional Measures, Order of 25 October 2013) ITLOS Reports 2013, 230, 232–33 [9].

settlement forms part of the agreement between the Netherlands and Russia on the prevention of and response to any future incident similar to the one in the *'Arctic Sunrise'* case.[13]

b) Contribution to international efforts against IUU fishing

With regard to the widespread phenomenon of illegal, unreported, and unregulated ('IUU') fishing, ITLOS's jurisprudence has contributed significantly to the international fight against this scourge. In *M/V 'Virginia G' (Panama/Guinea-Bissau)*, ITLOS held that the regulation by a coastal State of bunkering of foreign vessels fishing in its exclusive economic zone is among those measures the coastal State may take in the zone to conserve and manage its living resources under Article 56 of UNCLOS read together with Article 62(4) thereof, requiring nationals of other States fishing in the exclusive economic zone to comply with the conservation measures and with the other terms and conditions established in the laws and regulations of the coastal State. Besides, Article 58 of UNCLOS, stipulating the rights and duties of other States in the exclusive economic zone, is to be read together with Article 56, to the effect that Article 58 does not prevent coastal States from regulating, under Article 56, bunkering of foreign vessels fishing in their exclusive economic zones—such competence derives from the sovereign rights of coastal States to explore, exploit, conserve, and manage natural resources.[14] In ITLOS's view, it is apparent from the list in Article 62(4) of UNCLOS that for all activities which may be regulated by a coastal State there must be a direct connection to fishing, and

---

[13] 'Russia to Award $3M to Greenpeace in Settlement' *Moscow Times* (17 May 2019) <www.themoscowtimes.com/2019/05/17/russia-to-award-3mln-to-greenpeace-in-settlement-a65632>; Joint statement by the Russian Federation and the Kingdom of the Netherlands on cooperation in the Arctic zone of the Russian Federation and dispute settlement, dated 17 May 2019 <www.mid.ru/ru/foreign_policy/news/-/asset_publisher/cKNonkJE02Bw/content/id/3651941?p_p_id=101_INSTANCE_cKNonkJE02Bw&_101_INSTANCE_cKNonkJE02Bw_languageId=en_GB> accessed 30 March 2020.

[14] *M/V 'Virginia G' (Panama/Guinea-Bissau)* (Judgment) ITLOS Reports 2014, 4, 69 [217], 70 [222]. See also Anastasia Telesetsky, 'The International Tribunal for the Law of the Sea: Seeking the Legitimacy of State Consent' in Nienke Grossman and others (eds), *Legitimacy and International Courts* (Cambridge University Press 2018) 197.

such connection exists for the bunkering of foreign vessels fishing in the exclusive economic zone since this enables them to continue their activities without interruption at sea.[15] ITLOS concludes the bunkering of foreign vessels engaged in fishing in the exclusive economic zone is an activity which may be regulated by the coastal State concerned, but the coastal State does not have such competence with regard to other bunkering activities, unless otherwise determined in accordance with UNCLOS.[16]

In *M/V 'Virginia G' (Panama/Guinea-Bissau)*, ITLOS rejected the counterclaim by Guinea-Bissau, the coastal State in that case, that Panama, as the flag State of the 'Virginia G', violated Article 91 of UNCLOS by granting its nationality to a ship without any genuine link to Panama, thereby facilitating the practice of illegal actions of bunkering without permission in Guinea-Bissau's exclusive economic zone, and that Guinea-Bissau was entitled to claim from Panama all damages and costs caused by the 'Virginia G' to Guinea-Bissau as a result of Panama granting the flag of convenience to the ship.[17] This concern by the coastal State as expressed by Guinea-Bissau in that case has been fully addressed by ITLOS' Advisory Opinion in *Request for Advisory Opinion submitted by the Sub-Regional Fisheries Commission*[18] in which ITLOS defines the flag State's obligations to take necessary measures, including those of enforcement, to ensure compliance by vessels flying its flag with the laws and regulations enacted by the coastal State in this regard, as well as the extent to which the flag State may be held liable for IUU fishing activities conducted by vessels sailing under its flag.

Indeed, ITLOS's *Sub-Regional Fisheries Commission* Advisory Opinion has elucidated several important international rules governing the fisheries regime under UNCLOS and produced concrete outcomes for the Member States of the Sub-Regional Fisheries Commission ('SRFC') in the West African region. In particular, the flag State shall take necessary measures, including those of enforcement, to ensure compliance by vessels flying its flag with the laws/regulations of the coastal State as regards marine living resources within their maritime zones. The flag State shall also adopt the

---

[15] *M/V 'Virginia G'* (Judgment) (n 14) 68 [215]. Art 62(4) enumerates the list of coastal States' laws and regulations consistent with UNCLOS that nationals of other States fishing in its exclusive economic zone must comply with, including 'enforcement procedures'.

[16] *M/V 'Virginia G'* (Judgment) (n 14) 70 [223].

[17] *M/V 'Virginia G' (Panama/Guinea-Bissau)* Order of 2 November 2012, ITLOS Reports 2012, 309, 311–12 [16]; *M/V 'Virginia G'* (Judgment) (n 14) 44–46 [110]–[118], 111 [407].

[18] *Request for Advisory Opinion submitted by the Sub-Regional Fisheries Commission* (Advisory Opinion) ITLOS Reports 2015, 4.

necessary administrative measures to ensure that fishing vessels flying its flag are not involved in illegal fishing in other States. However, these obligations by the flag State are 'due diligence' obligations of conduct and not of result. They require the flag State to deploy adequate means, exercise its best possible efforts, and do the utmost to fulfil them, and the liability of the flag State does not arise merely from a failure of vessels flying its flag to comply with the laws and regulations of the coastal State against IUU fishing.

With regard to the implementation of this Advisory Opinion,[19] four SRFC Member States have adopted new legislation to implement the Advisory Opinion: Guinea,[20] Mauritania,[21] Senegal,[22] and Sierra Leone.[23] In August 2016, the SRFC developed a subregional plan to implement ITLOS's Advisory Opinion with five priority areas of action. First, the institutional and legal frameworks at the national and subregional levels must be reinforced and fisheries governance enhanced. Second, monitoring, control, and surveillance of fisheries activities must be reinforced. Third, traditional fisheries must be supported and protected against the impact of IUU fishing. Fourth, shared stocks and/or stocks of common interest must be sustainably managed. Lastly, the SRFC must provide information, raise awareness, and mobilize in relation to IUU fishing and the management of shared stocks and stocks of common interest. Also in August 2016, the 27th Extraordinary Session of the Coordinating Committee of the SRFC adopted the draft Convention on Monitoring, Control, and Surveillance and its additional protocols on the subregional register of industrial fishing vessels including the list of IUU fishing vessels, on the exchange of information between Member States, and on the subregional observers programme. All the SRFC Member States except Guinea-Bissau have become party to the 2009 FAO Agreement on Port State Measures to Prevent, Deter, and Eliminate Illegal, Unreported, and Unregulated Fishing.[24]

---

[19] Source: Information on the Implementation of the Advisory Opinion in Case No 21 (ITLOS/46/7/Rev1, 9 July 2018).

[20] Maritime Fisheries Code of 14 September 2015 (Law No 2015/026/AN); Decree No A/ 2016 003/MPA/CAB of 8 January 2016 concerning approval of the plan for fisheries development and management for the year 2016.

[21] Maritime Fisheries Code of 29 July 2015 (Law No 2015–017 concerning the Maritime Fisheries Code).

[22] Maritime Fisheries Code of 13 July 2015 (Law No 2015–18 concerning the Maritime Fisheries Code).

[23] Fisheries and Aquaculture Act 2017.

[24] See <http://www.fao.org/fileadmin/user_upload/legal/docs/037t-e.pdf> accessed 31 October 2019.

c) Guidance on responsibility and liability regarding activities in the Area

The questions in *Responsibilities and obligations of States with respect to activities in the Area*—the first and only Advisory Opinion by the Seabed Disputes Chamber to date—arose out of two applications to the International Seabed Authority in 2008 for approval of a plan of work for exploration in the deep seabed areas reserved for the conduct of activities by the Authority through the Enterprise or in association with developing States pursuant to UNCLOS Annex III, Article 8.

These applications were submitted by Nauru Ocean Resources Inc (sponsored by Nauru) and Tonga Offshore Mining Ltd (sponsored by Tonga). Nauru proposed that an advisory opinion be sought from the Chamber regarding the responsibility and liability of sponsoring States, bearing in mind the fact that Nauru, like many other developing States, did not yet possess the technical and financial capacity to undertake seafloor mining in international waters. To participate effectively in activities in the Area, these States had to engage entities in the global private sector (in much the same way as some developing countries require foreign direct investment). Not only did some developing States lack the financial capacity to execute a seafloor mining project in international waters, but some also could not afford exposure to the legal risks potentially associated with such a project. Recognizing this, Nauru's sponsorship of Nauru Ocean Resources Inc was originally premised on the assumption that Nauru could effectively mitigate (with a high degree of certainty) the potential liabilities or costs arising from its sponsorship. This was important, as these liabilities or costs could far exceed the financial capacities of Nauru (as well as those of many other developing States). Ultimately, if sponsoring States are exposed to potential significant liabilities, Nauru, as well as other developing States, may be precluded from effectively participating in activities in the Area, which is one of the purposes and principles of Part XI of UNCLOS.[25]

The Chamber's Advisory Opinion effectively provides crucial guidance on the interpretation of the relevant sections of Part XI pertaining to responsibility and liability, so that developing States can assess whether it is within their capabilities to effectively mitigate such risks and in turn

---

[25] *Responsibilities and obligations of States with respect to activities in the Area* (Advisory Opinion) ITLOS Reports 2011, 10, 16–17 [4].

make an informed decision on whether or not to participate in activities in the Area.

d) Development of procedural rules and substantive law in international adjudication

ITLOS has also contributed significantly to the development of procedural rules of international adjudication[26] as well as substantive law, as in *M/V 'Norstar' (Panama v Italy)*, the first case in which a party raised preliminary objections to ITLOS's jurisdiction and admissibility as preliminary questions to be dealt with in incidental proceedings, the decision upon which was requested before any further proceedings on the merits. The case involved the arrest and detention by Italy of the M/V 'Norstar', a Panamanian-flagged oil tanker—owned by a Norwegian company and chartered to a Maltese company with an Italian company acting as a broker—which had been supplying gasoil to mega yachts beyond the territorial sea of any State. The vessel was seized in September 1998 for probative purposes (*corpus delicti*) while in a Spanish port at Italy's request for tax avoidance against Italy's fiscal law.

ITLOS clarified rules of procedure and evidence, the scope of the good faith obligation under Article 300 of UNCLOS, the causal link between a wrongful act and the damage, the duty to mitigate damage, and the scope of the freedom of navigation under Article 87 of UNCLOS. In particular, ITLOS held that no State may exercise jurisdiction over a foreign ship on the high seas. While the coastal State may regulate bunkering of foreign vessels engaged in fishing in its exclusive economic zone, it has no competence regarding other bunkering activities in the exclusive economic zone and on the high seas as part of a freedom of navigation under Article 87 of UNCLOS. Any act of interference, physical or otherwise, with navigation of foreign ships or any exercise of jurisdiction over such ships on the high seas is a breach of the freedom of navigation, unless justified by UNCLOS or other international treaties. The principle of exclusive flag jurisdiction on the high seas prohibits not only the exercise of enforcement jurisdiction on the high seas by States other than the flag State but also the extension of prescriptive jurisdiction to lawful activities conducted by foreign ships on the

---

[26] Niki Aloupi, 'ITLOS Procedural Rules: Between Change and Stability' (2019) 61 Questions of Int'l L 21.

high seas. Even when enforcement is carried out in internal waters, Article 87 may still be applicable and be breached if a State extends its criminal and customs laws extraterritorially to activities of foreign ships on the high seas and criminalizes them. The freedom of navigation does not include a right to sail towards the high seas from a port of the coastal State, though.[27]

There are several lessons learned from the *M/V 'Norstar'* case. Apparently there is no mathematical formula as to how long a ship can be detained, all depending on the circumstances. The seizing authority should keep an inventory of the items on the seized vessel and the vessel's condition at the time of seizure, whereas the ship owner and the charterer must also keep a copy of invoices, orders, and other documents proving how the vessel and its business operations are at the time of the seizure. ITLOS left open the question as to who has the duty to keep the maintenance of the seized vessel. ITLOS also left untouched two crucial international legal issues. First, ITLOS did not address the issue of the *general* obligation to promptly notify the flag State after the arrest or detention of a vessel flying its flag beyond Article 27(3) (regarding criminal jurisdiction on board a foreign ship passing through the territorial sea of the coastal State) and Article 73(4) (on the coastal State's arrest and detention of foreign vessels in the enforcement of laws and regulations in its exclusive economic zone), neither of which was applicable in the *M/V 'Norstar'* context. Second, Italy deliberately waited until the 'Norstar' was in a Spanish port before it requested Spain to execute the Decree of Seizure issued by Italy. Spain complied with Italy's request despite the fact that the M/V 'Norstar' had not committed and was not committing an offence against Spanish law and Panama, the flag State, was not party to the mutual legal assistance agreements binding on Italy and Spain. ITLOS did not address the legality or otherwise of enforcement jurisdiction of the port State against a foreign vessel in the context of this case.

e) Upholding human rights at sea

As regards human rights protection, ITLOS has consistently held that '[c]onsiderations of humanity must apply in the law of the sea, as they do

---

[27] *M/V 'Norstar' (Panama v Italy)* (Merits) ITLOS Judgment of 10 April 2019 paras 212–30. *Contra*: the joint dissenting opinion of Judges Cot, Pawlak, Yanai, Hoffmann, Kolodkin, and Lijnzaad, and Judge ad hoc Treves.

in other areas of international law'[28] and applied this principle whenever occasions arise.

The underlying legal basis for this pronouncement is Article 293(1) of UNCLOS stipulating that it shall apply UNCLOS 'and other rules of international law not incompatible with [UNCLOS]'. In M/V 'Saiga' (No 2), in considering the force used by the respondent in the arrest of the M/V 'Saiga' ITLOS took into account the circumstances of the arrest in the context of the applicable rules of international law. Although UNCLOS does not contain express provisions on the use of force in the arrest of ships, international law, which is applicable by virtue of Article 293 of UNCLOS, requires that the use of force must be avoided as far as possible and, where force is unavoidable, it must not go beyond what is reasonable and necessary in the circumstances—considerations of humanity must apply in the law of the sea, as they do in other areas of international law.[29] As ITLOS has also pointed out in this connection, States are required to fulfil their obligations under international law, in particular human rights law, and considerations of due process of law must be applied in all circumstances.[30]

ITLOS's constant jurisprudence in this respect could have a far-reaching implication for the law of the sea, including the ongoing crisis of irregular migration at sea. As stated unequivocally by the Grand Chamber of the European Court of Human Rights in Medvedyev and Others v France,

the special nature of the maritime environment ... cannot justify an area outside the law where ships' crews are covered by no legal system

---

[28] M/V 'Saiga' (No 2) (Saint Vincent and the Grenadines v Guinea) (Merits) ITLOS Reports 1999, 4, 61–62 [155]; 'Juno Trader' (Saint Vincent and the Grenadines v Guinea-Bissau) (Prompt Release) [2004] ITLOS Rep 17, 38–39 [77]; 'Enrica Lexie' (Italy v India) (Provisional Measures, Order of 24 August 2015) ITLOS Reports 2015, 182, 204 [133]. This echoes the pronouncement of the International Court of Justice in Corfu Channel (UK v Albania) (Merits) [1949] ICJ Rep 4, 22 about the existence of 'certain general and well recognized principles' that include 'elementary considerations of humanity', which is subsequently quoted by the ICJ in Military and Paramilitary Activities in and against Nicaragua (Nicaragua v USA) (Merits) [1986] ICJ Rep 14, 112 [215]. See also Francesca Delfino, '"Considerations of Humanity" in the Jurisprudence of ITLOS and UNCLOS Arbitral Tribunals' in Angela Del Vecchio and Roberto Virzo (eds), Interpretation of the United Nations Convention on the Law of the Sea by International Courts and Tribunals (Springer 2019) 421–27, 428–35, 441–43.

[29] M/V 'Saiga' (No 2) (Merits) (n 28) 61–62 [155]. Followed, but with an opposite outcome, in M/V 'Virginia G' (Judgment) (n 14) 101–03 [359]–[362].

[30] M/V 'Louisa' (Saint Vincent and the Grenadines v Kingdom of Spain) (Merits) [2013] ITLOS Rep 4, 46 [155], citing 'Juno Trader' (n 28) 38–39 [77]; 'Tomimaru' (Japan v Russian Federation) (Prompt Release) ITLOS Reports 2005–07, 74, 96 [76]. cf Andrea Cannone, 'The Provisional Measures in The "Enrica Lexie" Incident Case' in Del Vecchio and Virzo (n 28) 164–65.

capable of affording them enjoyment of the rights and guarantees protected by the European Convention on Human Rights[31] which the States
have undertaken to secure to everyone within their jurisdiction . . .[32]

f) Strengthening marine environment protection and preservation

In the field of marine environment, ITLOS has concretized and strengthened Part XII of UNCLOS on the protection and preservation of the marine
environment in numerous judgments, orders, and advisory opinions.[33]

Whereas preventive measures are based on scientific knowledge, precaution is addressed where there exists no sufficient scientific certainty.[34] Thus,
in dealing with the protection of the environment such as the atmosphere,
consideration of precaution is inevitable. Precautionary *measures* involve
administrative measures implementing the rules of precaution. The precautionary *principle*, by contrast, is 'a legal principle to be applicable before a
court of law, the main function of which is to shift the burden of proof from
the party alleging the existence of damage to the defendant party, who is
required to prove non-existence of the damage.'[35] While a few conventions
provide for a precautionary principle, international courts and tribunals
have thus far never recognized the precautionary principle as customary
international law, although it has been invoked several times by claimants.[36]

In ITLOS's Order on the provisional measures of 27 August 1999 in
Southern Bluefin Tuna (New Zealand v Japan; Australia v Japan), ITLOS
considered the conservation of the living resources of the sea to be an
element in the protection and preservation of the marine environment'.[37]
It, therefore, required the parties to 'act with prudence and caution to ensure effective conservation measures [were] taken to prevent serious harm
to the stock of southern blue fin tuna', but ITLOS avoided referring to the

---

[31]   ETS 5.

[32]   App no 3394/03 (29 March 2010) para 81. See also Kriangsak Kittichaisaree, *International Human Rights Law and Diplomacy* (Edward Elgar 2020) ch 8.2.

[33]   See, generally, Alexander Proelss, 'Contributions of the ITLOS to Strengthening the Regime for the Protection of the Marine Environment' in Del Vecchio and Virzo (n 28).

[34]   International Law Commission Special Rapporteur's Third Report on the Protection of the Atmosphere, Doc A/CN4/692 (25 February 2016) para 39.

[35]   ibid.

[36]   ibid.

[37]   *Southern Bluefin Tuna (New Zealand v Japan; Australia v Japan)* (Provisional Measures, Order of 27 August 1999) ITLOS Reports 1999, 280, 295 [70].

'precautionary principle' invoked by the applicants.[38] 'Prudence and caution' were also referred to by ITLOS in provisional measures proceedings in *MOX Plant (Ireland v United Kingdom)*,[39] *Land Reclamation by Singapore in and around the Strait of Johor (Malaysia v Singapore)*,[40] *M/V 'Louisa' (Saint Vincent and the Grenadines* v. *Kingdom of Spain)*,[41] and *Delimitation of the Maritime Boundary in the Atlantic Ocean (Ghana/Côte d'Ivoire)*.[42]

In its Advisory Opinion on *Responsibilities and obligations of States with respect to activities in the Area*, the Seabed Disputes Chamber considers the link between an obligation of due diligence and the 'precautionary approach' implicit in ITLOS's Order on the prescription of provisional measures in the *Southern Bluefin Tuna* case that the parties should in the circumstances act with prudence and caution to ensure that conservation measures were taken, that there was scientific uncertainty regarding measures to be taken to conserve the stock of southern bluefin tuna, and that although ITLOS could not conclusively assess the scientific evidence presented by the parties, it found that measures should be taken as a matter of urgency.[43] In the Chamber's opinion, the 'precautionary approach' has been incorporated into a growing number of international treaties and other instruments, many of which reflect the formulation of Principle 15 of the 1992 Rio Declaration on Environment and Development,[44] thereby initiating 'a trend towards making this approach part of customary international law'.[45] The obligation to apply the precautionary approach as reflected in Principle 15 of the Rio Declaration and set out in the International Seabed Authority's Nodules Regulations and Sulphides Regulations is also to be considered an integral part of the 'due diligence' obligation of the sponsoring State and applicable beyond the scope of the two Regulations.[46] The Seabed Disputes

---

[38] ibid 296 [77].

[39] *MOX Plant (Ireland v United Kingdom)* (Provisional Measures, Order of 13 November 2001) ITLOS Reports 2001, 95, 110 [84].

[40] *Land Reclamation in and around the Straits of Johor (Malaysia v Singapore)* (n 6) 10, 26 [99].

[41] *M/V 'Louisa'* (Provisional Measures, Order of 23 December 2010) ITLOS Reports 2008–10, 58, 70 [77].

[42] *Delimitation of the Maritime Boundary in the Atlantic Ocean (Ghana/Côte d'Ivoire)* (Provisional Measures, Order of 6 March 2015) ITLOS Reports 2015, 146, 160 [72].

[43] *Responsibilities and Obligations of States with respect to Activities in the Area* (n 25) 46–47 [132], quoting *Southern Bluefin Tuna* (Provisional Measures) (n 37) 274 [77], [79], [80].

[44] (1992) 31 ILM 874.

[45] *Responsibilities and Obligations of States with respect to Activities in the Area* (n 25) 47 [135].

[46] ibid 75 [242]. See also Tiago Vinicius Zanella, 'The Application of the Precautionary Principle: The Role of the International Tribunal for the Law of the Sea' in Tafsir Malick Ndiaye

Chamber thus reaffirms the obligation to conduct an environmental impact assessment as a direct obligation under UNCLOS and a general obligation under customary international law.[47]

In its Advisory Opinion in *Request for Advisory Opinion submitted by the Sub-Regional Fisheries Commission*, ITLOS reiterates that living resources and marine life are part of the marine environment and, as stated in the *Southern Bluefin Tuna* case, 'the conservation of the living resources of the sea is an element in the protection and preservation of the marine environment'.[48] ITLOS elaborates the legal regime under UNCLOS regulating this integral relationship between the marine environment and marine fisheries resources,[49] as explained in Chapter 4.

g) Delimitation of continental shelf extending beyond 200 nm

With respect to maritime boundary delimitation other than the one concerning the continental shelf beyond 200 nm, ITLOS affirms the established jurisprudence of international courts and tribunals in the field, thereby avoiding possible fragmentation of international law.[50]

Furthermore, ITLOS was the first international judicial body to have rendered its judgment on the delimitation of the continental shelf beyond 200 nautical miles. ITLOS and its special chamber have held they can delimit the continental shelf beyond 200 nm if there is no doubt that

and Rodrigo Fernandes More (eds), *Prospects of Evolution of the Law of the Sea, Environmental Law and the Practice of ITLOS* (SAG Editoração 2018) 189–200.

[47] *Responsibilities and Obligations of States with respect to Activities in the Area* (n 25) 50 [145]. See further, Duncan French, 'From the Depths: Rich Pickings of Principles of Sustainable Development and General International Law on the Ocean Floor: The Seabed Disputes Chamber's 2011 Advisory Opinion' (2011) 26 Int'l J Marine & Coastal L 252.

[48] *Request for Advisory Opinion submitted by the Sub-Regional Fisheries Commission* (n 18), 68.

[49] ibid 63, 66–67, 68.

[50] Millicent McCreath and Zoe Scanlon 'The Dispute Concerning the Delimitation of the Maritime Boundary Between Ghana and Côte d'Ivoire: Implications for the Law of the Sea' (2019) 50 ODIL 1, 4–13, 16; Jérome Sautier, 'Délimitation de la frontière maritime entre le Ghana et la Côte d'Ivoire' (2017) 23 Annuaire du droit de la mer 64, 73–112, 116–19. cf Edwin E Egede and Lawrence Apaalse, 'Dispute Concerning the Delimitation of the Maritime Boundary between Ghana and Côte d'Ivoire in the Atlantic Ocean: Lesson from Another Maritime Delimitation Case Arising from the African Region' (2019) 29 Indiana Int'l & Comp L Rev 55, 80–89.

such a continental shelf exists.[51] While the Annex VII arbitral tribunal in *Arbitration between Barbados and the Republic of Trinidad and Tobago* had jurisdiction to decide upon the delimitation of a maritime boundary in relation to that part of the continental shelf extending beyond 200 nm, the single maritime boundary which that tribunal determined was such that, as between Barbados and Trinidad and Tobago, there was no single maritime boundary beyond 200 nm for the arbitration to deal with.[52]

ITLOS held in *Delimitation of the Maritime Boundary in the Bay of Bengal (Bangladesh/Myanmar)* that it had jurisdiction to delimit the continental shelf in its entirety after quoting the reasoning of the arbitral tribunal in *Arbitration between Barbados and the Republic of Trinidad and Tobago*, positing that the dispute included the outer continental shelf which either formed part of or was sufficiently closely related to the dispute, and that in any event there was in law only a single continental shelf rather than an inner continental shelf and a separate extended or outer continental shelf.[53] In examining the issue of whether ITLOS should refrain from exercising its jurisdiction to delimit the continental shelf beyond 200 nm until such time as the outer limits of the continental shelf had been established by each party or at least until such time as the Commission on the Limits of the Continental Shelf had made recommendations to each party on its submission and each party had had the opportunity to consider its reaction to the recommendations, ITLOS pointed out that the absence of established outer limits of a maritime zone did not preclude delimitation of that zone.[54]

As clarified by ITLOS, there is a clear distinction between the delimitation of the continental shelf under Article 83 of UNCLOS and the delineation of its outer limits pursuant to Article 76 thereof. Under Article 76, the Commission is assigned the function of making recommendations to coastal States on matters relating to the establishment of the outer limits

---

[51] *Delimitation of the Maritime Boundary in the Bay of Bengal (Bangladesh/Myanmar)* ITLOS Reports 2012, 4, 115–16 [444]–[449]; *Dispute Concerning the Delimitation of the Maritime Boundary between Ghana and Côte d'Ivoire in the Atlantic Ocean (Ghana/Côte d'Ivoire)* (Merits) Judgment of 23 September 2017 paras 491, 496. cf Egede and Apaalse (n 50) 112–16; Lan Ngoc Nguyen, 'UNCLOS Tribunals and the Development of the Outer Continental Shelf Regime' (2018) 67 ICLQ 425.

[52] *Arbitration between Barbados and the Republic of Trinidad and Tobago, relating to the Delimitation of the Exclusive Economic Zone and the Continental Shelf between them* (Award) PCA 11 April 2006 RIAA, vol XXVII, 147, para 368.

[53] *Delimitation of the Maritime Boundary in the Bay of Bengal* (n 51) 96–97 [362]–[363], quoting *Arbitration between Barbados and the Republic of Trinidad and Tobago* (n 52) para 213. See also Massimo Lando, *Maritime Delimitation as a Judicial Process* (CUP 2019) ch 3.

[54] *Delimitation of the Maritime Boundary in the Bay of Bengal* (n 51) 98 [369]–[370].

of the continental shelf, but it does so without prejudice to delimitation of maritime boundaries. The function of settling disputes with respect to delimitation of maritime boundaries is entrusted to dispute settlement procedures under Article 83 and Part XV of UNCLOS, which include international courts and tribunals, and there is nothing in UNCLOS or in the Rules of Procedure of the Commission or in its practice to indicate that delimitation of the continental shelf constitutes an impediment to the performance by the Commission of its functions.[55]

ITLOS considers that its decision not to exercise its jurisdiction over the dispute relating to the continental shelf beyond 200 nm would not only fail to resolve a long-standing dispute, but also would not be conducive to the efficient operation of UNCLOS whose object and purpose is to resolve the existing impasse. Inaction by the Commission and ITLOS, two organs created by UNCLOS to ensure the effective implementation of its provisions, would leave the parties in a position where they may be unable to benefit fully from their rights over the continental shelf.[56]

In order to fulfil its responsibilities under section 2 of Part XV of UNCLOS, ITLOS has an obligation to adjudicate the dispute and to delimit the continental shelf between the parties beyond 200 nm. Such delimitation is without prejudice to the establishment of the outer limits of the continental shelf in accordance with Article 76(8) of UNCLOS.[57] In this connection, the International Court of Justice subsequently held in *Maritime Delimitation in the Indian Ocean (Somalia v Kenya)* that

[a] lack of certainty regarding the outer limits of the continental shelf, and thus the precise location of the endpoint of a given boundary in the area beyond 200 nautical miles, [did] not ... necessarily prevent either the States concerned or the Court from undertaking the delimitation of

---

[55]   ibid 99 [376]–[377].
[56]   ibid 102 [391]–[392].
[57]   ibid 103 [394]. UNCLOS Art 76(8) reads:

Information on the limits of the continental shelf beyond 200 nautical miles from the baselines from which the breadth of the territorial sea is measured shall be submitted by the coastal State to the Commission on the Limits of the Continental Shelf ... [which] shall make recommendations to coastal States on matters related to the establishment of the outer limits of their continental shelf. The limits of the shelf established by a coastal State on the basis of these recommendations shall be final and binding.

the boundary in appropriate circumstances before the [Commission on the Limits of the Continental Shelf] [had] made its recommendations.[58]

This line of reasoning is of practical importance bearing in mind the Commission's current workload. As of 26 March 2019, 71 States Parties to UNCLOS had made submissions either individually or jointly and more were expected to be received in the coming years. In addition, the scientific and technical components of the submissions far exceed the complexity originally envisaged by the Third UN Conference on the Law of the Sea. Such situation is related, in part, to evolving knowledge and technologies and, in part, to the efforts of coastal States to support the proposed delineation with comprehensive data and information. While the Commission had already issued 32 sets of recommendations as of 5 April 2019, including four of the revised submissions, 45 submissions were still pending consideration. At the current stage, the waiting time between the making of a submission and the establishment of a subcommission to consider it is approximately 10 years and is expected to increase even further. Given the workload, the remaining work of the Commission may last several more decades.[59]

Nevertheless, ITLOS is careful when it posits that the fact that the outer limits of the continental shelf beyond 200 nm have not been established does not imply that ITLOS must refrain from determining the existence of the entitlement to the continental shelf and from delimiting the continental shelf between the parties concerned.[60] In ITLOS's view, as Article 76 of UNCLOS contains elements of law and science, its proper interpretation and application require both legal and scientific expertise which may include dealing with uncontested scientific materials or require recourse to experts.[61] In *Delimitation of the Maritime Boundary in the Bay of Bengal* itself the parties did not differ on the scientific aspects of the seabed and subsoil of the Bay of Bengal, but on the interpretation of Article 76, in particular the meaning of 'natural prolongation' in paragraph 1 of that Article and the relationship between that paragraph and paragraph 4 concerning the establishment by the coastal State of the outer edge of the continental margin.

---

[58] *Maritime Delimitation in the Indian Ocean (Somalia v Kenya)* (Preliminary Objections) [2017] ICJ Rep 3, 38 [94].

[59] Letter dated 5 April 2019 from the Chair of the Commission on the Limits of the Continental Shelf addressed to the President of the 29th Meeting of States Parties to UNCLOS, Doc SPLOS/29/6 (8 April 2019) paras 10–11.

[60] *Delimitation of the Maritime Boundary in the Bay of Bengal* (n 51) 107 [410].

[61] ibid 107 [410]–[411].

While the Parties agreed on the geological and geomorphologic data, they disagreed about their legal significance in the present case. Because the question of the parties' entitlement to a continental shelf beyond 200 nm raised issues which were predominantly legal in nature, ITLOS resolved that it could and ought to determine entitlements of the parties in that particular case.[62] As acknowledged in the course of negotiations at the Third Conference and confirmed in the experts' reports presented by Bangladesh during the proceedings before ITLOS in that particular case, which were not challenged by Myanmar, the Bay of Bengal is a unique situation. The sea floor of the Bay of Bengal is covered by a thick layer of sediments some 14 to 22 kilometres deep originating in the Himalayas and the Tibetan Plateau, having accumulated in the Bay of Bengal over several thousands of years. Moreover, in view of uncontested scientific evidence regarding the unique nature of the Bay of Bengal and information submitted during the proceedings, ITLOS was satisfied with the proven existence of a continuous and substantial layer of sedimentary rocks extending from Myanmar's coast to the area beyond 200 nm. ITLOS accordingly concluded that both Bangladesh and Myanmar had entitlements to a continental shelf extending beyond 200 nm, and that their entitlements overlapped in the area in dispute.[63]

Delimitation of the Maritime Boundary in the Bay of Bengal was also the first case in which an international court or tribunal deliberated on a 'grey area' arising from the delimitation of the continental shelf beyond 200 nm that gives rise to an area of limited size located beyond 200 nm from the coast of one party but within 200 nm from the coast of the other party, yet on the former party's side of the delimitation line.[64] Such an area results when a delimitation line which is not a line of equidistance reaches the outer limit of one State's exclusive economic zone and continues beyond it in the same direction, until it reaches the outer limit of the other State's exclusive economic zone.[65]

---

[62]   ibid 107–08 [412]–[413].

[63]   ibid 115–16 [444]–[449].

[64]   For a criticism of ITLOS's approach as regards grey areas, see Lando (n 53) 132–42.

[65]   Or, as described by one commentator, 'grey zones' are said to materialize in cases where a slice of maritime space on State A's side of a provisional equidistance line is more than 200 nm from its baselines but within 200 nm of State B's baselines and above a geologically existing continental shelf appertaining to State A. In the absence of State A having rights in the water column in this 'grey zone', they are allocated to State B, thereby creating 'an inconvenient result where seabed rights vest in State A and water column rights vest in State B': Douglas Guilfoyle in Review of Lando's *Maritime Delimitation as a Judicial Process* (2020) 69 ICLQ 499.

As between Bangladesh and Myanmar, the grey area occurs where the adjusted equidistance line used for delimitation of the continental shelf goes beyond 200 nm off Bangladesh and continues until it reaches 200 nm off Myanmar.[66] The boundary delimiting the area beyond 200 nm from Bangladesh but within 200 nm of Myanmar is a boundary delimiting the continental shelves of the parties, since in this area only their continental shelves overlap. There is no question of delimiting the exclusive economic zones of the parties as there is no overlap of those zones. The 'grey area' arises as a consequence of delimitation, but any delimitation may give rise to complex legal and practical problems, such as those involving transboundary resources. It is not unusual in such cases for States to enter into agreements or cooperative arrangements to deal with problems resulting from the delimitation. The legal regime of the continental shelf has always coexisted with another legal regime in the same area. By virtue of Article 56(3) of UNCLOS, the rights of the coastal State with respect to the seabed and subsoil of the exclusive economic zone shall be exercised in accordance with Part VI (continental shelf) of UNCLOS, which includes Article 83 on delimitation of the continental shelf. Furthermore, Article 68 provides that Part V on the exclusive economic zone does not apply to sedentary species of the continental shelf as defined in Article 77 of UNCLOS. In the area beyond Bangladesh's exclusive economic zone that is within the limits of Myanmar's exclusive economic zone, the maritime boundary therefore delimits the parties' rights with respect to the seabed and subsoil of the continental shelf but does not otherwise limit Myanmar's rights with respect to the exclusive economic zone, notably those with respect to the superjacent waters. Under UNCLOS, as a result of maritime delimitation there may also be concurrent exclusive economic zone rights of another coastal State. In such a situation, pursuant to the principle reflected in the provisions of Articles 56 (rights, jurisdiction, and duties of the coastal State in the exclusive economic zone), 58 (rights and duties of other States in the exclusive economic zone), 78 (legal status of the superjacent waters and air space and the rights and freedoms of other States), and 79 (submarine cables and pipelines on the continental shelf) and in other provisions of UNCLOS, each coastal State must exercise its rights and perform its duties with 'due regard' to the rights and duties of the other. There are many ways in which the parties may ensure the discharge of their obligations in this

---

[66] *Delimitation of the Maritime Boundary in the Bay of Bengal* (n 51) 119 [463]–[464].

respect, including the conclusion of specific agreements or the establishment of appropriate cooperative arrangements—it is for the parties to determine the measures they consider appropriate for this purpose.[67]

h) Hydrocarbon activities in disputed areas before delimitation

The special chamber of ITLOS in the *Ghana/Côte d'Ivoire* case addressed the important practical question as to whether hydrocarbon activities carried out by a State in a disputed area before the area in question was delimited by adjudication could give rise to international responsibility when these activities were carried out in a part of the area attributed by the judgment to the other State.

In the special chamber's view, in a case of overlap both States concerned had an entitlement to the relevant continental shelf on the basis of their relevant coasts, and only a decision on delimitation had a constitutive effect in giving one entitlement priority over the other by establishing which part of the continental shelf under dispute appertained to which of the claiming States. Therefore, maritime activities undertaken by a State in an area of the continental shelf which was subsequently attributed to another State by an international judgment could not be considered to be in violation of the sovereign rights of the latter if those activities were carried out before the judgment was delivered and if the area concerned was the subject of claims made in good faith by both States.[68] Even assuming that some of those activities had taken place in areas attributed to Côte d'Ivoire by the present judgment, the special chamber rejected the argument advanced by Côte d'Ivoire that the hydrocarbon activities carried out by Ghana in the disputed area constituted a violation of the sovereign rights of Côte d'Ivoire.[69]

---

[67] ibid 120–21 [471]–[476]. The operative clauses of the judgment in that case do not mention this grey area and ITLOS's explanation, however. See also Tafsir Malick Ndiaye, 'The Judges, Maritime Delimitation and the Grey Areas' (2015) 55 Indian JIL 493.

[68] *Dispute Concerning the Delimitation of the Maritime Boundary between Ghana and Côte d'Ivoire in the Atlantic Ocean* (Merits) (n 51) paras 589–92.

[69] ibid paras 593–94, citing also the 'convergent decision' of the ICJ in *Territorial and Maritime Dispute (Nicaragua v Colombia)* (Merits) [2012] ICJ Rep 624, 718 [250]. In that case, Nicaragua requested the ICJ to declare that Colombia was not acting in accordance with its obligations under international law by stopping and otherwise hindering Nicaragua from accessing and disposing of her natural resources to the east of the 82nd meridian in their disputed area. The ICJ observed that this request was made in the context of proceedings regarding a maritime boundary which had not been settled prior to the decision of the ICJ, and that the consequence of the ICJ's judgment was that the maritime boundary between

2. Future

a) State of Palestine's maritime claims

In September 2019, the third maritime delimitation dispute was submitted to ITLOS.[70] More should be coming before ITLOS in the near future.

In this connection, on 31 August 2015 the State of Palestine proclaimed its 12-nm territorial sea, 24-nm contiguous zone, 200-nm continental shelf, and 200-nm exclusive economic zone.[71] Where its maritime zones overlap with those of other States, 'delimitation of the boundaries between the maritime zones should be resolved on the basis of equity and the principles of international law, and with reference to the Statute [*sic*] of the International Court of Justice and the International Tribunal for the Law of the Sea'.[72] If agreement cannot be reached, 'recourse may be had to the competent international court or body for a final decision'.[73]

On 24 September 2019, the State of Palestine deposited a second Declaration with the UN Secretary-General to specify the geographical coordinates of its maritime zones as well as those of the baselines from which these zones are measured, with a sketch map attached thereto.[74] The maritime zones claimed by the State of Palestine are generated from the coast of the land area controlled by the Palestinian National Authority and they appear to overlap with those claimed by its neighbours, in particular Egypt,

---

Nicaragua and Colombia throughout the relevant area was now delimited as between the parties. In this regard, the judgment did not attribute to Nicaragua the whole of the area which it claimed and, on the contrary, attributed to Colombia part of the maritime spaces in respect of which Nicaragua sought a declaration regarding access to natural resources. In this context, the ICJ considered Nicaragua's claim to be unfounded. But cf McCreath and Scanlon (n 50) 13–14; Sautier (n 50) 119–22; Bin Zhao, 'The Curious Case of Ghana/Côte d'Ivoire: A Consistent Approach to Hydrocarbon Activities in the Disputed Area?' (2020) 10 Asian JIL 94.

[70] *Dispute Concerning Delimitation of the Maritime Boundary between Mauritius and Maldives in the Indian Ocean (Mauritius/Maldives)* ITLOS Case No 28.

[71] Declaration of the State of Palestine regarding the Maritime Boundaries of the State of Palestine in accordance with the United Nations Convention on the Law of the Sea, dated 31 August 2015, enclosed in Note No 15-15362(E) dated 31 August 2015 from the President of the State of Palestine and Chair of the Executive Committee of the Palestine Liberation Organization addressed to the UN Secretary-General.

[72] ibid para 11.

[73] ibid para 12.

[74] Declaration of the State of Palestine regarding its maritime boundaries in accordance with the United Nations Convention on the Law of the Sea <www.un.org/Depts/los/LEGISLATIONANDTREATIES/PDFFILES/PSE_Deposit_09-2019.pdf> accessed 22 October 2019.

Israel, and Cyprus.[75] In addition, Lebanon's exclusive economic zone claim overlaps with that of 'Palestine' (meaning Israel, which Lebanon does not officially recognize).[76]

The State of Palestine is party to UNCLOS and is, therefore, entitled to have a recourse to ITLOS to settle its maritime boundaries overlapping with those of other States in the region which are also parties to UNCLOS. At the time of its ratification of UNCLOS, Egypt declares, pursuant to Article 287 of UNCLOS, its acceptance of the Annex VII arbitral procedure as the procedure for the settlement of any dispute which might arise between Egypt and any other State relating to the interpretation or application of UNCLOS, but Egypt excludes from the scope of application of this procedure those disputes referred to in Article 297 of UNCLOS. However, Egypt does not declare, in accordance with Article 298(1)(a)(i) of UNCLOS, that it does not accept compulsory dispute settlement procedures with respect to disputes concerning the interpretation or application of Articles 15, 74, and 83 of UNCLOS relating to sea boundary delimitations, or those involving historic bays or titles. The State of Palestine, Cyprus, and Lebanon have not made such declaration under Article 298(1)(a)(i) either, whereas Israel is not party to UNCLOS, does not accept the ICJ's compulsory jurisdiction, and may not accept the State of Palestine's proclamation insofar as it deviates from the 1994 Agreement on Gaza Strip and Jericho Area concluded between the Israeli Government and the Palestine Liberation Organization,[77] which also governs the conduct of maritime activities off the land territory under the Agreement. The situation is further complicated by the fact that Article 34(1) of the ICJ Statute stipulates unequivocally that only States may be parties in cases before the ICJ. Much will depend on how the ICJ interprets this Article in relation to the State of Palestine in *Relocation of the United States Embassy to Jerusalem (Palestine v United States of America)* now pending before it. If a dispute over the overlapping maritime claims between the State of Palestine and any State Party to UNCLOS is submitted to ITLOS, ITLOS should have no problem with its jurisdiction over the dispute, while taking into consideration the interest of Israel as a third party to

---

[75] James Stocker, 'No EEZ Solution: The Politics of Oil and Gas in the Eastern Mediterranean' (2012) 66 Middle East Journal 579, 587–92; Nicholas A Ioannides, 'Palestine Takes to the Sea: A Commentary on Palestine's Declaration concerning its Maritime Claims' (*The NCLOS Blog*, 20 November 2019) <https://site.uit.no/nclos/2019/11/20/palestine-takes-to-the-sea-a-commentary-on-palestines-declaration-concerning-its-maritime-claims/> accessed 31 October 2020.

[76] Stocker (n 75) 586.

[77] (1994) 33 ILM 622.

the dispute even though Israel is not party to UNCLOS. However, the extent to which Israel's interest impact on the delimitation itself would be very significant. Let us wait and see how the parties concerned will settle this extremely complex situation, hopefully with ITLOS's assistance.

b) Underutilized protection under Article 73 of UNCLOS

It is much regretted that several provisions of UNCLOS have been breached without the injured State Parties seeking redress from ITLOS as diligently as they should have, especially as regards violations of paragraphs 3 and 4 of Article 73.

By virtue of Article 73(1) of UNCLOS, the coastal State may, in the exercise of its sovereign rights to explore, exploit, conserve, and manage the living resources in the exclusive economic zone, take such measures, including boarding, inspection, arrest, and judicial proceedings, as may be necessary to ensure compliance with the laws and regulations adopted by it in conformity with UNCLOS. Pursuant to Article 73(2), arrested vessels and their crews shall be promptly released upon the posting of reasonable bond or other security. Under Article 73(3), coastal State penalties for violations of fisheries laws and regulations in the exclusive economic zone may not include imprisonment, in the absence of agreements to the contrary by the States concerned, or any other form of corporal punishment. In cases of arrest or detention of foreign vessels, Article 73(4) requires the arresting/detaining coastal State to promptly notify the flag State, through appropriate channels, of the action taken and of any penalties subsequently imposed. ITLOS has held that the principle of reasonableness applies generally to enforcement measures under Article 73, and in applying enforcement measures due regard has to be paid to the particular circumstances of the case and the gravity of the violation.[78]

While Article 73(1) provides for the possibility of the coastal State sanctioning violations of laws and regulations concerning living resources in its exclusive economic zone, this provision makes no reference to confiscation of vessels. In ITLOS's view, Article 73(1) has to be interpreted in the light of the practice of coastal States and, in practice, many coastal States do

---

[78] *M/V 'Virginia G'* (Judgment) (n 14) 81 [270].

confiscate fishing vessels as a sanction for such violations. However, confiscation of a fishing vessel must not be used in such a manner as to upset the balance of the interests of the flag State and of the coastal State established in UNCLOS, and such a decision to confiscate should not be taken in such a way as to prevent the shipowner from having recourse to available domestic judicial remedies, or as to prevent the flag State from resorting to the prompt release procedure set forth in UNCLOS; nor should it be taken through proceedings inconsistent with international standards of due process of law. The principle of reasonableness applies generally to enforcement measures under Article 73 of UNCLOS, and in applying enforcement measures due regard has to be paid to the particular circumstances of the case and the gravity of the violation.[79]

In *M/V 'Virginia G'*, ITLOS held that the confiscation by the respondent Guinea-Bissau of the vessel and the gas oil on board in the circumstances of the case violated Article 73(1) as it was not necessary either to sanction the violation committed or to deter the vessels or their operators from repeating this violation measure against the M/V 'Virginia G'.[80] By contrast, the temporary measures of confinement taken by the respondent with regard to the crew members during a short period of initial detention of the M/V 'Virginia G' at sea and the subsequent stay of the vessel in the port of Bissau when the crew members were free to leave the vessel could not be interpreted as imprisonment. Similarly, the temporary holding of their passports could not be considered imprisonment within the meaning of Article 73(3). ITLOS concluded that there was no penalty of imprisonment imposed on members of the crew of the M/V 'Virginia G', and Guinea-Bissau therefore did not violate Article 73(3).[81] Nevertheless, by failing to notify Panama as the flag State of the detention and arrest of the M/V 'Virginia G' and subsequent actions taken against this vessel and its cargo, Guinea-Bissau violated the requirements of Article 73(4) and thus deprived Panama of its right as a flag State to intervene at the initial stages of actions taken against the M/V 'Virginia G' and during the subsequent proceedings.[82]

Due to the lack of bargaining power of the vessel owners and the crew vis-à-vis their respective flag States, no case has been submitted to ITLOS where some coastal States pursue vigilante justice by burning down or

---

[79]   ibid 77–81 [251]–[270], citing *'Tomimaru'* (n 30) 96 [72], [75], [76].
[80]   *M/V 'Virginia G'* (Judgment) (n 14) 82 [271].
[81]   ibid 90 [308]–[311].
[82]   ibid 93 [328].

destroying foreign vessels arrested for alleged illegal fishing in their exclusive economic zone without these coastal States' fulfilling their own obligation for prompt release of the vessels upon the posting of reasonable bond or other security; or where certain coastal States imprison foreign fishers found guilty of illegal fishing in its exclusive economic zone.[83] It is important to raise awareness about the existing possibilities for submitting these disputes to ITLOS so that the balance of the rights and obligations between coastal States and flag States as enshrined in Article 73 can be upheld.

c) Contentious cases before the Seabed Disputes Chamber

With respect to the Seabed Disputes Chamber, no contentious case has been submitted to it as of this writing, but potentials for contentious disputes are always there,[84] including disputes arising from the Mining Code, or regulations governing exploitation of mineral resources in the Area, scheduled to be adopted by the International Seabed Authority in 2020. Regulation 106 (Settlement of disputes) of the draft Mining Code requires disputes concerning the interpretation or application of these regulations and an exploitation contract to be settled in accordance with section 5 of Part XI of UNCLOS,[85] which accords jurisdiction to the Seabed Disputes Chamber, a special chamber of ITLOS, an ad hoc chamber of the Seabed Disputes Chamber, or compulsory commercial arbitration.

Beyond the context of 'activities in the Area', Article 82 of UNCLOS regulates payments and contributions by the coastal State with respect to the exploitation of the non-living resources of its continental shelf beyond 200 nm from the baselines from which the breadth of its territorial sea is measured. The payments and contributions shall be made annually with respect to all production at a site after the first five years of production at the site. For the sixth year, the rate of payment or contribution shall be one per cent of the value or volume of production at the site. The rate shall increase by one per cent for each subsequent year until the twelfth year and shall

---

[83] To this author's knowledge, no flag State has concluded an agreement with a coastal State to include imprisonment as a penalty for violations of fisheries laws and regulations in the latter's exclusive economic zone.

[84] cf Linlin Sun, 'Dispute Settlement Relating to Deep Seabed Mining: A Participant's Perspective' (2017) 18 Melbourne JIL 71, 78–94.

[85] Doc ISBA/25/C/WP1 (22 March 2019).

remain at seven per cent thereafter. Production does not include resources used in connection with exploitation. However, a developing State which is a net importer of a mineral resource produced from its continental shelf is exempt from making such payments or contributions in respect of that mineral resource. The payments or contributions shall be made through the International Seabed Authority, which shall distribute them to UNCLOS States Parties on the basis of equitable sharing criteria, taking into account the interests and needs of developing States, particularly the least developed and the landlocked among them. It is the Council of the Authority that recommends to the Assembly of the Authority for consideration and approval rules, regulations, and procedures on the equitable sharing of financial and other economic benefits derived from such payments and contributions.[86] Nonetheless, UNCLOS is vague on how to implement Article 82 in practice.[87] For example, it does not specify who determines the amount of contribution, the currency in which the contribution is to be made, whether 'annually' means a calendar year or 12 months, and how the payment or contribution obligations are to be determined where more than one coastal State is exploiting, on the continental shelf beyond 200 nm, resources straddling maritime zone limits and boundaries.[88]

Therefore, possible disputes relating to Article 82 may arise, first, between the coastal States making payments or contributions and other States Parties to UNCLOS; second, between the former and the Authority; and, third, between other States Parties to UNCLOS, in particular potential beneficiaries, and the Authority. In the first scenario, a related question is whether any State Party to UNCLOS or only a State Party that would benefit from the payments and contributions under Articled 82 has legal standing to bring the case before ITLOS. In the second scenario, it is debatable

---

[86] UNCLOS Art 162(2)(o)(i).

[87] Joanna Mossup, *The Continental Shelf Beyond 200 Nautical Miles: Rights and Responsibility* (OUP 2016) 123–47; Frida M Armas-Pfirter, 'Article 82 of UNCLOS: A Clear Outcome of the "Package Deal" Approach of the Convention Negotiation' in International Ocean Institute—Canada (ed), *The Future of Ocean Governance and Capacity Development: Essays in Honor of Elisabeth Mann Borgese (1918–2002)* (Brill/Nijhoff 2017) ; Aldo Chircop, 'Article 82' in Alexander Proelss (ed), *United Nations Convention on the Law of the Sea: A Commentary* (Hart 2017) 641, 647–48; David M Ong, 'The Continental Shelf beyond 200 Nautical Miles and Its Superjacent Waters' in Kenyuan Zhou (ed), *Global Commons and the Law of the Sea* (Brill/Nijhoff 2018) 199–206.

[88] International Seabed Authority, *A Summary of Outcomes of the 2009 ISA–Chatham House Seminar on the Implementation of Article 82 of the UN Convention on the Law of the Sea*, Informal Background Paper prepared by the Secretariat of the Authority, November 2012, paras 16, 18, 35.

whether the Seabed Disputes Chamber has jurisdiction over this kind of dispute which is not 'with respect to activities in the Area' as stipulated in Article 187 of UNCLOS on the scope of the Chamber's jurisdiction. In the third scenario, a question is whether such disputes can fall under Article 187 or whether the State concerned and the Authority have to conclude an agreement conferring jurisdiction on ITLOS by means of a special agreement related to the submission of a specific dispute only or through the dispute-settlement clause of a general agreement between the Authority and the State concerned. If the Authority wishes to request an advisory opinion regarding the implementation of Article 82, it is debatable whether the full-bench ITLOS or the Seabed Disputes Chamber has advisory jurisdiction regarding legal questions pertaining to Article 82.

There are other unresolved legal questions which may come before ITLOS or the Seabed Disputes Chamber, such as the questions of accommodation, compatibility, and coexistence between activities in the Area and the laying, operation, and so forth, of submarine cables in the same maritime location. If a legal question is one concerning the interpretation of the Article 87 freedom of the high seas to lay submarine cables and pipelines 'with due regard' for the rights under UNCLOS with respect to activities in the Area, this will come under Part XV of UNCLOS. However, if it concerns Article 147 requiring activities in the Area to be carried out 'with reasonable regard' for other activities in the marine environment, the Seabed Disputes Chamber will have jurisdiction over it.[89]

d) Sea-level rise and the law of the sea

Natural phenomena unforeseen at the time of the Third UN Conference on the Law of the Sea may pose challenging legal questions for ITLOS to answer, foremost among which is the impact of sea-level rise on maritime entitlement of insular features or even national survival of small island States.[90]

---

[89] International Seabed Authority, *Deep Seabed Mining and Submarine Cables: Developing Practical Options for the Implementation of the 'Due Regard' and 'Reasonable Regard' Obligations under UNCLOS*, ISBA Technical Study No 24 (2018) 7–25 and passim.

[90] See International Law Association, *Report of the Sydney Conference (2018) on International Law and Sea Level Rise* (Sydney, August 2018) https://www.ila-hq.org/images/ILA/DraftReports/DraftReport_SeaLevelRise.pdf; International Law Association, *Baselines under the International Law of the Sea* (Final Report, August 2018) https://www.ila-hq.org/images/ILA/DraftReports/DraftReport_Baselines.pdf; International Law Commission, 'Report of the International Law Commission on the work of its 70th Session' (30 April–1

Article 7(2) of UNCLOS is the only provision regarding the effects of highly unstable coastlines—it allows the use of a straight baseline because of the presence of a delta or other natural conditions. Articles 11 and 12 of UNCLOS stipulate that offshore installations and artificial islands do not possess the status of islands; hence, no territorial sea of their own, and their presence does not affect the delimitation of the territorial sea, the exclusive economic zone, or the continental shelf. By virtue of Article 121(1) of UNCLOS, islands generate maritime zones as measured from their baseline, whereas Article 13 of UNCLOS allows the use of low-tide elevations as baselines only where the low-tide elevations are within 12 nm off the coast.

Commentators have diverging views on the impact of sea-level rise on maritime entitlement. For some of them, the coastal baseline under Article 5 of UNCLOS can shift as a result of natural conditions of the coastline— the limits of maritime zones are therefore ambulatory, except for the permanently delineated outer limit of the continental shelf the charts and relevant information of which have been duly deposited with the UN Secretary-General pursuant to Article 76(9) of UNCLOS. Others argue that settled maritime boundaries between States entail the 'finality of the frontier' among the States concerned.[91] It is also contended that a maritime boundary settled through judicial means has the force of *res judicata* and enjoys continuity. On the other hand, a view is expressed that the foregoing cannot prejudice the rights of third States not party thereto, and that, under the cardinal principle of 'the land dominates the sea', only where there is land can be there a maritime zone generated from that land; otherwise the sea is the high seas. Options suggested so far include artificially conserving baselines, for example, by engineering structures such as sea walls, which are expensive; and preserving the existing maritime zones once determined in accordance with UNCLOS by freezing the existing baselines, freezing the

June and 2 July–10 August 2018) UN Doc A/73/10, Annex B (Sea-level rise in relation to international law).

[91] cf *Territorial and Maritime Dispute (Nicaragua v Colombia)* (Preliminary Objections) [2007] ICJ Rep 832, 861 [89]:

> ... Even if the Court were to find that the 1928 Treaty has been terminated, as claimed by Nicaragua, this would not affect the sovereignty of Colombia over the islands of San Andrés, Providencia, and Santa Catalina. The Court recalls that it is a principle of international law that a territorial régime established by treaty 'achieves a permanence which the treaty itself does not necessarily enjoy' and the continued existence of that régime is not dependent upon the continuing life of the treaty under which the régime is agreed (*Territorial Dispute (Libyan Arab Jamahiriya/Chad)*, Judgment, ICJ Rep 1994 p 37 paras 72–73).

outer limit of the territorial sea, or freezing the outer limit of the exclusive economic zone.[92]

In 2011, Palau and the Marshall Islands intended to call on the UN General Assembly to seek, on an urgent basis and pursuant to Article 96 of the UN Charter, an advisory opinion from the ICJ on the responsibilities of States under customary international law and Article 194(2) of UNCLOS to ensure that activities emitting greenhouse gases carried out under their jurisdiction or control do not damage other States. These two States considered it was time for the ICJ to determine what the international rule of law means in the context of climate change.[93] As of this writing, the UN General Assembly has not submitted to the ICJ such a request for an advisory opinion, understandably because the issue of State responsibility for climate change is politically sensitive. Instead, the States concerned may find it wise to ask ITLOS to render an advisory opinion to guide them which direction they should take under UNCLOS and other rules of international law not incompatible with UNCLOS so as to alleviate potentially adverse effects of sea-level rise and climate change.

According to some commentator, disputes concerning climate-related impacts on the marine environment are within compulsory jurisdiction under Part XV of UNCLOS since Articles 286 and 288 of UNCLOS cover any dispute concerning interpretation and application of UNCLOS unless excluded by Article 297 or 298 thereof, and neither Article excludes a dispute concerning interpretation and application of Article 192 (on the general obligation to protect and preserve the marine environment), Article 194 (on measures to be taken to prevent, reduce, and control pollution of the marine environment), Article 207 (on the obligation to reduce marine pollution from land-based sources), nor Article 212 (on the obligation to prevent, reduce, and control pollution of the marine environment from or through the atmosphere). Any State Party to UNCLOS may, according to this view, institute contentious proceedings for non-compliance by another

---

[92] See further, Clive Schofield and David Freestone, 'Islands Awash Amidst Rising Seas: Sea Level Rise and Insular Status under the Law of the Sea' (2019) 34 Int'l J Marine & Coastal L 391; Nilüfer Oral, 'International Law as an Adaptation Measure to Sea-Level Rise and Its Impacts on Islands and Offshore Features' 34 Int'l J Marine & Coastal L 415; Catherine Redgwell, 'Treaty Evolution, Adaptation and Changes: Is the LOSC "Enough" to Address Climate Change Impacts on the Marine Environment?' 34 Int'l J Marine & Coastal L 440; Kate Purcell, *Geographical Change and the Law of the Sea* (OUP 2019).

[93] Address by Mr Johnson Toribiong, President of the Republic of Palau, before the UN General Assembly, 22 September 2011, Doc A/66/PV16 pp 27–28.

State Party with Part XII (Protection and Preservation of the Marine Environment).[94]

e) Marine biological diversity of areas beyond national jurisdiction

In negotiating an agreement under UNCLOS on the conservation and sustainable use of marine biological diversity of areas beyond national jurisdiction ('BBNJ'), States have various proposals on the procedures for settlement of disputes under the agreement. One option is to follow the dispute settlement formula under the 1995 UN Agreement for the Implementation of the Provisions of the UN Convention on the Law of the Sea of 10 December 1982 relating to the Conservation and Management of Straddling Fish Stocks and Highly Migratory Species Fish Stocks ('FSA'),[95] which, as Chapter 3 has shown, is still subject to varying interpretations, and the negotiations leading to the FSA preceded ITLOS's existence. Another option is to resort to ITLOS as a default, fallback, mechanism instead of an Annex VII arbitral tribunal as provided for in Part XV of UNCLOS. Yet another option is for ITLOS to establish a standing special chamber for BBNJ disputes, which is permissible under Article 15(1) of the ITLOS Statute. Some States propose that ITLOS may render advisory opinions on BBNJ matters, as provided for in Article 21 of the ITLOS Statute and Article 138 of its Rules, while other States are against it.

Part IX (Settlement of Disputes) of the revised draft text of a BBNJ agreement as presented by the President of the BBNJ conference on 18 November 2019 has two articles. Draft Article 54 (Obligation to settle disputes by peaceful means) provides: 'States Parties have the obligation to settle their disputes by negotiation, inquiry, mediation, conciliation, arbitration, judicial settlement, resort to regional agencies or arrangements, or other peaceful means of their own choice.' The whole draft Article 55 (Procedures for the settlement of disputes) is in square brackets. It reads:

[1. The provisions relating to the settlement of disputes set out in Part XV of [UNCLOS] apply *mutatis mutandis* to any dispute between States Parties to this Agreement concerning the interpretation or

---

[94] Alan Boyle, 'Litigating Climate Change under Part XII of the LOSC' (2019) 34 Int'l J Marine & Coastal L 458, 475, 477–81.
[95] 2167 UNTS 88.

application of this Agreement, whether or not they are also Parties to [UNCLOS].]

[2. Any procedure accepted by a State Party to this Agreement and [UNCLOS] pursuant to Article 287 of [UNCLOS] shall apply to the settlement of disputes under this Part, unless that State Party, when signing, ratifying or acceding to this Agreement, or at any time thereafter, has accepted another procedure pursuant to Article 287 for the settlement of disputes under this Part.]

[3. A State Party to this Agreement that is not a Party to [UNCLOS], when signing, ratifying or acceding to this Agreement, or at any time thereafter, shall be free to choose, by means of a written declaration, one or more of the means set out in Article 287, paragraph 1, of [UNCLOS] for the settlement of disputes under this Part. Article 287 shall apply to such a declaration, as well as to any dispute to which such State is a party that is not covered by a declaration in force. For the purposes of conciliation and arbitration in accordance with annexes V, VII and VIII to [UNCLOS], such State shall be entitled to nominate conciliators, arbitrators and experts to be included in the lists referred to in annex V, article 2, annex VII, article 2, and annex VIII, article 2, for the settlement of disputes under this Part.][96]

There is hardly anything innovative in Part IX of this draft Agreement. Owing to the time constraint imposed on the BBNJ Conference, delegations have not been able to devote more time to Part IX of the draft text of the BBNJ Agreement. Draft Article 54 closely follows the general obligation to settle disputes by peaceful means as stipulated in Article 33(1) of the UN Charter,[97] whereas draft Article 55 copies verbatim Article 30(1), (3), and (4) of the FSA. If Part IX is finally adopted with no substantive changes thereto, the dispute settlement regime under Part XV of UNCLOS as well as the role of ITLOS as elucidated in the preceding chapters of this book will apply *mutatis mutandis* to any dispute between States Parties to the BBNJ Agreement concerning the interpretation or application of the BBNJ Agreement, whether or not they are also parties to UNCLOS.

---

[96] Doc A/CONF232/2020/3 (18 November 2019).
[97] UN Charter Art 33(1): 'The parties to any dispute, the continuance of which is likely to endanger the maintenance of international peace and security, shall, first of all, seek a solution by negotiation, enquiry, mediation, conciliation, arbitration, judicial settlement, resort to regional agencies or arrangements, or other peaceful means of their own choice.'

Index

For the benefit of digital users, indexed terms that span two pages (e.g., 52–53) may, on occasion, appear on only one of those pages.

Tables are indicated by *t* following the page number